Asien- und Afrika-Studien
der Humboldt-Universität
zu Berlin

Band 68

2025
Harrassowitz Verlag · Wiesbaden

Studies on Buddhist Monastic Cultures

German-Japanese Collaboration

Edited by
Annette Schmiedchen, Petra Kieffer-Pülz
and Taiken Kyuma

in collaboration with
Satoshi Ogura

2025
Harrassowitz Verlag · Wiesbaden

The present publication is a result of the project DHARMA 'The Domestication of "Hindu" Asceticism and the Religious Making of South and Southeast Asia.' This project has received funding from the European Research Council (ERC) under the European Union's Horizon 2020 research and innovation programme (grant agreement no 809994). The papers in this book reflect only the respective authors' view. The funding body is not responsible for any use that may be made of the information it contains.

Bibliographic information published by the Deutsche Nationalbibliothek
The Deutsche Nationalbibliothek lists this publication in the Deutsche Nationalbibliografie; detailed bibliographic data are available on the internet at https://www.dnb.de/.

For further information about our publishing program consult our website
https://www.harrassowitz-verlag.de/

Published by Otto Harrassowitz GmbH & Co. KG, Wiesbaden 2025
Kreuzberger Ring 7c-d, 65205 Wiesbaden, produktsicherheit.verlag@harrassowitz.de
Printed on permanent/durable paper.
Printing and binding: docupoint GmbH
Printed in Germany

ISSN 0948-9789
eISSN 2750-1388
DOI: 10.13173/0948-9789

ISBN 978-3-447-12424-9
eISBN 978-3-447-39712-4
DOI book 10.13173/9783447124249

Table of Contents

Introduction
The Editors and Taiken Kyuma

Vihāra, *ārāma* and *āvāsa* in Early Pāli Literature
Petra Kieffer-Pülz

Vihāra, *mahāvihāra*, *vihāramaṇḍala*: The Terminology for Buddhist Monasteries and Nunneries in Indian Epigraphical Sources from Late Antiquity to the Early Medieval Period
Annette Schmiedchen

DOI: 10.13173/9783447124249.V

Written Evidence of Buddhism in 15th-Century Eastern India: Dated Colophons of Sanskrit Manuscripts in Old Bengali Script
Shin'ichirō Hori

Preface

In 2021 and 2022 two workshops titled *Studies on Buddhist Monastic Cultures. German-Japanese Collaboration* (Parts 1 and 2), were jointly organised by the Indology Department of the Seminar for South Asian Studies and Indology at Martin Luther University Halle-Wittenberg, and the Japanese Vihāra project. These two institutions had cooperated already earlier when Walter Slaje still held the chair of Indology. It was one of the worldwide initiatives to make the international networking of Indology in Halle visible. As the chair of Indology at Martin Luther University was vacant since the retirement of Walter Slaje in 2019, Indology was represented by the deputy professors Petra Kieffer-Pülz in 2021, and Philipp A. Maas in 2022. On the Japanese side, Taiken Kyuma from the Faculty of Humanities, Law and Economics of Mie University, and Satoshi Ogura from the Research Institute of Languages and Cultures of Asia of the Institute of Languages and Cultures of Asia and Africa at the Tokyo University of Foreign Studies, represented the Japanese Vihāra Project. Due to the pandemic both workshops took place online.[1] In addition to Welcoming and Closing Addresses, an Overview of the Japanese Vihāra Project, and the Q & A sections, there were eight lectures all in all, four each in 2021 and 2022.

On March 17, 2021, Annette Schmiedchen[2] opened the first workshop with her paper "*Vihāra*, *mahāvihāra*, and *vihāramaṇḍala* – the Terminology for Buddhist Monasteries and Nunneries in Sanskrit Epigraphy from Late Antiquity to the Early Medieval Period". Based on inscriptions from various Indian regions (mainly Gujarat, Bengal, and Andhra Pradesh), she investigated potential structural differences between monasteries called *vihāra*, *mahāvihāra* ('great monastery'), or *vihāramaṇḍala* ('monastic complex'). Her contribution is contained in the present volume, pp. 57–103.

1 March 17, and 24, 2021, 09.00–12.00; and March 16, and 23, 2022, 09.00–12.00 (CET).

2 Humboldt University Berlin, Institute for Asian and African Studies, ERC Synergy Grant DHARMA; Martin Luther University Halle-Wittenberg, Oriental Institute, Seminar for South Asian Studies and Indology, Indology.

DOI: 10.13173/9783447124249.VII

Hiroko Matsuoka[3] continued the session with a contribution to the "Biographical Data on Yamāri". Evaluating Tibetan and Sanskrit sources, she updated both biographical and bibliographical data of this late Buddhist Vijñānavādin, who wrote a major commentary on Prajñākaragupta's *Pramāṇavārttikālaṅkāra*. In addition, she provided new information about Yamāri's direct teacher and the original Sanskrit title of his work and reported on the then current state of the "Yamāri Project" (headed by Eli Franco, since 2014, at Leipzig University in cooperation with the China Tibetology Research Center). Her article is going to appear as "Biographical and Bibliographical Data on Yamāri and the *Pramāṇavārttikālaṅkāranibandha*", in *Sanskrit Manuscripts in China IV*, ed. by HORST LASIC and FRANCESCO SFERRA, Beijing: China Tibetology Publishing House.

On the second day of the first workshop (March 24, 2021), Petra Kieffer-Pülz[4] spoke about "The Meaning of *vihāra* in Pāli Literature", tracing the development of the meaning of the word *vihāra* in canonical and commentarial Pāli literature, in comparison to the terms *ārāma* and *āvāsa*. Her contribution is found in the present volume, pp. 1–55.

Ryuta Kikuya[5] continued the programme with his presentation on "Scripture and Commentary – the transmission of **Mahāmantrānudhāriṇī* in Indian Tantric Buddhism". He investigated the *Mahāmantrānusāriṇī* and its other version, the **Mahāmantrānudhāriṇī* – very different as to content – which both have been counted among the Five Protections (*Pañcarakṣā*) or Five Great Dhāraṇīs (gZungs chen po lnga). In this connection, he also attempted to describe the relationship between the lineage of *sādhana* literature and *vihāra*. Unfortunately, due to other obligations of the author, this article is neither contained in the present volume, nor being published elsewhere.

The second workshop started on March 16, 2022, with Charlyn Edwards'[6] lecture "New Perspectives on Late Indian Buddhism, and Our Methods for Understanding It, from a Nālandā Inscription by a Lineage from Somapura *Mahāvihāra*". She presented new discoveries and further questions about late Indian Buddhism in the *mahāvihāra*, and discussed our methods for

3 Austrian Academy of Sciences, Institute for the Cultural and Intellectual History of Asia; Leipzig University, Faculty of History, Art and Area Studies, Institute for Indology and Central Asian Studies.

4 Martin Luther University Halle-Wittenberg, Oriental Institute, Seminar for South Asian Studies and Indology, Indology; Academy of Sciences and Literature, Mainz.

5 Kyoto University, The HAKUBI Center / The Institute for Research in Humanities.

6 PhD candidate Department of Indology and Tibetology, Asia and Africa Institute, University of Hamburg.

understanding it. Her investigations were connected with a new edition and interdisciplinary commentary on "The Nālandā Stone Inscription of Vipulaśrīmitra", an inscription, from perhaps the last *vihāra* at Nālandā, that reflects centuries of Indian traditions, textual and non-textual, and not exclusively 'Buddhist'. The donor of the Nālandā *vihāra* is from Somapura *mahāvihāra*; each of the members of his teaching lineage is portrayed with a different Buddhist textual tradition. He is said to have made donations at many locations. His donations are presented as *vidyādāna*, gifts of knowledge, as described, for instance, in the Purāṇas. Due to personal circumstances, Charlyn Edwards was not able to provide us with a final version of her article.

Philipp A. Maas[7] continued the programme with a presentation of the "Spatial and Somatic Aspects of Early Buddhist and Non-Buddhist Meditations". Starting from the earliest unambiguous textual references to meditation practice in premodern South Asia, that is, brief stock phrases preserved in the Pāli canon, the origin of which is dateable to the earliest phase of Buddhism, i.e., to the lifetime of the historical Buddha or shortly thereafter (around 400 BCE), he drew upon the commentarial literature of the Pāli canon, artefacts, the Mūlasarvāstivāda *Vinaya* and Aśvaghoṣa's *Buddhacarita*, in order to identify the Buddhist meditation posture as performed at least from the first century of the Common Era onwards. In addition, he analysed quite comprehensive accounts of Buddhist meditation from the *Śrāvakabhūmi* and the *Mahāprajñāpāramitāśāstra* to draw a more complex picture of the spatial and somatic aspects of early Buddhist meditation. He also compared the emerging conceptions of the early Buddhist meditation posture and the appropriate locations for its practice with early non-Buddhist accounts contained in the *Bhagavadgītā*, the *Śvetāśvatara Upaniṣad*, the *Pātañjalayogaśāstra* and its *Vivaraṇa*, the *Nyāyabhāṣya* and Kālidāsa's *Kumārasambhava*, concluding that the early non-Buddhist meditation practice may have been profoundly influenced by its Buddhist analogue. Unfortunately, due to other obligations of the author, this article is neither contained in the present volume, nor published elsewhere.

On March 23, 2022, Shin'ichirō Hori,[8] presented a paper on "Evidence of Buddhism in 15th-Century Eastern India: Dated Colophons of Sanskrit Manuscripts in Old Bengali Script". Based on dated colophons of several

7 Martin Luther University Halle-Wittenberg, Oriental Institute, Seminar for South Asian Studies and Indology, Indology; Leipzig University, Faculty of History, Art and Area Studies, Institute for Indology and Central Asian Studies.

8 International College for Postgraduate Buddhist Studies, Tokyo.

Sanskrit manuscripts in Old Bengali script, Hori showed that despite the destruction of the major Buddhist monasteries in Eastern India by Turkic Muslims around the turn of the 13th century, Buddhists still survived in some rural areas in Bihar until the middle of the 15th century. He established the exact dates of four manuscripts, attempted to identify the village names recorded in the colophons, and dealt with personal names and titles including the name of a king unknown elsewhere. His contribution is contained in the present volume, pp. 105–135.

Concluding the second workshop, Chao-jung Ching[9] spoke on "Buddhist Monasteries to the South of the Tianshan Mountains in the 5th–8th Centuries CE". Her lecture focused on the complexes of Buddhist monasteries situated towards the northern rim of the Tarim Basin (Xinjiang Uygur Autonomous Region, China) and their development as traceable from the evidence of Chinese literature, historical texts and unearthed documents. In addition, she examined in depth the economic base of a few sites around today's Turfan and Kucha and traced their institutional change after the conquest of the Tang 唐 Dynasty (618–907). She intended to publish her contribution elsewhere.

Originally, the organisers of the two events had decided to publish the contributions to these two workshops in a joint volume of the *Studia Indologica Universitatis Halensis*. Due to the sudden closure of the Indological Department at Halle University and the drying-up of financial resources this plan had to be given up. Fortunately, Annette Schmiedchen offered to accept the volume for publication in the series *Asien- und Afrika-Studien der Humboldt-Universität zu Berlin*. Some of the contributors, however, have either published their work already in other places, had binding contracts with other publishers, or due to other obligations were not able to revise their presentations for publication in the present volume. Therefore, only three of the originally eight contributions are assembled here. In addition, Prof. Taiken Kyuma presents a short statement concerning the Japanese Vihāra Project.

The Editors
September 2025

9 Kyoto University, The HAKUBI Center / The Institute for Research in Humanities.

Indology in Halle (Saale) and the Vihāra Project
A Note

Taiken Kyuma

It is my great pleasure to be able to publish the results of our research activities in the series of the *Asien- und Afrika-Studien der Humboldt-Universität zu Berlin*, since the plan to have them published in the series *Studia Indologica Universitatis Halensis* of the Indological Department at Martin Luther University Halle-Wittenberg had to be given up due to the closure of that department. The starting point of the Japanese Vihāra Project (supported by the Japanese Society for the Promotion of Science) was to reconsider the decline of Indian Buddhism. The decline of Indian Buddhism has often been associated with the rise of tantric Buddhism. Nevertheless, recent studies clearly show that the system of tantric Buddhism developed to its fullest extent in late Indian Buddhism, even though it was under the influence of Hinduism. It is also a well-known fact that a certain number of great monasteries were still functioning around the 13th century. To reconstruct the history of Indian Buddhism more precisely, it is necessary to challenge and relativise the stereotyped assumption that Indian Buddhism showed a downward curve after the rise of tantric Buddhism.

We have been trying to shed more light on the decline of Indian Buddhism from different angles, focusing on the tradition of Buddhist monasteries from the Gupta period onward. Thanks to the project members, who performed their research very energetically during the first research term,[1] we were able to proceed to the next stage of the project,[2] which will be dedicated to elucidating the relationship between Buddhist monasteries and secularity from the Gupta period onward. As a methodological hypothesis, the concept of secularity is divided into the following three elements: la-

1 FY2018–2021, JSPS KAKENHI Grant No. 18H03569.
2 FY2022–2025, JSPS KAKENHI Grant No. 22H00002.

DOI: 10.13173/9783447124249.XI

ity, secular power, and tantric Buddhism (of course they are closely related to one another). The first two elements existed before the rise of tantric Buddhism, but we may also say that the secular aspect of Indian Buddhism clearly revealed itself within tantric Buddhism. Starting from the boundary (*sīman*) of a monastery (*vihāra*), we aim to expand our horizons for Buddhist monastic activities in the secular world. Further details of the project are given in our *Vihāra Newsletter.*[3]

There are several research teams in the Vihāra Project, one of which is the team of evaluation. The chief of this team[4] was Prof. Satoshi Ogura, who once studied in Halle, under the guidance of Prof. Walter Slaje. This research team is expected to evaluate the research discipline of the project and provide continuous feedback to the project from "outside", i.e., from the viewpoints of Buddhism before the Gupta period (including early Buddhism), Buddhism in neighboring regions (such as Central Asia, Southeast Asia, and West Asia), and other religious traditions (such as Hinduism). Here I would like to express my deepest gratitude to the kind support of Indology in Halle (Saale), which enabled the Vihāra Project (especially the team of evaluation) to co-organize the abovementioned two successful workshops. I am proud that both workshops were rich in contents and helpful in considering various issues of Buddhist monasteries from different perspectives.

On this occasion I would also like to introduce another important publication relevant to the Vihāra Project: Walter Slaje, *Brahmā's Curse: Facets of Political and Social Violence in Premodern Kashmir,* Halle: Universitätsverlag Halle-Wittenberg, 2019 (Studia Indologica Universitatis Halensis. 13). The second chapter of this book ("What Does it Mean to Smash an Idol? Iconoclasm in Medieval Kashmir as Reflected by Contemporaneous Sanskrit Sources", pp. 23–44) is based on Prof. Slaje's paper read at a workshop organised by the evaluation team with the title "Temples/Monasteries and Political Power in Medieval India", on March 7, 2019, at the Tokyo University of Foreign Studies.[5] In this chapter, Prof. Slaje clarifies the different dimensions of the concept of an idol from the viewpoints of Hinduism, Buddhism, and Islam. In doing so, he discusses how to understand the religious situation in medieval Kashmir, as well as the decline of Buddhism in this region.

As is well known, Halle's Indology is founded on the long-established tradition of philology and philosophy as methodological bases. In addition,

3 Published online in both English and Japanese, search "newsletter" at https://mie-u.repo.nii.ac.jp/.
4 FY2018–2021.
5 For more details, cf. *Vihāra Newsletter* vol. 2.

it covers a very wide range of subjects from early Buddhism to Islam in Kashmir, as is clearly shown by a number of publications in the series of the *Studia Indologica Universitatis Halensis*. Combining both these characteristics is a desideratum in present-day Indology and Buddhist Studies, since scholars are required to focus on global and interdisciplinary studies according to the progress of information technology. In that sense, Halle's Indology offers us an archetype of modern Indology and Buddhist Studies, and shows us how modern Indologists and Buddhologists should act in this age.

Vihāra, *ārāma* and *āvāsa* in Early Pāli Literature

Petra Kieffer-Pülz

1. Introduction

In the beginning of Buddhism monastics were essentially wandering mendicants who only during the rains sought shelter in natural caves, rock-cut chambers, self-made huts, or sponsored buildings of different qualities. Over time the periods during which monastics were settled in one and the same place became longer,[1] and finally led to permanently inhabited monastic compounds. Hence, a transition from a peripatetic lifestyle to a settled form of monasticism has taken place at some time.[2] The exact date is disputed.[3]

One of the main terms rendered as "monastery" or "monastic compound" is *vihāra*. But this word can refer to single dwellings, to various building types or to monasteries of different sizes and complexity. To know when it refers to what, it is necessary to investigate the relevant references. In the present contribution I will examine the usage and meanings of *vihāra* in Pāli literature, beginning with the canonical writings and proceeding with the commentarial layer of the *Aṭṭhakathā* commentaries (ca. 4th or 5th centuries CE up to the 10th century CE). To cover the whole spectrum of complexes that could be subsumed under the term "monastery", it is necessary to also consider the terms *mahāvihāra*, and *ārāma*.[4] Another important term in this context is the word *āvāsa*, commonly translated as "residence", which origi-

1 For instance, by the introduction of the Kaṭhina period beginning after the rains retreat, monks were enabled to prolong their stay for a further four months.

2 This must not have happened at the same time everywhere, and it also does not exclude that some monastics retained a peripatetic life-style.

3 For a discussion of this topic from an archaeological point of view, see SHAW 2011; from a text historical view, see BRONKHORST 2011: 18–19, SCHOPEN in several of his articles (e.g. 1994: 527–554 [2004a: 45–90]; 2006a), see also n. 230.

4 In 1997 Gustav Roth published a small monograph discussing the terms *ārāma*, *vihāra* and *mahāvihāra*, based on Pāli and Buddhist Sanskrit as well as Sanskrit material. He,

DOI: 10.13173/9783447124249.001

nally referred to an undefined but quite large area within which monks and nuns spent the rains.

Before we start with the investigation of the usage of these terms in Pāli sources, we will briefly look at the situation in the field of epigraphical and archaeological studies.

1.1 Epigraphical sources

The earliest references to a *vihāra* in epigraphical sources date from around the beginning of the Christian era.[5] According to Albery who examined inscriptions of the Indic North and Northwest between the second century BCE and the third century CE, in inscriptions the term *vihāra* appears as a single word,[6] and combined with the donors' names as proper names of *vihāras*.[7] Here *vihāra* can stand for mere dwellings[8] or monasteries.[9] In addition to *vihāra*, the words *ārāma*,[10] *saṅghārāma*,[11] and *araṇya*, "wilderness location", are used, the latter of which according to Albery (2020, 501 and n. 4) comes to replace the term *saṅghārāma* during the Kuṣāṇa period. The earliest dated inscription mentioning a *vihāra* stems from the last quarter of the first century CE.[12] Several earlier undated inscriptions are placed into the

---

however, did not differentiate between the canonical and commentarial texts, and the various strata of the canonical material.

5 BRONKHORST 2011: 18 and n. 25; SCHOPEN 2006b: 316; 2007: 61.

6 ALBERY 2020: Fig. 9.1 (no. 9, 46).

7 Busavihāra, ca. 1st century CE, see ALBERY 2020: 149 (Fig. 4.2, no. 31); 338 (Fig. 9.1, no. 3); 503 (Fig. 12.1, n. 3); Śirivihāra in Mathura, ca. 1st century CE, see ALBERY 2020: 338 (Fig. 9.1, no. 6); 372; 503 (Fig. 12.1, no. 5); for further names see fig. 12.1. ALBERY 2020: 511 states that a "monastery is typically named after the person or group by whom it was established", but he also states that in some cases the names of monasteries could be toponyms. SALOMON 1999: 241 (based on A. M. Shastri, *An Outline of Early Buddhism*) states that for Mathura the names of more than a dozen *vihāras* are preserved in inscriptions of the Kuṣāna period.

8 ALBERY 2020: 357 (in *Avadāna* and *Vinaya* texts), 501 (in Brāhmī and Kharoṣṭhī inscriptions); FOGELIN 2003: 15, uses the term for a row of monastic cells that share a common veranda, which strictly is a dwelling place. This architecture is typical for the Andhra region (see KIEFFER-PÜLZ 1994: 352–353).

9 ALBERY 2020: 223, 501 (in Brāhmī and Kharoṣṭhī inscriptions).

10 ALBERY 2020: 150 (Fig. 4.2, no. 43), 151 (Fig. 4.2, no. 44), 158, 269 (Fig. 8.2, no. 19), 280 (Fig. 8.3, no. 15). Albery (2020: 105 n. 5, 158) translates *ārāma* as "garden". For *ārāma* as part of the name of an *ārāmā*, see for instance, Ghoṣitārāma in Kauṣāmbī (ALBERY 2020: 104, 416, 501, 503 [Fig.12.1, no. 1], 506 [Fig. 12.1, no. 31]), see also below, n. 175.

11 ALBERY 2020: 147 (Fig. 4.2, no. 12), 149 (Fig. 4.2, no. 31), 158, 223, 503 (Fig. 12.1, nos. 2–3), 504 (Fig. 12.1, no. 8), 603 (Fig. 14.1, no. 1), 604 (Fig. 14.1, no. 5), 607.

12 ALBERY 2020: Fig. 9.1, no. 9, 373–374 (a reliquary inscription of the Year 126 of Azes (78/79 CE), linked to the Mahīśāsaka.

first century CE on palaeographical grounds.[13] The donor inscriptions from Sanchi and Bharhut of the second to first centuries BCE, many of which document donations by monastics,[14] do not contain references to *vihāras*, and the monks and nuns who made donations do not identify themselves by reference to a monastery or a specific community.[15] The earliest inscriptions that state donations of land to *vihāras*, are the Alluru inscription (1st/2nd centuries CE)[16] and the Mathura Lion Capital Inscription (No. 25, 1st century CE).[17] Thus, epigraphically there seem to exist no references to *vihāras* and no donations of land to *vihāras* that predate the first century CE.[18]

1.2 Archaeological sources

In the beginning monks used free-standing buildings (houses or huts) and natural caves, later also rock-cut chambers sculpted out of the rock as shelters. With respect to the rock-cut caves in Western India,[19] Zukas (2023: 65f.) determines altogether nine phases. His Phase 1 covers natural caverns which are only slightly modified to work as monastic dwellings. His Phase 2 (up to 150 BCE) covers single cells and small shrines allowing individual veneration (ZUKAS 2023: 70–74). Zukas (2023: 74–78) notes a major change between this second and his third Phase (150–100 BCE). In the latter the first monumental shrines and multi-celled dwellings appeared, which both indicate the presence of larger communities dwelling there and communal instead of individual worship. In his Phase 4 (100–50 BCE) the "monastic multi-celled residences set around a communal hall", i.e. the courtyard *vihāra*, "become the norm" (ZUKAS 2023: 78–81). In Phase 5 (50–0 BCE), "earlier monumental shrine-halls" are "converted into an apsidal monastic resi-

13 Busavihāra (Mathura Lion Capital, no. 25; ALBERY 2020: 375), Śirivihāra (Bodhisattva statue of Dharmaka; ALBERY 2020: 372), Ālānakavihāra (Pedestal Donation for Mahāsāmghika; ALBERY 2020: 375).

14 SCHOPEN 1985 [= 1997: 30–31]; 1996a: 60 [= 2004a: 383].

15 DEHEJIA 1992: 36–37; SCHOPEN 1994: 550 [= 2004a: 77]: "In none of the hundreds of donative records from Bhārhut, Sāñcī, and Pauni does the term (i.e. *vihāra*) occur. The scores of monk and nun donors at these sites identify themselves never as from or residents of any *vihāra* but rather—*exactly like lay donors*—by their natal or residential villages."

16 SCHOPEN 1994: 532 [= 2004a; 52, 89 n. 100].

17 ALBERY 2020: 149 (Fig. 4.2, no. 31), 352, 607–608, 777–778.

18 ALBERY 2020: 501. For a list of monasteries in donative inscriptions, see ALBERY 2020: 502 and Fig. 12.1. See also SCHOPEN 1994: 552 and n. 100 [= 2004a: 89, n. 100].

19 These caves differ regarding their size, the number of cells and their layout. For a short overview over the development, see HUNTINGTON & CHANDRASEKHAR 2000: 56–59. More details concerning the caves in Bhaja, Bedsa and Karla are found in ZUKAS 2023: 61–92. See also REES 2010.

dence". The remaining Phases 6 to 9 established by him are not relevant for our present investigation.[20]

In Bhaja, Zukas notes the existence of single-cell caves[21] that were later reused as access to newly excavated larger caves behind the original cells (ZUKAS 2023: 72–74). It is quite likely that similar changes can also be observed in other cave areas. Concerning early monasteries in the caves of Western India, Rees assumes that caves that "have been organized into discrete spatially bounded groups separated by distances not usually less than 200 m" constitute a monastery.[22] Normally they comprised several dwelling caves, which Rees mentions as *vihāra*, and one worship cave, called *caitya* by him, and in some cases, additionally a larger room for assemblies or as a refectory, which he refers to as *maṇḍapa* (REES 2010: 63). As we will see, these assumed monasteries could well correspond to what is named an *āvāsa* in the canonical Pāli texts.

Concerning free-standing monastic buildings, only few early monasteries are traced. The absence of monasteries at early Buddhist sites, has often been explained as resulting from the fact that they had been built with perishable materials,[23] and it has long been assumed that the oldest free-standing monasteries are found in the northwest (Taxila) and date from the first and second centuries CE.[24] Based on her investigations in the frame of the Sanchi Survey Project, Julia Shaw distinguished four types of free-standing monasteries in

20 In the remaining of the nine phases differentiated by Zukas the size of the shrine-halls as well as additional buildings such as cisterns, rest-halls, dams, water-tanks, etc., make the differences.

21 His caves 6A, 7A, 9A, etc. which he assigns to Phase 2, i.e. up to the middle of the second century BCE.

22 REES 2010: 60. Alternatively, Rees (2010: 60 and n. 12) calls such monasteries *leṇa*, basing himself on Sukumar Dutt's description of the development of permanent monasteries (DUTT 1962: 93). Dutt's description is, however, severely flawed, because he gives *āvāsa* and *ārāma* as a starting point for a development leading to *leṇa*s, for which there is no basis in the texts.

23 Gregory Schopen's main argument against this hypothesis are the irregularly sized rooms of the oldest structural monasteries (SCHOPEN 1994: 547–550 [= 2004a: 74–77]) – he mentions especially Taxila –, and the "lack of order or standardization" of the early phases of the early rock-cut monasteries, where "no two caves or *vihāras* are organized the same way" (SCHOPEN 1994: 548–549 [= 2004a: 75]). Shaw (2009: 124) criticizes Schopen stating that the "most obvious problem with this line of reasoning is its underlying normative model of spatial order". Even though she certainly is right in assuming that there is not only a single layout for monasteries in all parts of India, the different sizes of the early rock cut monasteries and the varying arrangement of the cells around a hall clearly show that this type of courtyard monastery was not yet completely developed in the most cases.

24 MARSHALL 1951: 315. These monasteries are of the courtyard type, with cells arranged around an open courtyard. The courtyards measure 31 x 41 or 52 x 44 meters with circa 21 cells surrounding it. The size of these monasteries and their arrangement clear-

Sanchi and its surroundings, which because of the proximity to Sanchi phase II she dates to the second century BCE,[25] namely the (1) 'courtyard monastery',[26] (2) a 'platformed monastery',[27] (3) rectangular structures arranged around a series of interconnected courtyards which may represent "an early experimental phase of the courtyard model in the Sanchi area" (SHAW 2009: 124), and (4) "simple single- or double-roomed rectangular structures" which Shaw also considers as possible prototypes of the courtyard monasteries. According to her the courtyard model in a fully developed form is found in the Deccan already in the second century BCE. As an example, she refers to Cave 4 in Pitalkhora,[28] which she dates to the mid-second century BCE. This dating might, however, be less secure than Shaw suggests.[29] In addition, Mitra states that Cave 4 is one of the "grandest pre-Christian monasteries" and concerning its fine execution "unparalleled in the pre-Christian caves".[30] So it seems Cave 4 is not a representative of an average monastic building. Applying Zukas' Phases of rock-cut monastic dwellings, Cave 4 possibly belongs at the

---

ly show that they are already more developed monasteries hosting communities with larger numbers of monks or nuns, and therefore are later than the early caves.

25 SHAW 2009: 124. "Their proximity to Phase II stūpas implies a second century BCE date." This seems a little vague as an argument.

26 SHAW 2011: 115, describes it as "with single or double occupancy cells arranged around a central courtyard".

27 SHAW 2009: 120; 2011: 115; Sanchi Building 8 and examples in Morel khurd, Satdhara, Sonari, Andher and Mawasa, which she dates to Phase II. The 'platformed monastery' consisted in platforms with stairways set into the body of the structure on which monasteries were erected with bricks and probably covered by timber superstructures (SHAW 2009: 122 and n. 18). As an argument for her hypothesis, she refers to the fact that, for instance, Cave 4 at Pitalkhora imitates such building structures in that the *vihāra* is built in a cave that is reached from a front court below via a staircase of eleven steps (SHAW 2009: 123).

28 See DESHPANDE 1959: pl. 46, for floor plans of the caves. It consists of a central hall with three rows of pillars, seven cells at the back and some (perhaps also six, nowadays largely destroyed) on the right side, all with barrel-vaulted roofs.

29 SHAW 2009: 123 (referring to MITRA 1971: 173, and *Indian Archaeology — A Review*, 1957–8: 65–6); 2011: 117 (with n. 27 giving the same references). Mitra (1971: 172) dates the inscriptions connected with Cave 3, which is contemporaneous with Cave 4, "to dates between 150 and 50 B.C." She does not give a separate date for Cave 4 on p. 173. *Indian Archaeology —A Review*, 1957–8: 65–6, does not contain any date. So, it is to be assumed that Shaw adopted the earlier of the dates given by Mitra. Deshpande (1959: 70) states that there are inscriptions in Cave 3 which on palaeographical grounds "may be assigned to the second century B.C.", and newly found inscriptions in Cave 4 he ascribes to the "second-first century B.C." and "*circa* second century B.C." (DESHPANDE 1959: 76). No details concerning these datings are provided. If there are no other substantiated datings elsewhere, the dating to the middle of the second century BCE cannot be regarded as a secure date.

30 MITRA 1971: 173–174.

earliest to his Phase 3 (150–100 BCE) but considering its size and execution more probably to Phase 4 (100–50 BCE).[31]

Falk (2012: 507–509) hinted at inscriptions which show that in the Mathura area even in the early second century CE the Buddha is worshipped in the form of his seat (*āsana*) situated at some lake or in villages, but not in a monastery. This indicates that there may have been huge differences concerning the existence of monastic compounds as centers of Buddhist monastic life in various regions.

All in all, the archaeological findings hint at the beginning of the creation of monastic dwellings or units of such dwellings in the two centuries before the common era, but the differences in size and arrangement of the caves and of the free-standing buildings indicate a development from single cells to small irregular monasteries, to more regular and larger monasteries, the latter probably only around the 1st century BCE.

1.3 Literary Sources: the Pāli canon and commentaries

The textual transmission taken as a basis for the present investigation of the term *vihāra* is the Pāli literature of the Theravāda tradition.[32] The reason for this choice is that the canon of this school was redactionally closed earlier than that of most other Buddhist schools.[33] According to the Chronicle of the Island (*Dīpavaṃsa*, ca. 4th century CE) and the Great Chronicle (*Mahāvaṃsa*, ca. 6th century CE) the writing down of the Pāli canon, the Tipiṭaka, took place in the first century BCE in present day Sri Lanka in the reign of King Vaṭṭagāmaṇi Abhaya (103 and 89–77 BCE).[34] Even if that is not accepted as a historical fact, the Pāli texts themselves show that they reflect very early layers of the development of the Buddhist tradition. Though there is a consensus that the *Vinaya* of the Mūlasarvāstivādins — which was redactionally closed later — also contains very old material, older and younger strata are mixed, and it is more difficult to sort out what belongs to which time. Also, much of what is found in this monastic law code is not contained in the canonical texts of the Pāli tradition, but only in the commentaries (*aṭṭhakathā*) from the fourth or fifth

31 Other scholars more generally assume that monasteries were constructed not earlier than the first century BCE. FOGELIN 2003: 95 for the monastery of Thotlakonda; more general FOGELIN 2015: 104ff.; ALBERY 2022: 501.

32 It is the heritage of the Mahāvihāra school that originated in present day Sri Lanka in the third century BCE. All the Pāli texts handed down to date are of this school, which was one of three schools established in Sri Lanka. The written heritage of the other schools is lost except for the one or other quotation and some translations (COUSINS 2012).

33 Concerning Buddhist schools with their own *Vinaya*, see CLARKE 2015: 60–87.

34 Dīp 20.20–21; Mhv 33.100–101. For a discussion of this passage, see BECHERT 1992.

centuries CE onwards.[35] These *Aṭṭhakathā*-commentaries made use of earlier now lost commentaries, and therefore partly also reflect developments that occurred between the writing down of the Pāli canon and the compilation of the *Aṭṭhakathās*, that is, roughly during the first half of the first millennium CE. Since information is spread over canon and commentaries, developments can be traced more easily. The main words used in the context of Buddhist monastic compounds or dwellings are the terms *vihāra*, *mahāvihāra*, and *ārāma*.[36] The term *assama* which corresponds to Sanskrit *āśrama*, "hermitage", is used most often in connection with ascetics of other traditions, that is, of Jaṭilas and Brāhmins,[37] and thus can be excluded here.[38]

Speaking of monasteries, we must clarify what we understand under monastery in the Buddhist context. Roughly, a complex monastery would be a compound consisting of the living quarters of the monastics, accompanied by several buildings for different purposes like an assembly hall, a refectory, bathrooms, toilets, storage rooms, etc. After the Buddha's *parinirvāṇa* a ritual space with a *caitya* (Pāli *cetiya*) or *thūpa* (skt. *stūpa*), and in later times an image house with statues of the Buddha is added as well. In some traditions the Bodhi tree also is an indispensable part of a monastery. At earlier stages no such permanent and fully developed monasteries existed, but probably places still rudimentary with a few dwellings that enabled monastics to stay in one area during the rains and perhaps with smaller shrines which enabled them to worship.[39] While archaeological remains allow to sketch the development of such monastic sites via their size and the facilities offered, an absolute dating is difficult. Also, the texts may show what served as a determining factor in the life of the monastics

35 For instance, the differentiation of a *sīmā* into a *mahāsīmā* and *khuddaka sīmā* found in the *Vinaya* of the Mūlasarvāstivādins (KIEFFER-PÜLZ 1992: 371–375). In the Pāli tradition this differentiation of *sīmās* can only be traced in the commentary as *mahāsīmā* and *khaṇḍasīmā* (KIEFFER-PÜLZ 1992: 242–259). Also, unlike the Mūlasarvāstivāda *Vinaya* the Pāli *Vinaya* does not yet know "the office of Elder and of Provost" (SCHOPEN 1994: 547 [=2004a: 73]); it also does not yet know a bathing costume for monks (the *udakasāṭikā* is only meant for nuns), and to my knowledge the rains robe also is not described as being used as a bathing robe as it seems to be in the Dharmagupataka tradition (HEIRMAN & TORCK 2012: 30). For further differences see also FIORUCCI 2023: 70–76 and n. 240, 241, 261 (with older literature).

36 Albery (2020: 357 and 501) understands *vihāra* to refer to dwellings of single monastics as well as to monasteries; Karashima (2012: III 486–487 [reference list]) in his study of the *Abhisamācārika*, a part of the *Vinaya* of the Mahāsāṅghikas, also distinguishes between *vihāra* in the meaning "monastery" and *vihāra* in the sense "the cell where some monks live".

37 Brāhmaṇas: M I 160.$_{26}$, 161.$_{12,13,14–15,17,19,24}$; Jaṭilas: D II 340.$_{9,11}$; M II 146 [omitted in E^{e}] = Sn 105.$_{8,9,}$ 111.$_{3}$; Vin I 24.$_{19}$, 26.$_{1}$, 246.$_{26}$; IV 108.$_{26}$, 109.$_{2}$.

38 For a discussion of *āśramas*, see BRONKHORST 2016a: 137–160.

39 For an overview, see FOGELIN 2015: 124–145, especially 129–130.

and played a role in the administrative life of local communities. To answer this question, I will first examine the use of the term *vihāra* and variants in the Pāli canon, followed by the terms *ārāma* and *āvāsa*. I then turn to their use in the *Aṭṭhakathā* literature and finally point out the differences.

2. The Pāli Canonical Texts

The first layer of texts to be consulted are the canonical scriptures (*tipiṭaka*), and here the baskets of the monastic law code (*Vinayapiṭaka*) and the discourses of the Buddha (*Suttapiṭaka*). Both collections show various chronological strata, of which the earliest may date back to the time of the Buddha or shortly after, while others originated later.[40] Roughly the canon may cover the period between the fourth to first centuries BCE. Concerning the *Suttapiṭaka*, attempts to stratify the various collections were not successful. But in general, the first four *nikāya*s of the *Suttapiṭaka* are considered older than the *Vinayapiṭaka*.[41] Commentaries like the *Niddesa*s belong to the younger portions, and the *Apadāna* collection is considered one of the youngest additions. The *Vinayapiṭaka* is divided into three parts, the *Suttavibhaṅga* centered around the *Pātimokkha*, the *Khandhaka*s with the formulas for legal acts (*kammavācā*) at their center, and the *Parivāra*, an Appendix added as the last part to the *Vinaya*. Within the *Suttavibhaṅga* the oldest stratum is represented by the *Pātimokkha* rules.[42] They were supplemented later with introductory stories giving the alleged incident for the enactment of the rule, by a word commentary (the *padabhājaniya*), and casuistries.[43] Each rule ends with a non-offence-clause (*anāpatti-vāra*) which was long considered the youngest part. But a still more recent section may be the cases listed as *vinītavatthu* and added to the first nine rules (Pār 1–4, Sgh 1–5). The *Khandhaka*s center around the formulas for legal acts (*kammavācā*). They contain younger and older parts and may have originated largely at the same time as the introductory stories etc. of the *Suttavibhaṅga*. The *Parivāra* was probably completed only in Sri Lanka in the first century BCE or CE, and the fact that it contains information not found in the rest of the *Vinaya* shows that it is the youngest part.[44]

---

40 For a discussion of this literature and its dating, see VON HINÜBER 1996: §§ 12–45 and 46–128; concerning the relation of *Vinaya* and *Suttapiṭaka*, see especially §§ 33–39.

41 VON HINÜBER 1996: § 51 (based on the material culture as reflected in these texts).

42 The investigation of these rules by VON HINÜBER 1999, has shown that the *Pātimokkha* already passed through a period of formation before it constituted the core of the *Suttavibhaṅga*.

43 KIEFFER-PÜLZ 2020–2021: 161–165.

44 VON HINÜBER 1996: §§ 22–42; KIEFFER-PÜLZ 2020–2021: 154–155.

In considering from which texts or text portions references come, it becomes possible to show whether a term was already established early or came into being only at a later stage. This enables us to sketch a more differentiated picture of the development of the usage of the word *vihāra*, etc.

2.1 Vihāra

The verb *viharati* (*vi* + √*har*) is very common in Pāli literature expressing among others "to stay, abide, dwell, sojourn (in a certain place)".[45] The noun *vihāra* accordingly means "spending one's time (sojourning or walking about), staying in a place", etc.[46] In this meaning *vihāra* is used in many compounds in Pāli literature.[47] But the meaning important in our context is the third one listed in the PED, which again is subdivided into three subcategories (a–c):

a) a habitation for a Buddhist mendicant, an abode in the forest (*arañña°*), or a hut; a dwelling, habitation, lodging (for a bhikkhu), a single room (Vin II 207[48]);
b) place for convention of the bhikkhus, meeting place; place for a rest & recreation (in garden or park);[49]
c) (later) a larger building for housing bhikkhus, an organized monastery, a Vihāra, Vin I 58,[50] III 47;[51] S I 185 (°*pāla* the guard of the monastery);[52] J

45 CHILDERS 1976: s.v. *viharati*: "to dwell, sojourn, live"; PED, s.v. *viharati*: "to stay, abide, dwell, sojourn (in a certain place); in general: to be, to live; appl[d]: to behave, lead a life ...".

46 CHILDERS 1976: s.v. *vihāro*: "Rambling, roaming, recreation; a Buddhist monastery or convent; state of life, condition; stopping, staying, sojourn, living, abiding, dwelling." PED, s.v. *vihāra*: "1. (as m. & adj.) spending one's time (sojourning or walking about), staying in a place, living; place of living, stay, abode (in general) ...; 2. (appl[d] meaning) state of life, condition, mode of life ...; 3. (a)–(c)" as quoted above.

47 It also is the meaning it has in Classical Sanskrit (NWS s.v. *vihāra*), and in Aśoka's inscriptions (FALK 1997: 118–119; SCHOPEN 2006a: 487 and n. 3), and even in a Jain context. Bronkhorst (2016b: 473) hints at the fact that despite some scholars' claim "*vihāra* in early Jainism does not mean 'monastery', but rather 'roaming' ... 'itinerary'." According to him the possibly oldest inscription where *vihāra* is used for a monastery of the Jainas is the Paharpur copper-plate inscription from 479 CE (BRONKHORST 2016b: 474 n. 34). See also Schmiedchen, below, p. 58 n. 5.

48 Vin II 207.$_{10}$, describes the building type *vihāra* that may be used as a dwelling place inside an *ārāma*.

49 No references are given for this definition. But these are the meanings the word has in Classical Sanskrit at least since the Mahābhārata (PW s.v.; see also ROTH 1997: 7–9). The same meaning ("park") it still has in 15 c. Kashmir, see SLAJE 2022: 493 n. 359, 866, 867.

50 Vin I 58.$_{19-20}$: *atirekalābho vihāro aḍḍhayogo pāsādo hammiyaṃ guhā.*

51 Vin III 47.$_{28-29}$ *vihāraṭṭhaṃ* listed in a line with *ārāma°*, *vihāra°*, *khetta°*, *vatthu°*, etc. to define *bhumaṭṭhaṃ* "[an object to be stolen] being in/on the earth". This passage gives no information concerning the *vihāra*, only that it is positioned between a park (*ārāma*) and a field (*khetta*).

52 S I 185.$_{7}$, *vihārapāla* "guard of the *vihāra*" which is the dwelling place of the monk Vaṅgīsa and his preceptor at Āḷavi at the Aggāḷava shrine. This seems to be the only reference in

I 126;[53] Miln 212;[54] Vism 292; DhA 1.19 (°*cārikā* visit to the monastery), 49 (°*pokkharaṇī*), 416; Mhvs 19, 77; PvA 12, 20, 54, 67, 141, 151; and passim.

Though the third meaning (c) is characterized as "later", the references given for it partly come from the canonical texts. Checking these references has shown that *vihāra* is not used for a permanent monastic compound there or that its actual meaning cannot be deduced from the respective passages (see the notes to the references).

The translators who translate *vihāra* by "monastery" probably do so without pondering much about the implications this has for a given context.[55] According to my research, *vihāra* in the canonical texts does not refer to a permanent Buddhist monastery in the sense of a building or complex of buildings within which a defined community of monks or nuns is permanently settled, and therefore should not be translated as "monastery".[56] In all the canonical references given in the PED, *vihāra* can be understood as a residential building[57] to be used as a dwelling place by one or several monks or for other purposes.[58] In the *Suttapiṭaka* the word *vihāra* is mostly used incidentally, that

the *Suttavibhaṅga*. The compound *vihārapāla* otherwise appears only twice in the *Vinaya*, in younger textual strata, namely in the introductory story to the rule Nissaggiya 5 (Vin III 208.$_{22}$) and in the *anāpatti*-clause of Pācittiya 42 (Vin IV 94.$_{7}$).

53 J I 126.$_{21}$, *vihārapaccante vasati*. This reference is part of the commentary, and thus late (5th/6th century CE). *Vihāra* here probably stands for the monastery, adjacent to which the landlord lives who ordained as a novice after the death of his wife.

54 Mil 212.$_{5}$ *vihāra* refers to dwelling places. All the remaining references given either belong to the Sinhalese chronicle *Mahāvaṃsa* or to the *Aṭṭhakathā* layer.

55 In the various translations of the canonical writings the term *vihāra* is partly left untranslated (HORNER, BD I: 38, 60, 76, etc.), sometimes translated by "cell" (NORMAN 2007: 30, 46 [Th vv. 222, 223, 385]); sometimes by "abode" (NORMAN 2007: 44 [Th vv. 365–366]), sometimes by "dwelling" (BODHI 2002: 729 [M II 119.$_{24,31}$]; WALTERS 2022: 777 [Ap II 418.$_{27}$]), sometimes by "monastery" (NORMAN 2007: 55 [Th v. 477]; WALTERS 2022: 322 [Ap I 202.$_{12}$]; 777 n. 5014 [Ap II 418.$_{27}$]). See also n. 197.

56 See also GRÄFE 1974: 50–53. LAMOTTE 1988: 342, also states that "[i]n the early literature, *vihāra* always or nearly always designated 'the dwelling, personal apartment of a single monk'".

57 In the old commentary in the *Vinaya vihāra* is defined as follows: Vin III 156.$_{22}$; IV 47.$_{28}$: *vihāro nāma ullitto vā hoti avalitto vā ullittāvalitto vā*. "Vihāra means it is smeared inside or it is smeared outside, or it is smeared inside and outside" (BD I 267). This shows that at the time of this old commentary *vihāra* is understood as referring to a building.

58 Concerning the other purposes, see below, p. 22. *Vihāra* is also used in Sanskrit texts, where it too is often translated by "monastery". Schopen (2000c: 151–152) in translating the *Śayanāsanavastu* notes: "I have not translated *vihāra* = *gtsug lag khang* here or elsewhere in the text. It is commonly translated by 'monastery,' but such a rendering is misleading and conceals the fact that the precise nature of the structures that are referred

is in introductory passages of Suttas or stories. This however throws light on how *vihāras* were used and gives a background to the more detailed information on the construction of *vihāras* contained in the monastic law code.

2.1.1 An individual's vihāra

In the *Suttapiṭaka* it is often stated that the Buddha or some monk enter the or a *vihāra* after a dhamma talk, giving the impression that they enter their own dwelling.[59] Alternatively, they sit down on a prepared seat in a *vihāra* (M I 332.$_{10}$; II 158.$_{10-11}$; etc.) or outside a *vihāra* in its shade,[60] or prepare a sleeping place in a *vihāra*.[61] A *vihāra* is further mentioned as the dwelling place of various monastics.[62] Comparable dwellings of worldly persons (kings, brahmins, *gahapatis*) are designated as *nivesana*.[63] In some passages a *vihāra* is described as a specific monk's dwelling when it is said that the monks each went to their respective *vihāras*,[64] or when a *vihāra* is specified as a monk's own *vi-*

to by the term is, in most cases, not actually determinable. The term in fact—as, for example, our passage makes abundantly clear—is applied to a wide range of structures of various sizes and configurations. ... How vague the term is can be seen in the definition it is given in the *Vibhaṅga* (Derge Ca 249b.3): '*vihāra* means: where there is room for the four bodily postures—walking, standing, sitting and lying down.' The history of Buddhist monastic architecture is, moreover, especially in its early periods, badly understood; (see G. Schopen, 'Doing Business for the Lord: Lending on Interest and Written Loan Contracts in the *Mūlasarvāstivāda-vinaya*,' *Journal of the American Oriental Society* 114 (1994) esp. 547ff), and for this reason, if no other, it is worth noting that in our passage the *vihāra* has not yet been reduced to what became a single quadrangular type (cf. Et. LAMOTTE, *Histoire du bouddhisme indien. Des origines à l'ère śaka* (Louvain : 1958) 197)."

59 A person – the Buddha, some monk or lay person – enters/entered (*paviṭṭho/pavisitvā/pavisissāmī/pāvisi*) a *vihāra* (for instance, D II 7.$_{31}$; M I 13.$_{35}$; 110.$_{7.10,28-29,32}$; 111.$_{32}$; 113.$_{1}$; S I 107.$_{13-14}$; Vin I 87.$_{16}$; etc.).

60 D I 152.$_{4-5.7}$; Vin I 180.$_{14-15}$, etc.: *vihārapacchāyāya(ṃ) āsanaṃ paññāpehi/paññāpesi*. D I 152.$_{8-9}$; S V 153.$_{4}$; Vin I 180.$_{15-16}$, etc.: *vihārā nikkhamma (or nikkhamitvā) vihārapacchāyāya(ṃ) paññatte āsane nisīdi.*

61 The Blessed One enters a *vihāra* and lies down on his right side in the lion pose (S I 107.$_{13-14}$; etc.); the Buddha enters a *vihāra*, puts down his outer robe (*saṅghāṭī*) and prepares his bed (*seyya*) Th 40.$_{25}$ [v. 366]; the Buddha wants the monk Soṇa to spend the night in the same *vihāra* he is going to stay (Ud 59.$_{11-17}$ = Vin I 196.$_{22-30}$), showing on the one side that there was a specific *vihāra* where the Buddha stayed, and on the other that there was sufficient space for at least two persons.

62 For instance, as the dwelling place of a preceptor (*upajjhāya*, Vin I 47.$_{31}$ = II 224.$_{33}$), of a teacher (*ācariya*, Vin I 61 = II 23 [both abbreviated in Vin]), of a pupil of a preceptor (i.e. the *saddhivihārika*, Vin I 52.$_{19}$), or of an *ācariya* (i.e. the *antevāsika*; Vin I 61 [abbreviated in Vin]).

63 Vin III 10.$_{33}$; IV 158.$_{35}$; D II 180.$_{17}$; S V 176.$_{23,32}$; 177.$_{3}$; 344.$_{19,28,32}$; etc.

64 Literally, as the *vihāras* were situated (*yathāvihāraṃ agamaṃsu*, S IV 290.$_{11}$; A III 299.$_{11,25}$; *yathāvihāraṃ gacchanti*, Vin IV 15,$_{28}$; *yathāvihāraṃ pavisiṃsu/paviṭṭhā*, Vin I 291.$_{17,24}$).

hāra (*saka/attano vihāra*).[65] There are also references to *vihāras* of specific monks, such as the *vihāra* of the Sakyan Upananda,[66] Udāyī,[67] Sabbakāmi,[68] or Kappitaka.[69] In the widest sense this could mean that the respective monks lived in a specific *vihāra* for a sufficient long time period for that *vihāra* to be identified as theirs by others. This does not necessarily imply that they owned these *vihāras*, which, however, cannot be excluded either. [70] Possibly they could also be named after them.[71] That they could be and in fact were named after their donors can be deduced from the formula (*kammavācā*) used to assign construction work (*navakamma*) on a *vihāra* to a specific monk. In that formula the respective *vihāra* is identified by a householder's name,[72] which very likely is that of the donor who then also is its owner (*sāmi, sāmika*).[73] And since such formulas serve as a template for all legal procedures with which such a task is to be performed, the connection of a *vihāra* with a householder's (i.e. donor's) name must have been quite common and stable.[74]

---

65 "The venerable Mahaka went to his own *vihāra*" (*āyasmāpi Mahako sakaṃ vihāraṃ agamāsi*, S IV 290.$_{12}$); "a resolve arose in my mind when I had entered my cell" (NORMAN 2007: 30) (*vihāraṃ me paviṭṭhassa cetaso paṇidhī ahū*, Th v. 222); "a monk had a wall of his own *vihāra* shored up" with a piece of wood belonging to the Saṅgha (*attano vihārassa kuḍḍaṃ upatthambhesi*, Vin III 65.$_{20-21}$); "a monk had had a *vihāra* built for himself" (*bhikkhunā ... attano atthāya vihāro kārāpito*, Vin I 141.$_{31}$ and 142.$_{2}$); "build a *vihāra* for me" (Vin III 157.$_{10,13,17,24,30}$); "they built a *vihāra* for him" (Vin III 157.$_{10-11,15,20,26,31}$).

66 Vin IV 168.$_{14-15}$: *yenāyasmato Upanandassa Sakyaputtassa vihāro ten' upasaṅkami.*

67 Vin III 127.$_{24-25,29}$: *āyasmā Udāyi araññe viharati, tassāyasmato vihāro abhirūpo hoti ... icchāma mayaṃ bhante ayassa vihāraṃ pekkhitun ti.*

68 Vin II 303.$_{31,35-36}$: *yasmiṃ vihāre Sabbakāmī thero viharati ...*

69 Vin IV 308.$_{23-25}$: *... āyasmato Kappitakassa vihāraṃ pāsāṇehi ca leḍḍūhi ca ottharāpetvā, "mato Kappitako" ti pakkamiṃsu.*

70 The owner of a *vihāra* normally is the donor, whether he gives a *vihāra* to an individual monk or to the Saṅgha. Only if a monk has built the hut or *vihāra* with his own means can he be understood to be the owner. A *vihāra* given to the Saṅgha, a *saṅghika vihāra*, will be assigned by the Saṅgha to a monk who is going to use it. The donor (= owner) of this *vihāra* is obliged to provide that monk with the requisites required for maintaining the *vihāra*. For more details concerning the *vihāra* owner in the Pāli tradition, see KIEFFER-PÜLZ 2022.

71 It remains unclear whether references to specific monks' *vihāras* by the monks' names (Upananda's, Udāyi's, etc. *vihāra*, see above n. 66–69) imply that these were the *vihāras*' names.

72 Vin II 160.$_{15-17}$: *yadi saṃghassa pattakallaṃ saṅgho itthannāmassa gahapatino vihāraṃ itthannāmassa bhikkhuno navakammaṃ deti. ...* "If it seems right to the Saṅgha, the Saṅgha grants [responsibilities for] renovation of the *vihāra* of the householder So-and-so to the monk So-and-so."

73 See below, pp. 19–20.

74 This is confirmed by epigraphical sources, see above, pp. 2–3.

Potential cases for such a usage in the Pali canon could be the *vihāras* of the Sakyan Kāḷakhemaka[75] or the Sakyan Ghāṭāya.[76] In the formulas with which specific functions of a *vihāra* are determined – for instance as an "observance house" (*uposathāgāra*), as a "place for allowable goods" (*kappiyabhūmi*) or as a "storage place" (*bhaṇḍāgāra*) – the *vihāra* is mentioned as "the *vihāra* having such and such a name" (*itthannāma-vihāra*).[77] This leaves open what a *vihāra* is named after, but shows that they normally bore names.

There are references mentioning that laymen wanted to build a *vihāra* for a specific monk.[78] Whatever the exact role of the donor regarding such a *vihāra*, the recipient in such a case is an individual. In younger texts such *vihāras* are called "*vihāras* belonging to an individual" (*puggalika vihāra*), but in canonical literature *puggalika vihāra* is not yet used.[79]

---

75 M III 109.$_{24-25,26-27,28}$, 110.$_{2,11,14}$: *Kāḷakhemakassa Sakkassa vihāro/e.* This must have been a larger dwelling, since it is stated that there several lodgings (*sambahula senāsana*) were prepared, and several monks (*sambahulā bhikkhū*) stayed there, because it was the time of robe making. The Buddha takes this as a starting point for saying that a "bhikkhu does not shine by delighting in company". In the *Aṭṭhakathā* layer this *vihāra* is said to having been part of the Nigrodhārāma, enclosed by a wall (*pākārena parikkhipitvā*) and provided with its own entrance gate, pavilions, and a dining hall (Ps IV 155.$_{4-9}$).

76 M III 110.$_{6,8}$: *Ghaṭāya-Sakkassa vihāre/o.* According to the *Aṭṭhakathā* this *vihāra* also formed part of the Nigrodhārāma (Ps IV 157.$_{16-17}$).

77 Vin I 107.$_{13-14}$: *yassāyasmato khamati itthannāmassa vihārassa uposathāgārassa sammuti, so tuṇh' assa ...*; Vin I 239.$_{15-17}$: *... itthannāmassa vihārassa kappiyabhūmiyā sammuti ...* ; Vin I 284.$_{25-27}$: *... itthannāmassa vihārassa bhaṇḍāgārassa sammuti ...*

78 In Vin III 155.$_{29-30}$ (Sgh 7) a supporting householder (*upaṭṭhāko gahapati*) wants to have a *vihāra* built for the Venerable Channa. In M II 163.$_{13-28}$ the brahmin Ghoṭamukha wishes to give money to the monk Udena. Since he is told that this is not suitable for a monk, he suggests having a *vihāra* built for Udena. *Vihāra* here means a dwelling place for that monk, because Udena then tells the brahmin, if he wants to have a *vihāra* built for him, he shall rather have an assembly hall (*upaṭṭhānasālā*) built for the Saṅgha in Pāṭaliputta. The brahmin is pleased that Udena suggests he should donate to the Saṅgha instead of to him personally, even though this is – as becomes visible from the subsequent explanations – more expensive for the brahmin. In A V 347.$_{13}$ the householder Dasama has a *vihāra* built for *Ānanda* that is worth 500 *kahāpaṇas* (*Ānandassa pañcasataṃ vihāraṃ kārāpesī ti*). In Vin I 140.$_{7ff.}$ we have an enumeration that laymen have *vihāras* built for several monks, for one monk, for the nuns' saṅgha, several nuns, a single nun, for novices, etc. This is then extended to all buildings mentioned in the various enumerations of monastic buildings.

79 In the youngest part of the *Vinaya*, in the *Parivāra*, five qualities are enumerated that cause a resident monk (*āvāsika*) to be doomed to the Niraya hell. The fifth point is that he uses property of the Saṅgha according to the usage of individual property (*saṅghikaṃ puggalikaparibhogena paribhuñjati*, Vin V 204.$_{2}$), and he is consigned to heaven, if he does not use saṅgha property according to the usage of individual property (*saṅghikaṃ na puggalikaparibhogena paribhuñjati*, Vin V 204.$_{6-7}$). This shows that the differentiation between *puggalika* and *saṅghika* objects becomes more nuanced in later times. The term *puggalikavihāra/*

Even monastics of all types — monks and nuns down to male and female novices — could build *vihāras* for a Saṅgha, other monks, nuns, probationers, novices or for themselves.[80] Since the fully ordained are not prohibited to have their own money or wealth they could use their own means.[81] Alternatively they could use what they obtained from begging (see below, p. 20). In the definition of an owner of a *vihāra* in the old commentary to the seventh Saṅghādisesa, among others a *pabbajita*, "one who has gone out from home", is mentioned.[82] This term also includes Buddhist monks and thus makes explicit that Buddhist monastics also could be owners of *vihāras*.[83] For "huts" (*kuṭi*), which are less durable dwellings,[84] this is proved by a reference in the *Pātimokkha* itself (Vin III 149.$_{10}$, Sgh 6), and confirmed by references from other parts of the canon, where it is reported that monks built *kuṭis* and donated them to the Saṅgha of the four quarters (*cātuddisa saṅgha*; i.e. to the Saṅgha as a whole, not to a specific local Saṅgha).[85]

puggalika vihāra is rarely used in Pāli literature, and except for a few references in the *Vinayaṭṭhakathā* (Sp VI 1237.$_{1-2}$; 1247.$_{19}$; for Sp VI 1246.$_{14}$–1247.$_{5}$, where some aspects of individual ownership are discussed, see VON HINÜBER 2006: 20 [2009: II 886]), mostly in the younger layers, that is in subcommentaries.

80 Vin I 141.$_{31}$–142.$_{2}$: *idha pana bhikkhave bhikkhunā saṃghaṃ uddissa, bhikkhuniyā saṃghaṃ uddissa, sikkhamānāya saṃghaṃ uddissa, sāmaṇerena saṃghaṃ uddissa, sāmaṇeriyā saṃghaṃ uddissa, sambahule bhikkhu uddissa, ekam bhikkhuṃ uddissa, bhikkhunīsaṃghaṃ uddissa sambahulā bhikkhuniya uddissa, ekaṃ bhikkhuniṃ uddissa, sambahulā sikkhamānāya uddissa, ekaṃ sikkhamānaṃ uddissa, sambahule sāmaṇere uddissa, ekaṃ sāmaṇeraṃ uddissa, sambahulā sāmaṇeriyo uddissa, ekaṃ sāmaṇeriṃ uddissa, attano atthāya vihāro kārāpito hoti* ... "In case a *vihāra* has been caused to be built by a monk for a Saṅgha, by a nun for a Saṅgha, by a probationer for a Saṅgha, by a male novice for a Saṅgha, by a female novice for a Saṅgha, by [a monk, nun, etc. as before] for several monks, for one monk, for a nuns' Saṅgha, for several nuns, for one nun, for several probationers, for one probationer, for several male novices, for one male novice, for several female novices, for one female novice, for his own use ... ."

81 There did not exist a vow of poverty in Buddhism (VON HINÜBER 1995a: 11 [= 2009: 192]); 2004: 27; 2006: 16 [= 2009: II 882]; SCHOPEN 1996a: 60–61 [= 2004a: 383]) and as the non-offence clauses to various rules of the *Pātimokkha* show, if a monk or nun transgress the respective rule using their own wealth (*attano dhanena*) there is no offence (Vin III 213.$_{23}$; 215.$_{7-8}$; 217.$_{22-23}$; etc.). See also SCHOPEN 1995: 106 [= 2004a: 173–174]; 1996a: 61 and n. 7 [= 2004a: 383, 393n7].

82 See below, n. 115

83 This is again confirmed by the reasons why a monk might interrupt his rains retreat for a matter requiring his absence for a period of at most seven days, which includes the gift of a *vihāra* by a monk, nun, etc., to a Saṅgha, monks, etc. (Vin I 141.$_{31ff.}$; see above, n. 80).

84 Among the *kuṭis* there may have been further differences depending on the materials with which they were made. Huts made of grass (*tiṇakuṭi*) by the monks themselves for the rains may have been especially fragile. The monks destroyed them before they left after the rains retreat (Vin III 41.$_{2-9}$).

85 Pv 18.$_{13}$ [v. 123]: *catasso kuṭiyo katvā saṅghe cātuddise adā, kuṭiyo annapānañ ca mātu dakkhiṇam ādisī.* "He (i.e. Upatissa) built four huts and he gave those huts together with food and drink to

2.1.2 *A Saṅgha's vihāra*

The Saṅgha is another possible recipient for the donation of a *vihāra*.[86] There are several references showing that lay-followers, etc., build or have built *vihāras* for the Buddhist community (*saṅgha*),[87] for the Buddhist community of the four quarters (*cātuddisa saṅgha*),[88] or for the Buddhist community of the four quarters, present and to come (*āgatānāgata cātuddisa saṅgha*).[89] The latter two dedications imply that these *vihāras* are intended for all Buddhist monks that exist or will exist in future, and not for residents of a specific monastery.[90] *Vihāras* given to the Saṅgha are called *saṅghika vihāras*.[91] There are no references for a *saṅghika vihāra* in the *Suttapiṭaka*, except for one in the relatively recent *Apadāna* collection.[92] But there is evidence for a *saṅghika vihāra* in four *Pātimokkha* rules (Pāc 15–18).[93] All other references in the *Vinaya* – distributed over *Cullavagga* and *Parivāra* – only take up these same four rules.[94] However, the idea that objects belong to the Saṅgha or individuals is clearly present in the casuistries to various *Pātimokkha* rules, as is the judgment concerning a monk's behaviour depending on whether some-

---

the Saṅgha of the four quarters and then dedicated that donation to his mother" (Masefield 1980: 87). Pv 50.$_{31}$ [v. 426]: *thero paṇṇakuṭiṃ katvā saṅghe cātuddise adā*, "When the elder had built a hut of leaves, he gave it to the Saṅgha of the four quarters" (Masefield 1980: 192).

86 See also above, n. 80.

87 Vin I 139.$_{6,27–28}$; IV 287.$_{17–18}$; Vv 67.$_{28}$ [v. 788].

88 D I 145.$_{11–12}$; A IV 395.$_{4,24–25}$. Such a gift is considered of very great fruit and advantage.

89 Vin II 147.$_{25–26–27,27–29}$: *tvaṃ gahapati/Rājagahako seṭṭhi ... te saṭṭhiṃ vihāre patiṭṭhāpehī ti/patiṭṭhāpesi*. The same wording we find for the Jetavana, though there *vihāras* are not mentioned, Vin II 164.$_{21–22,23–25}$: *tvaṃ gahapati/Anāthapiṇḍiko gahapati Jetavanaṃ āgatānāgatacātuddisassa saṅghassa patiṭṭhāpehī ti/patiṭṭhāpesi*.

90 Albery (2020: 346 n. 1) interprets the *cātuddisasaṅgha* in this context as an idealized entity.

91 *saṅghika* is defined always in the same manner in the old commentary: *saṅghiko nāma vihāro saṅghassa dinno hoti pariccatto*, Vin IV 41.$_{26}$; 43.$_{12}$; 45.$_{3}$; 46.$_{20}$; *saṅghikaṃ nāma saṅghassa dinnaṃ hoti pariccattaṃ*, Vin III 266.$_{1}$; IV 40.$_{4}$; 154.$_{31}$; 156.$_{23}$; etc.

92 Ap II 488.$_{9}$ [v. 30]. Translated as "Assembly monasteries" by Walters (2017: 926; 2022: 924) even though this refers to *vihāras* of the Saṅgha which a monk who suffers from illness does not use as his dwelling.

93 These rules do not belong to the earliest corpus of rules of the *Pātimokkha*. This is obvious from their not being formulated as locative rules (misbehavior in the locative, offence in the nominative), as the oldest rules are. Also they are not placed in the beginnings of the decades in which the 92 Pācittiya rules are divided, where the locative rules stay. For these and more details concerning the genesis of the *Pātimokkha*, see von Hinüber 1999: 32–38.

94 Vin IV 41.$_{6,10,14–15,18,21}$ (Pāc 15; corresponds to Vin V 15.$_{22,25}$; 38.$_{12}$); 43.$_{7}$ (Pāc 16; corresponds to Vin V 15.$_{28}$; 38.$_{16}$); 44.$_{15,21–22,24,31–32}$ (Pāc 17; corresponds to Vin II 166.$_{19,25–26,28,31,34}$, and Vin V 15.$_{35,38}$; 38.$_{19}$); 46,$_{16}$ (Pāc 18; corresponding to Vin V 16.$_{3}$; 38.$_{22}$).

thing is *saṅghika* or *puggalika*.[95] This is expressed in general with regard to "possessions" (*lābha*),[96] or beds[97] and beddings.[98] All in all, this suggests that the differentiation of material objects in *puggalika* and *saṅghika* had started at the time of the casuistries, but that its application to buildings used as dwellings, etc., still was in its infancy.

The donation of a *vihāra* (*vihāradāna*) to the Saṅgha is considered an important gift, as becomes obvious from five stanzas transmitted in the *Cullavagga*, in connection with the allowance of the five types of shelter (*leṇa*, see below, 2.1.5). A merchant of Rājagaha had sixty *vihāras* built, which were not accepted by the monks because *vihāras* were not yet allowed by the Buddha. When the merchant spoke to the Buddha, the Buddha asked him whether these *vihāras* were intended for the "Saṅgha of the four quarters, present and to come", which was answered in the affirmative. This shows that such *vihāras* were intended for all Buddhist monks, present and future, and not for specific local Saṅghas or monasteries. The Buddha accepted the *vihāras* and thanked the merchant with five verses in which he praised the gift of a *vihāra* to the Saṅgha (I quote only three of them central to our topic):

> Praised as chief by the Buddha is the gift of a *vihāra* to the Saṅgha, for shelter (*leṇattha*), for (providing) comfort, to meditate and to gain insight.
>
> Therefore, a wise man, considering his own welfare, should have delightful *vihāras* built [and] should have those who have heard much (i.e. learned ones) dwell/stay there;
>
> to them he should give food and drink, clothes and beds and seats, with a confident heart concerning those who are of upright character.[99]

---

95 Vin IV 41.$_{21}$ (Pāc 15); 43.$_{7}$ (Pāc 16); 44.$_{31-32}$ (Pāc 17); 46.$_{16}$ (Pāc 18). In the casuistries to these four rules a monk commits the full offences when he acts with regard to something belonging to the Saṅgha (*saṅghike*), but only an offence of wrong-doing (*dukkaṭa*) when he acts with regard to something belonging to another individual (*aññassa puggalike*), and there is no offence if it is with regard to his own individual possession (*attano puggalike*, f.i. Vin III 34.$_{4-17}$).

96 Vin III 265.$_{31}$ (Niss 30); IV 154.$_{21}$ (Pāc 81); 156.$_{18}$ (Pāc 82; *saṅghikaṃ lābhaṃ*).

97 Vin IV 39.$_{25}$: *saṅghikaṃ mañcaṃ vā pīṭhaṃ vā bhisiṃ vā kocchaṃ vā ...*

98 Vin II 170.$_{9-10,11,13,1517,18-19,21}$; 171.$_{6-7,9,20-21,25,27-28,30-31}$.

99 Vin II 147.$_{34}$–148.$_{2}$ = II 164.$_{30-35}$:
leṇatthañ ca sukhatthañ ca jhāyituñ ca vipassituṁ
vihāradānaṁ saṁghassa aggaṁ Buddhena vaṇṇitaṁ.
tasmā hi paṇḍito poso sampassaṁ attham attano
vihāre kāraye ramme vāsayettha bahussute.
tesaṁ annañ ca pānañ ca vatthasenāsanāni ca.
dadeyya ujubhūtesu vippasannena cetasā.

These stanzas make plain that giving *vihāras* — which were intended for dwelling of monastics — to the Saṅgha is considered an eminent donation. They also show that there are further obligations associated with such a gift, since the donors needed to support the residents of these *vihāras* by providing them with the necessities of daily life. At the latest from the times of the *Aṭṭhakathās* onwards this also includes the maintenance and repair (*navakamma*) of *vihāras*, because the monks living in them seek out the donor when they need tools or building materials for carrying out repairs.[100] In various *Aṭṭhakathās* of later centuries the verses from the *Cullavagga* are cited or referred to[101] showing that *vihāradāna* is understood as referring to dwelling places for single monks there as well,[102] not to monastic complexes.[103] Comparable to the praise of the gift of a *vihāra* to the Saṅgha in the monastic law code, is the praise of building a *vihāra* for the Saṅgha of the four quarters (*cātuddisaṃ saṅghaṃ uddisa vihāraṃ karoti*) in the *Dīghanikāya* (*Kūṭadantasutta*). It is listed in a row of sacrifices (*yañña*), of which the sacrifices mentioned before are more difficult to perform and of lesser fruit, whereas those mentioned subsequently to the *vihāradāna* are each less difficult, but of greater fruit, namely taking refuge to the Buddha, undertaking the training rules, and entering the four kinds of absorption (D I 145.$_{11ff.}$).

2.1.3 The Buddha's vihāra

During the Buddha's lifetime he stayed in *vihāras* just like the monks. This is obvious from various discourses where the Buddha is said to have gone to his *vihāra*, to have come out of it, etc. But a Buddha, either one of the earlier

---

These verses are also discussed by ROTH 1997: 28–29. A similar statement is made with respect to hermitages (*assama*) in the *Saṃyuttanikāya* (S I 100.$_{8-22}$; BODHI 2000: 191).

100 Sp VI 1246.$_{14ff.}$; Spk III 107.$_{20-29}$; see KIEFFER-PÜLZ 2022: 195–196.

101 Sv I 304.$_{5-15}$; Ps III 26.$_{10-20}$; Spk III 51.$_{10-20}$; Ud-a 419.$_{27}$–420.$_{6}$; referred to in It-a I 91.$_{26}$.

102 In the post-canonical *Milindapañha* two advantages of giving a *vihāra* (*vihāradāna*) are described without the recipient being mentioned. According to that someone who gives a dwelling-place is praised by all Buddhas, and will be utterly freed from birth, ageing, and dying. Second when there is a dwelling-place nuns can [meet] at an appointed place with experienced [monks], and it is easy for those who want to see them to do so; (Mil 212.$_{19-25}$: *vihāradānaṃ nāma sabbabuddhehi vaṇṇitaṃ ..., taṃ te vihāradānaṃ datvā jātijarāmaraṇā parimuccissantī ti. ...vihāre vijjamāne bhikkhuniyo byattasaṅketā bhavissanti, sulabhaṃ dassanaṃ dassanakāmānaṃ, ...*)

103 Dhp-a I 416.$_{16}$–417.$_{6}$. Here *vihāradāna* is exemplified by the building type of a *pāsāda*, *senāsanadāna* by bed and stool (*mañcapīṭha* etc.), *bhojanadāna* by food, *cīvaradāna* by cloth and *bhesajjadāna* by medicine. In various *Aṭṭhakathās* *vihāra* in this context is identified with *āvāsa*, which at the time of the commentary refers to an individual dwelling (see below, 3.3).

Buddhas[104] or the historical Buddha, is also mentioned in a few references as the recipient of the gift of a *vihāra*,[105] or a *kuṭi*.[106] These references are found in the younger text collections of the *Suttapiṭaka*.[107] *Vihāra* and *kuṭi* here might be understood as a precursor of the term *gandhakuṭi* ("perfumed chamber") of the Buddha which is used for the shrine of the Buddha[108] included in monasteries at a later time. This term appears in younger inscriptions and in the *Vinaya* of the Mūlasarvāstivādins, but not in the Pāli canon, except for several times in the *Apadāna* collection.[109] Later the term is used in the *Aṭṭhakathā* layer.[110]

2.1.4 Ownership of vihāras

In the Theravāda texts the ownership of *vihāras* is not discussed explicitly.[111] *Vihāras* of lay-followers,[112] and of one or several families[113] are mentioned in the monastic law code without further information. But from the descriptions in the *Sutta-* and *Vinayapiṭaka*, it is obvious that a donor of *vihāras* had obligations concerning his donated buildings, such as providing the inhabitants with food and daily requisites,[114] and later also with tools and building materials to restore dilapidated *vihāras* (see below, p. 19). Thus, the donors obviously had financial responsibilities regarding the *vihāras* they donated which are considered the tasks of owners. The sixth and seventh

---

104 Thī 174.$_4$ [v. 518] = HALLISEY 2015: 236 [v. 521] = Ap II 512.$_7$ *sakhiyo tisso janiyo vihāradānaṃ adāsimha*, report the donation of a *vihāra* (*vihāradāna*) by a woman (Sumedhā) to the Buddha Koṇāgamana when he was in his new residence (*navanivesa*) in a *saṅghārāma*.

105 Vv 114.20–21 [v. 1136]: *ahaṃ Andhakavindasmiṃ Buddhass' Ādiccabandhuno, vihāraṃ satthu kāresiṃ sehi pāṇihi*, "For the teacher, for the Buddha, for the one related to the sun, I, devoted, in Andhakavinda, built a *vihāra* with my own hands" (MASEFIELD 2015: 466); 114.23 [v. 1137]: *vihāraṃ satthuno 'dāsiṃ*. "A *vihāra* I ... gave to the teacher" (MASEFIELD 2015: 466).

106 Ap 229.$_{10-11}$: *paṇṇasālaṃ karitvāna adāsiṃ aparājite, ekanavute ito kappe yaṃ paṇṇakuṭikaṃ adaṃ*, ... WALTERS 2022: 367–368: "Fashioning a hall of leaves, I gave [it] for the Unconquered One. In the ninety-one aeons since I gave that hut of leaves [to him] ..."

107 Concerning the *Apadāna*, see NORMAN 1983: 90; VON HINÜBER 1996: § 121; concerning the *Vimānavatthu*, see NORMAN 1983: 70; VON HINÜBER 1996: § 102.

108 For the *gandhakuṭi*, see STRONG 1977.

109 Ap 60.$_{20,21}$; 186.$_3$; 489.$_{23}$; 509.$_{17}$.

110 Ps II 268.$_6$; III 347.$_{20,21}$; Spk I 310.$_{16}$; Dhp-a III 62.$_{1,2-3,4-5,6}$; etc.

111 The topic is dealt with in some detail in the *Vinaya* of the Mūlasarvāstivādins. See HU-VON HINÜBER 2018: 201 n. 3; SCHOPEN 1996b [= 2004a: 219–259].

112 Vin II 174.$_{4-5}$ = III 65.$_{38}$–66.$_1$: *bhikkhū aññatarassa upāsakassa vihāraparibhogaṃ senāsanaṃ aññatra paribhuñjanti*. "Monks made use elsewhere of lodging(s) to be made use of in a dwelling-place of a certain lay-follower." Also taken as a proof by SCHOPEN (1996b: 87 [= 2004a: 222]) that a *vihāra* may be a layman's property.

113 *ekakulassa vihāra* (Vin III 202.$_1$); *nānākulassa vihāra* (Vin III 202.$_{4-5}$).

114 See 3.1, for references in the *Aṭṭhakathā* layer; see also KIEFFER-PÜLZ 2022.

Saṅghādisesas of the *Pātimokkha* throw further light on this. Saṅghādisesa six deals with a hut (*kuṭi*) that has no owner (*assāmikā*) and Saṅghādisesa seven with a *vihāra* that has an owner (*sassāmika*).[115] Saṅghādisesa six in addition relates that the monk who has the ownerless hut built, does so by his own begging (*saññācikāya*). The old commentary explains that this means that he asks for tools, men and material.[116] In Saṅghādisesa seven which tackles a *vihāra* with an owner, the question of finances is not touched upon. So, the difference seems to be that in the case of an ownerless *kuṭi* the monk who builds it must find materials, tools, and workers himself, whereas in the case of an owned *vihāra* the owner is responsible for providing them. The donors, who are also the owners, are designated as *vihārasvāmin* in inscriptions since the second century CE,[117] as well as in the monastic law code of the Mūlasarvāstivādins,[118] but not yet in the Pāli canon. In the commentarial layers of the Theravādins they are called *vihārasāmi*, *vihārasāmika*, or *āvāsasāmika*.[119] Taken all together, the references looked at so far show that *vihāra* in the canonical scriptures refers to a building used mainly for dwelling. Its usage for specific tasks like storing of cloth or food, etc., is only just beginning, as a few references in the *Vinaya* indicate. *Vihāra* does not yet stand for a permanent monastic compound. The *vihāras* are given to individuals as well as to the Saṅgha, and the donors have obligations to care for the *vihāras* and for those who live in them.

115 Vin III 156.$_{15-20}$; the old commentary in the Vinaya (Vin III 156.$_{24-25}$) defines *sassāmika* "having an owner", as a certain owner (*añño koci sāmiko*), be it a woman (*itthi*), a man (*purisa*), a house resident (*gahaṭṭha*) or someone who had gone forth (*pabbajita*), which also includes Buddhist monks.

116 Vin III 149.$_{19-22}$: *saṃyācikāya nāma sayaṃ yācitvā purisam pi purisatthakaraṃ pi goṇaṃ pi sakaṭaṃ pi vāsiṃ pi pharasuṃ pi kuthāriṃ pi kuddālaṃ pi nikhādanaṃ pi ... pa ... tiṇaṃ pi mattikaṃ pi.* "By begging means oneself begging for a man, for a servant, for an ox, for a wagon, for a knife, for a hatchet, for an axe, for a spade, for a chisel ... for *tiṇa*-grass, for clay" (based on BD I 254). For more details in the commentary of the *Aṭṭhakathā* layer, see NORMAN et al. 2018: 144.

117 ALBERY 2020: 406, notes seven inscriptions where a *vihārasvāmin* is mentioned.

118 See SCHOPEN 1996b: 83–88 [= 2004a: 220–223].

119 Sp IV 777.$_{18}$: *yena vihāro kārito* (Kkh-nṭ *kārāpito*) *so vihārasāmiko*. For a detailed discussion of the references in the *Aṭṭhakathā* layer, see KIEFFER-PÜLZ 2022: 191–196.

2.1.5 *Vihāra* as a building type

Five types of shelters (*leṇa*, v.l. of the Siamese edition *senāsana*) are allowed to the monks (Vin II 146.$_{28-29}$), a *vihāra*, an *aḍḍhayoga*,[120] a palace (*pāsāda*),[121] a *hammiya*,[122] (and) a cave (*guhā*).[123] The same five abodes are listed as an extra acquisition (*atirekalābha*) for monks after their ordination, and after the basic expectancies have been told, which in the case of habitation consisted in lodging at the foot of a tree (*rukkhamūlasenāsana*),[124] at least during the eight

120 *aḍḍhayoga*. This type of building is mentioned only a few times in the canon, namely in the *Vinaya*, the *Niddesa* and once in the *Paṭisambhidāmagga*. In the *Vinaya* it is nearly exclusively mentioned in enumerations of the above named five shelters (Vin I 58.$_{19-20}$ = 96.$_{9}$; 107.$_{7}$; 139.$_{33}$; 140.$_{9,18}$; 141.$_{12}$; 239.$_{9}$; 284.$_{19}$; II 146.$_{29}$; 177.$_{33}$). In only one passage in the *Cullavagga*, stating for how long restoration work (*navakamma*) on different building types may be assigned to a bhikkhu, a little more can be learned concerning an *aḍḍhayoga*. The *aḍḍhayoga* is larger than a small *vihāra*, and smaller than a large *vihāra*, since *navakamma* in the case of an *aḍḍhayoga* may be assigned to a bhikkhu for six to eight years (Vin II 172.$_{26-30}$; 179.$_{5}$). In the *Suttapiṭaka* the word is mentioned in a list of the same five shelters as in the *Vinaya* in the explanation of "lodging" (*sayana* = *senāsana*) or a place where to lie down, or of "house" (*āgāra*, Nidd I 377.$_{6-7}$ = 467.$_{3-4}$ = 481.$_{18}$; 493.$_{11-12}$; Paṭis I 176.$_{23-24}$). Otherwise it is mentioned in an enumeration of places within a *saṅghārāma* that, in addition to the list of the five shelters we have seen in the *Vinaya*, contains some more places (*pariveṇa, vihāra, aḍḍhayoga, pāsāda, hammiya, guhā, leṇa, kuṭi, kūṭāgāra, aṭṭa, māḷa, uddaṇḍa, upaṭṭhānasāla, maṇḍalamāḷa, rukkhamūla*, Nidd I 226.$_{21}$ = 463.$_{17ff.}$; 374.$_{8-17}$ = Nidd II B^{e} 286), beginning with *vihāra* (Nidd I 67.$_{11ff.}$ = 476.$_{21ff.}$ = Nidd II B^{e} 247, 297). Thus, all in all the *aḍḍhayoga* seems to not really have played a role in the Buddhist monastic context and is simply listed as one of the architecturally present building types of the day.

121 *pāsāda*; a building type also common in non-monastic architecture as a building owned by kings, or rich citizens (GRÄFE 1974: 53), and in this function comes up several times in the canon. In the *Vinaya* the *pāsāda* is mentioned in the same stereotype lists as the other types of buildings (see n. 120). Twice it is mentioned in the canon that a donor wants to build a *pāsāda* for the Saṅgha, once it is the King Bimbisāra and once Visākhā, Migāra's mother: Vin II 154.$_{17-20}$: ... *rājā Māgadho Seniyo Bimbisāro saṃghassa atthāya sudhāmattikālepanaṃ pāsādaṃ kārāpetukāmo hoti*. "King Seniya Bimbisāra of Magadha wanted to have a *pāsāda* with a smearing of plaster and clay built." Vin II 169.$_{24-26}$: *Visākhā Migāramātā saṃghassa atthāya sālindaṃ pāsādaṃ kārāpetukāmā hoti hatthinakhakaṃ*. "Visākhā, Migāra's mother, wanted to have a *pāsāda* with a veranda of the 'elephant-nail' type built for an/the Order" (based on BD V 237). The *pāsāda* is mentioned much more often than *aḍḍhayoga* and *hammiya*.

122 A building similar to a *pāsāda*, but with a flat roof. Only rarely used in the *Vinaya* and *Suttapiṭaka*, and mostly in the same lists as *aḍḍhayoga*.

123 *guhā* is only rarely used in the *Vinaya*, where it appears in the list of the five shelters (Vin I 58.$_{20}$ = 96.$_{9}$; 107.$_{7}$; 139.$_{34}$; 140.$_{9,18}$; 141.$_{12}$ [abbreviated]), and in three non-offence clauses of rules that deal with a *vihāra*, namely of Sgh 6–7 (Vin III 155.$_{21}$; 157.[abbreviated]) and Pāc 17 (Vin IV 48.$_{20-21}$).

124 Vin I 96.$_{7-9}$. See also VON HINÜBER 2006: 16 [= 2009: II 882].

months (Vin III 172.$_{3-4}$ = II 197.$_{25-26}$) outside the rainy season.[125] The number of references for these five shelters in the canon show that *vihāra* is the main building in a Buddhist monastic context, followed, at a great distance, by the *pāsāda*. The other three, *aḍḍhayoga, hammiya,* and *guhā*, are rarely mentioned, and then almost always in stereotypical phrases, which suggests that they had no major practical relevance. All five shelters can be used in a variety of functions: as dwellings for monks, as a storage place for clothes (*bhaṇḍāgāra*, Vin I 284.$_{18-20}$), as a place where to keep allowable things of the Saṅgha (*kappiyabhūmi*, Vin I 239.$_{7-10}$), and as a house for carrying out the observance (*uposatha*), that is, as an *uposathāgāra* (Vin I 107.$_{5-7}$). These functions are only mentioned in the *Vinayapiṭaka*, not in the *Suttapiṭaka*.[126] Apart from their use as dwellings, all other functions need to be assigned to the buildings by a local Saṅgha in a legal act (*kamma*) of the *ñattidutiya*-type (consisting of a motion and one proclamation), as the examples of the *bhaṇḍāgāra*, the *kappiyabhūmi*, and the *uposathāgāra* show.[127] If a *vihāra* does not serve as a dwelling, but has one of the above mentioned functions, it normally is not referred to as *vihāra*, but by the word which indicates its function, i.e. as *bhaṇḍāgāra, kappiyabhūmī,* and *uposathāgāra*. From this it can be concluded that most references to *vihāra* refer to buildings used as dwellings.

2.1.6 The construction of a vihāra

A *vihāra* was built on a piling made of bricks, stones, or wood, so that water could not flood in (Vin II 152.$_{5-9}$); a staircase of the same three materials with a balustrade could be added to allow access (Vin II 152.$_{10-12}$). Likewise, a veranda (*āḷinda, paghana*)[128] could be added to its front. It was thatched with grass (*tiṇa*, Vin II 148.$_{24}$; 152.$_{27-28}$) and leaves (*paṇṇa*, Vin IV 48.$_{12-13}$) or in the case of more solid constructions with bricks or stone tiles (*sīla*). It had a door (Vin II 148.$_{10}$), was protected by a canopy (*vitāna*, Vin II 152.$_{31-32}$), and the windows (Vin II 148.$_{28-30}$) had shutters.[129] The walls of a *vihāra* may have been

125 Vin I 152.$_{11ff.}$ prohibits spending the rains in a hollow tree (*rukkhasusīra*), in the forks of a tree (*rukkhaviṭabhi*), in the open air (*ajjhokāsa*), etc., which also implies the foot of a tree.

126 Such assignments only are useful when a Saṅgha is settled more permanently in a specific place. Nevertheless, a *bhaṇḍāgārika*, i.e. the person responsible for the *bhaṇḍāgāra*, is mentioned in a stereotype list there (A III 274.$_{30-31}$).

127 *Bhaṇḍāgāra* (Vin I 284.$_{15-29}$); *kappiyabhūmi* (Vin I 239.$_{10-19}$); *uposathāgāra* (Vin I 107.$_{7-17}$).

128 Vin II 153.$_{1-3}$. At least in front of the entrance there is a veranda (*ālinda*) which one needs to cross to reach the door (Vin I 248.$_{5}$).

129 This is reported for a large dwelling place (*mahallaka vihāra*) in the *Pātimokkha* (Pāc 19, Vin IV 47.$_{23}$).

wattle and daub walls,[130] or been made from stone, and could be smeared inside or outside or both (Vin III 156.$_{22}$).[131]

Two types of *vihāra* are mentioned in the monastic law code: (1) a small *vihāra* (*khuddaka vihāra*) appearing exclusively in the *Cullavagga*, and (2) a large *vihāra* named *mahallaka vihāra* dealt with in the *Pātimokkha*. A large *vihāra* named *mahāvihāra* is further mentioned in the introductory story to Pācittiya 17,[132] in the *Cullavagga* and the youngest part of the *Vinaya*, the *Parivāra*. In the *Suttapiṭaka* we find only three references of a *mahāvihāra*,[133] but none of a *mahallaka vihāra* or a *khuddaka vihāra*.

2.1.6.1 A small vihāra (khuddaka vihāra)

The small *vihāra* is intended as a dwelling place for one or two monks and may consist of a single room with or without a cell (*gabbha*).[134] If a cell was built, it had to be placed at one end, since otherwise there would not have been access (*upacāra*, Vin II 120.$_{23}$) to the remaining part of the room.[135] Repairs of dilapidated buildings and the erection of new buildings fall under the word *navakamma*, which is used in this sense only a few times in the younger parts of the *Suttapiṭaka*,[136] and in the *Vinayapiṭaka* in younger textual strata of the *Suttavibhaṅga* as well as seventy-seven times in the *Cullavagga*.[137] To care for *navakamma* became the task of a monk or nun who were installed in the position of a *navakammika* by a local community in a legal act (Vin II 160.$_{9-21}$).[138] They are asked for by lay people when these want to build *vihāras* for the

130 See above, n. 65.

131 For more details, see GRÄFE 1974: 50–53.

132 The introductory stories to the *Pātimokkha* rules are younger than the rules themselves, see VON HINÜBER 1996: § 23.

133 Ja IV 310.$_{13}$ [v. 87]; Vv 62.$_{34}$ [v. 731]; Vv 63.$_{23}$ [v. 740].

134 Two ordained monks, of which one is a *nāga*, live in one *vihāra* (Vin I 87.$_{8-15}$). When the *nāga* fell asleep, he filled the entire room. His companion monk who wanted to enter, saw that the *vihāra* was filled by the *nāga*. Thus, here the *vihāra* inhabited by two persons consisted of a single room without a cell.

135 Vin II 152.$_{19-23}$: *tena kho pana samayena bhikkhū khuddake vihāre majjhe gabbhaṃ karonti. upacāro na hoti. ... anujānāmi, ... khuddake vihāre ekam antaṃ gabbhaṃ kātuṃ, mahallake majjhe ti.* “At that time monks built a cell in a small *vihāra* in the middle; there was no access. ... I allow to make one end in a small *vihāra* to a cell, in a large [*vihāra*] in the middle.”

136 Ap I 251.$_{19,20}$; II 513.$_{21}$; Nidd I 372.$_{23}$; 388.$_{27}$; II B^{e} 258; 334.

137 Vin III 81.$_{23,28,32,36}$; 82.$_{4}$; 85.$_{31}$ (*Vinītavatthu* of Pār 3; one of the youngest textual strata); IV 32.$_{24}$; 34.$_{3}$; 48.$_{28}$ 118.$_{15}$ (introductory stories of Pāc 10, 11, 20, 57). The references in the *Cullavagga* are not listed but can easily be found via the CSCD. *Navakamma* otherwise appears only three times in the older parts of the *Suttapiṭaka* where it, however, means “new *kamma* [created by present acts]” (S IV 132.$_{20,22}$; 133.$_{11}$).

138 For what did belong and not belong to their tasks, see Vin II 172.$_{1}$–173.$_{3}$ (BD V 241–244).

Saṅgha (Vin IV 207.$_8$). The term *navakammika* in this meaning presupposes a local community that cares for a monastery. Therefore, it is telling that the term *navakammika* does not appear in this sense in the *Suttapiṭaka*, where it is used only for a builder who is not a monastic.[139] And in the *Vinaya* it appears only four times, twice in younger textual strata of the *Suttavibhaṅga*,[140] and twice in the *Cullavagga* (Vin II 15.$_{30}$; 160.$_{10}$). So, this office within the administration of the Saṅgha obviously was not yet long and well established at the time of the final redaction of the Pāli *Tipiṭaka.*

It was not allowed to assign the *navakamma* of two *vihāras* to a single monk (Vin II 172.$_{35-36}$). He could become responsible for single buildings, and for a limited time period which depended on the type respectively size of the building.[141] In the case of a small *vihāra* (*khuddaka vihāra*) the supervision may last five to six years at most.[142] In the *Aṭṭhakathā* layer this is justified with the measures of such a small *vihāra* which are given as consisting in four, five or six cubits (*hattha* = ca. 40 cm),[143] that is in 1.6 to 2.4 meters probably for the length of one side of a *khuddaka vihāra*, which then corresponded to between 2.6 and 5.8 square meters. Imagining two monks to stay in such a small *vihāra*, may seem difficult compared to present day measures, but in connection with the distribution of sleeping places we learn that a monk has the right for a sleeping place (*seyya*) to which is added an access space (*upacāra*).[144] The latter allows him to access his bed, without disturbing another monk. If we look at the measurements of the older rock-cut caves, as, for example cave 15A in Ajanta,[145] we see that this cave measures 2.5 by 2.4 meters which corresponds to 5 square meters. The cave is provided with two stone beds, each three quarters of a meter wide, and with a space in between the two beds of almost one meter (0.94). Thus, this cave, intended

139 See the *navakammika* Bharadvāja, a brahmin living in Kosala, who becomes a lay follower of the Buddha (S I 179.$_{26,28,35}$; 189.$_9$).

140 Vin IV 211.$_{8,16}$ (Introductory story of Pār 1 for nuns).

141 Similarly, in inscriptions *navakammikas* are mentioned who were responsible for a *vedikā*, for a *stūpa* or for the fire house (see KIEFFER-PÜLZ 2010: 78). The length of time a monk could function as a *navakammika* for a certain building was restricted, probably to avoid corruption, since this job possibly was related to the responsibility for and administration of the income of funds for *navakamma* activities.

142 Vin II 172.$_{24-27}$: *khuddake vihāre kammam oḷoketvā chappañcavassikaṃ navakammaṃ dātuṃ.*

143 Sp VI 1246.$_{3-6}$: ***khuddake vihāre kammaṃ oloketvā chappañcavassikan*** *ti kammaṃ oloketvā catuhatthavihāre catuvassikaṃ, pañcahatthe pañcavassikaṃ, chahatthe chavassikaṃ dātabbaṃ.*

144 Vin IV 43.$_{16-19}$. The measure of the access space is, however, only given in the commentary. For details, see KIEFFER-PÜLZ 2013: II 1320 and n. 3.

145 MITRA 1971: 33 Fig. 4 (Ajanta cave 15A, dated to the 2nd century BCE by Mitra).

for two monastics, in size approximately would equal the small *vihāra* of the Pāli monastic law code.

2.1.6.2 A large vihāra (mahallaka vihāra, mahāvihāra)

As stated, there are two expressions for a large *vihāra*, the older expression *mahallaka vihāra*[146] and the younger *mahāvihāra*. The *mahallaka vihāra* is the subject of two *Pātimokkha* rules, the first being Saṅghādisesa seven concerning the erection of a *mahallaka vihāra* by a monk, for his own usage.[147] It is characterized as having an owner.[148] Thus, the *mahallaka vihāra* which a monk had built for himself, obviously is a building someone else pays for (see above, 2.1.4), who consequently is the donor and therefore the owner of the building. If in such a *mahallaka vihāra* a cell was to be built, it could be placed in the middle (Vin II 152.$_{22-23}$).

The second *Pātimokkha* rule mentioning a *mahallaka vihāra* is Pācittiya 19, which regulates where a monk has to stand when plastering the walls around the door and the windows of a *vihāra* he is going to build, and how often he may plaster these areas. In the old word commentary to this rule *mahallaka* too is defined as a *vihāra* with an owner.[149] Nevertheless, even if a monk transgresses that rule, there is no offence according to the non-offence clause, if he does so with his own money (*attano dhanena*).[150]

Construction and repair work (*navakamma*) of a large *vihāra* (*mahallaka vihāra*) and a *pāsāda* may be given to a monk for at most ten to twelve years.[151] This shows that a *mahallaka vihāra* is equated with a *pāsāda* concerning its size,

146 *Mahallaka* from a linguistic point of view is the older form (VON HINÜBER 1995b: 193 and n. 32 [= 2009: I 487]). The corresponding sentence stands in the oldest stratum of the monastic law code, in the *Pātimokkha*, Pāc 19. In the *Pātimokkhas* of other Buddhist schools too *mahallaka* is used in the corresponding rule, except for the Mūlasarvāstivādins who use *mahāvihāra* instead. Both types of *vihāras* are also discussed by ROTH 1997: 44–45.

147 Vin III 156.$_{15-20}$. Like Sgh 6 the main point here is that the place where a *vihāra* shall be built needs to fulfill certain conditions and to be assigned for the construction of the *vihāra* by other monks.

148 Vin III 156.$_{21}$: *mahallako nāma vihāro sassāmiko vuccati*. Vin III 156.$_{24-25}$: ***sassāmikan*** *ti añño koci sāmiko hoti itthi vā puriso vā gahaṭṭho vā pabbajito vā*.

149 Vin IV 47.$_{27}$. In this case the introductory story and the old word commentary only speak of a *vihāra*. Concerning this rule, the introductory story and the rule do not go together which led to several misunderstandings in the translation of the rule itself (see NORMAN et al. 2018: 326 n. 1).

150 Vin IV 48.$_{21}$.

151 Vin II 172.$_{28-30}$: *mahallake vihāre pāsāde vā kammam oloketvā dasadvādasavassikaṃ navakammaṃ dātuṃ*. It certainly is not to be assumed that the construction work lasts ten to twelve years, but rather that a monk in the position of *navakammika* is responsible for such a period at most.

and that the length of being allowed to act as a *navakammika* is dependent on this size. The measures given for the *mahallaka vihāra* in the *Aṭṭhakathā* layer are ten by twelve *hattha*, that is 4 x 4.8 meters. If we assume that this refers to the length of one side of the building, we will have a building of between 16 and 23 square meters.

Larger than this *mahallaka vihāra*, is the *mahāvihāra* described in different contexts in younger strata of the monastic law code.[152] Here a group of seventeen monks repairs a *mahāvihāra* in a rains residence (*vassāvāsa*), because they want to spend the rains in it. The group of six bad monks who wants that same *vihāra* decides to wait till the seventeen have finished the renovation, and then tell them to leave, since this *vihāra* had been obtained by them. The seventeen ask whether that *vihāra* does not belong to the Saṅgha, which the six monks affirmed. Nevertheless, they insist that it is obtained by them. Obviously, there is no local Saṅgha staying in this *vihāra* which could have been asked. The seventeen monks then suggest that the *vihāra* is big (*mahallaka*) and should allow the group of seventeen and the group of six to spend the rains there together. The six monks reject this offer.

The story shows four things: first, the *vihāra* belongs to the Saṅgha; second, obviously it is not inhabited permanently by other monks; third, it could be used theoretically by different monks' groups, which, therefore, obviously were not yet affiliated with settled monasteries; and fourth, it is large enough for at least 23 monks (17 + 6). According to the smallest unit by which lodgings are assigned, that is, by a bed with an access space, which roughly would have covered 2.7 square meters, a *vihāra* for 23 monks would at a minimum have had 62 square meters for sleeping places.[153] If two monks shared one cell this would correspond to a monastery with four cells each on three sides, or three each on four sides. This is comparable to some of the larger monasteries in the rock cut monasteries in the Western Deccan.

---

152 In the introductory story to Pācittiya 17, and in the *Cullavagga* (Vin IV 44.$_{1ff.}$ = Vin II 166.$_{8ff.}$). One other reference in the *Cullavagga* refers to a great dwelling-place (*mahāvihāra*) that belonged to an order (*saṅghika*) and fell into decay (Vin II 174.$_{15}$).

153 This would roughly correspond to the early monasteries at Takt-i-bahi or Saidu Sharif (see ALBERY 2020: 514 and n. 4). The ground measures given by Shaw (2011: 120) for her platform monasteries at Mawasa, which she dates to the second to first centuries BCE, are six to ten times this size (SC662: 26 x 14 m = 364 square meter; SC659: 30 x 17 m = 510 square meter).

2.1.7 *Inheritance of a vihāra*

A *vihāra* and its building site as well as other real estate and further goods (*ārāma, ārāmavatthu; vihāra, vihāravatthu,*[154] etc.) belong to the category of so-called "heavy" or "valuable goods" (*garubhaṇḍa*) according to three references in younger parts of the *Vinaya.*[155] In the *Suttapiṭaka* the terms *ārāmavatthu* and *vihāravatthu* each only appear twice in the late *Mahāniddesa.* When such valuable goods belong to the Saṅgha they are indivisible (*avebhaṅgika/°iya*) and not to be given away (*avissajjika/°iya*).[156] In connection with the rules for the distribution of the heritage of a deceased monk it is regulated in the *Vinaya* that the "light" or "less valuable goods" (*lahubhaṇḍa*) of a deceased monk may be distributed among the Saṅgha that is present (*sammukhībhūtasaṅgha*). This is interesting insofar as the monks who may receive portions of this inheritance are not defined by their affiliation with the monastery of the deceased, but simply by their presence at the time of the distribution of his heritage. Concerning the valuable goods that might have been among the deceased monk's possessions, they are not allowed to be distributed, but come into the possession of the Saṅgha of the four quarters present and to come.[157] This

---

154 The term *ārāmavatthu* appears in the *Suttapiṭaka* only once, in the younger *Mahāniddesa* in the definition of *vatthu* (Nidd I 11.$_4$; 248.$_5$); for the rest it is used in the *Vinayapiṭaka* eleven times; once in a supplementary text portion (Vin III 50.$_{26}$) added later to the second Pārājika rule (KIEFFER-PÜLZ 2017: 5–8); once in the introductory story to the fourth Pārājika (Vin III 90.$_{13}$); seven times in stereotype lists of buildings or building-sites made by lay followers, etc., for a Saṅgha, etc., in the *Mahāvagga* (Vin I 140.$_{22,35}$; 142.$_{2-3}$ [most passages are abbreviated]) where grounds for interrupting the rains retreat for at most seven days are listed; and twice in the *Cullavagga* (Vin II 170.$_{26}$; 171.$_{36}$ [abbreviated]) when the objects that are indivisible and not to be given away are defined. Similarly it is with the term *vihāravatthu* that is also twice used in the same portion of the *Mahāniddesa* (Nidd I 11.$_5$; 248.$_6$); in the same sections of the *Vinaya* (Vin II 170.$_{29}$; 171.$_{36}$ [abbreviated]; III 50.$_{26}$; 90.$_{13}$); and in addition in the *vinītavatthu* section of Pār 3 (Vin III 80.$_{38}$; 81.$_5$) as well as in the introductory story, the word commentary and the casuistry to Sgh 7 (Vin III 155.$_{29,30}$; 156.$_{28,31,37}$ [many times, abbreviated].

155 In the *Vinaya* this term is used only three times. In addition to the regulation concerning the handling of the *garu-* and *lahubhaṇḍa* in the *Mahāvagga* (Vin I 305.$_{8.10-13}$, see n. 157), it is used in the introductory story to the fourth Pārājika (Vin III 90.$_{12}$) and in the *Parivāra* with respect to the rule of theft (Vin V 217.$_8$).

156 Vin II 170.$_{23-35}$. In that context the term *garubhaṇḍa* is not used, but the objects are enumerated.

157 Vin I 305.$_{8.10-13}$: *anujānāmi ... yaṃ tattha lahubhaṇḍaṃ lahuparikkhāraṃ taṃ sammukhībhūtena saṅghena bhājetuṃ, yaṃ tattha garubhaṇḍaṃ garuparikkhāraṃ taṃ āgatānāgatassa cātuddisassa saṅghassa avissajjikaṃ avebhaṅgikan ti.* "I allow that the order that is present divides whatever light goods, light requisites are there; whatever heavy goods, heavy requisites are there, that belong to the Order of the four quarters present and to come; they are not to be disposed of, not to be divided up."

implies that a monk could have owned real estate, plots of land, and so on.[158] The fact that his "valuable goods" were given to the Buddhist Saṅgha of the four quarters present and to come, shows that the deceased monk's heritage goes to the Buddhist Saṅgha as a whole. Thus, the deceased was obviously not considered to be affiliated with a specific monastery which could have inherited his valuable goods.

2.1.8 Vihāra as a recipient of donations

In the canonical texts we do not have a single reference for donations to *vihāras* as they exist in inscriptions since the first century CE (see above, p. 3). As recipients of donations individuals, the Saṅgha, and, in a younger stratum of the *Suttavibhaṅga*, a *cetiya* are mentioned.[159] This changes in the commentarial literature, where *vihāras* developed into recipients of donations that enabled Saṅghas to accept even objects not allowable for monastics or the Saṅgha.[160]

2.2 Ārāma

Ārāma[161] literally means "a place of pleasure; a pleasure grove"[162] and is used as a term for parks and pleasure grounds in the vicinity of settlements, where people went to amuse themselves and to enjoy the scenery.[163] In this sense

158 See also above, n. 81.

159 Vin III 266.$_{15-18}$ = IV 156.$_{32-35}$: *saṅghassa pariṇataṃ aññasaṅghassa vā cetiyassa vā pariṇāmeti, āpatti dukkaṭassa, cetiyassa pariṇataṃ aññacetiyassa vā saṅghassa vā puggalassa vā pariṇāmeti, āpatti dukkaṭassa.* "If one apportions [something] apportioned to a Saṅgha to another Saṅgha or to a shrine, there is an offence of wrong-doing. If one apportions [something] apportioned to a shrine to another shrine or a Saṅgha or an individual, there is an offence of wrong-doing." (See for a discussion KIEFFER-PÜLZ 2024: 31 and n. 25). Though it is not the donation which stands in the foreground here, it clearly shows that a shrine could be the recipient of something given.

160 See below, 3.1.

161 For the earliest epigraphical references, see ALBERY 2020: 105 n. 5; 158; ALI 2003: 222 n. 4; more often the term *saṅghārāma* seems to be used in the Northwest, see the references in ALBERY 2020: 223, 501 and n. 4, 611n1; see also Fig. 4.2 (12, 31); Fig. 12.1 (2, 3, 8); Fig 14.1 (1, 7).

162 CPD s.v. ^{2}*ārāma*; DoP s.v. *ārāma*; PED s.v. *ārāma*; ROTH 1997: 6–14 discusses a variety of references also from Sanskrit literature; UPĀSAK 2001: 30–31 s.v. *ārāma*: mentions first "a pleasure-garden or a private pleasure-park or a villa" in general, second the *ārāmas* or *uyyānas* given to the Saṅgha, third *ārāmas* as orchards. His statement that "these *Ārāmas* were changed into *Vihāras* or residential buildings for the Buddhist Order", is not correct. Likewise, the statement "[g]enerally speaking the entire compound of a *Vihāra* is known as *Ārāma*", is not correct concerning the canonical references.

163 Vin IV 298.$_{24-25}$: *ārāmo nāma yattha katthaci manussānaṃ kīḷituṃ ramituṃ kataṃ hoti.* (The same definition is given for an *uyyāna*, Vin IV 298:$_{25-26}$). Discussed also by ROTH 1997:

ārāma is used in the monastic law code when nuns are prohibited to go to see a king's house or a picture gallery or an *ārāma* or a garden (*uyyāna*) or a lotus pond (Vin IV 298.$_{18ff.}$), because these are places where the king and the people amuse themselves. Like a garden (*uyyāna*), an *ārāma* in the first place is a worldly space that is artificially created (*karoti*)[164] or as Pieruccini states a "structured" area.[165] Sometimes *uyyāna* ("garden") and *ārāma* are used for the same plots of land, especially when an *uyyāna* is given to the Saṅgha and thereby becomes an *ārāma* (see below). The vocabulary used when the donors made over *uyyānas/ārāmas* to the Saṅgha shows that such donations are legal contracts. When King Seniya Bimbisāra of Magadha intended to give the bamboo grove (Veḷuvana), designated as a garden (*uyyāna*), to the community of monks with the Buddha at its head, he took a golden ceremonial vessel (*bhiṅkāra*) and poured water (into the hand) of the Blessed One[166] with the words: "I give this Bamboo Grove, this garden (*uyyāna*), to the Order of monks with the Awakened One at its head." And the Buddha accepted the gift, which is reported as, "He accepted the *ārāma*".[167] Based on this, *ārāmas* were subsequently generally allowed.[168] Thus, the Buddha was offered an *uyyāna* and he accepted an *ārāma*. This could be interpreted to mean that *uyyāna* and *ārāma* are synonyms, but it also could mean that by its donation to the Saṅgha an *uyyāna* became an *ārāma*.[169] A very similar description we have for the donation of the Jetavana by the merchant Anāthapiṇḍika. The latter asked Prince Jeta for his garden (*uyyāna*) which he considered perfect as a dwelling place for the Saṅgha, saying "give me [your] garden to make [it] an *ārāma*" (*dehi me ...*

9–10. For a comparison of the *ārāma* as a pleasure ground and its usage for a monastery, see ALI 2003 and SCHOPEN 2006a.

164 The merchant Anāthapiṇḍika when on his way from Rājagaha to Sāvatthi asked the people on his way to build *ārāmas* (*ārāme ... karotha*), to establish *vihāras* (*vihāre patiṭṭhāpetha*) and to provide gifts (*dānāni paṭṭhapetha*), so that the Buddha, when on his way to Sāvatthi to spend the rains, would be able to pause there (Vin II 158.$_{20-21}$).

165 PIERUCCINI 2018: 63.

166 The pouring of water into the hand of the recipient, also called "donation water", is a rite documenting the legally binding act of the transfer of the *uyyāna* to the Buddhist Saṅgha. Another example is given in Dhp-a II 74.$_{11-12,14-15}$ (below, n. 201). See also KAJIHARA 2017: 18–21. For *dakkhiṇodaka*, see KIEFFER-PÜLZ 2013: II 1052, n. 14; BOLLÉE 2015: 127 with n. 412. Pouring of water over or in the recipient's hand is a general Indian custom in connection with donations, and not restricted to Buddhists (KAJIHARA 2017).

167 Vin I 39.$_{14-18}$: *atha kho rājā Māgadho Seniyo Bimbisāro sovaṇṇamayaṃ bhiṅkāraṃ gahetvā bhagavato onojesi 'etāhaṃ bhante Veḷuvanaṃ uyyānaṃ buddhapamukkhassa bhikkhusaṅghassa dammī' ti. paṭiggahesi Bhagavā ārāmaṃ.* Also quoted and translated by ROTH 1997: 1–2.

168 Vin I 39.$_{22}$: *anujānāmi bhikkhave ārāman ti.*

169 On this switch of the vocabulary, see also PIERUCCINI 2018: 65 with n. 11.

uyyānaṃ ārāmaṃ kātun ti, Vin II 158.$_{34-35}$).[170] But there are also cases where the donor directly gave an *ārāma*, like the courtesan Ambapālī.[171]

Only in a few cases is the donation of an *ārāma* to the Buddhist Saṅgha reported in the texts. These are the famous *ārāmas* given by royals, rich merchants, courtesans, etc.[172] They may be named after their donors[173] as, for instance, the *ārāma* of Anāthapiṇḍika,[174] the Ghositārāma,[175] the Kassapakārāma,[176] or the *ārāma* of queen Mallikā in Sāvatthi (D I 178.$_{5}$; M II 22.$_{29}$.), etc.[177]

The word *ārāma* is further used in the sense of "orchard" in the monastic law code, and differentiated into a fruit and a flower orchard,[178] that may belong to one or several families,[179] and may or may not have been fenced in.[180]

Since *ārāmas* were given to the Saṅgha for the dwelling of the Buddhist mendicants, *ārāma* also is used *pars pro toto* for the place where the Buddhist monks' community resides.[181] This does not, however, mean that the *ārāmas*

---

170 Cf. Dhp-a II 74.$_{11-12,14-15}$, below, n. 201. See also ROTH 1997: 41–42 who hints at the relief from Barhut where the donation of the Jetavana is documented. Roth mentions it as Jetavana Vihāra, an expression not contained in the canon, but only from the *Aṭṭhakathā* layer onwards.

171 D II 98.$_{3-5}$ ≠ Vin I 233.$_{5-7}$: *imāhaṃ bhante ārāmaṃ* (Vin *Ambapālivanaṃ*) *Buddhapamukhassa bhikkhusaṅghassa dammī ti. paṭiggahesi Bhagavā ārāmaṃ*. The wording is similar to that of the donation of King Seniya Bimbisāra.

172 See also PIERUCCINI 2018: 65.

173 For inscriptions, see ALBERY 2020: 511, see above n. 7.

174 *Anāthapiṇḍikassa ārāma*, D I 178.$_{3}$; 204.$_{3}$; II 1.$_{4}$; M I 146.$_{18,20-21,24}$; II 22.$_{27}$; III 201.$_{2}$; S III 235.$_{8,17}$; V 161.$_{27-28}$; Ud 7.$_{15}$; 58.$_{34}$; Vin I 158.$_{15}$; 196.$_{20}$; 253.$_{15}$; II 11.$_{25-26}$; 17.$_{35-36}$; III 181.$_{30-31}$.

175 The Ghositārāma is built by the merchant Ghosita in Kosambī, D I 157.$_{9}$; 159.$_{3}$; Vin II 292.$_{5}$; etc.

176 The Kassapakārāma (S III 124.$_{17-18}$) according to the commentary (Spk II 315.$_{15}$) is an *ārāma* made by the merchant Kassapa.

177 The mango *ārāma* belonging to king Seniya Bimbisāra of Māgadha (Vin II 108.$_{31-32}$). King Bimbisāra's Veḷuvana *uyyāna* (Vin I 39.$_{14-18}$, above n. 167) is mentioned as Veḷuvanārāma in commentarial literature (Dhp-a I 88.$_{13}$; Bv-a 21.$_{20,25}$; etc.).

178 A monk goes to a flower orchard (*pupphārāma*) to steal flowers (Vin III 61.$_{17,20}$); in an additional section of the rule on theft, where various spaces are defined, *ārāma* is defined as flower orchard or fruit orchard (*ārāmo nāma pupphārāmo phalārāmo*, Vin III 48.$_{36}$).

179 Vin III 201.$_{36-38}$: *ekakulassa ārāmo hoti parikkhitto ca ... aparikkhitto hoti. nānākulassa ārāmo hoti parikkhitto ca ... aparikkhitto hoti.*

180 See Vin II 154.$_{10-17}$ where for an unfenced *ārāma* (*ārāmo aparikkhitto*) three types of hedges were allowed (consisting of bamboo, thorns, or a ditch).

181 For instance, Vin II 158.$_{34-35}$; see also Vin I 76.$_{29}$, mentioning someone who goes to an *ārāma*, where he then is ordained as a novice; Vin I 84.$_{20,22}$ where novices are prohibited entrance into the *ārāma* as a penance for their misbehaviour. See also an *ārāma* mentioned as a place to which the Buddha, monks and lay people are heading (*ārāmagata*,

were immediately filled with buildings that constitute complex monastic compounds, even though in some cases an enumeration of the many buildings erected in such *ārāmas* follows, as in the case of Anāthapiṇḍika's *ārāma*. He had a variety of buildings built that constitute such a complex monastic compound. Listed are *vihāras* ("residential buildings"), *pariveṇas*[182] ("cells"), *koṭṭhakas*[183] ("gate houses, store rooms"), *upaṭṭhānasālās*[184] ("assembly halls"), *aggisālās*[185] ("fire houses"), *kappiyakuṭis*[186] ("huts for allowable

M I 28.$_{34-35,37}$; 29.$_{1-2,8,10-12}$; 451.$_{2}$; 452.$_{5}$; II 139.$_{25}$; 140.$_{1-2,18-19}$; S V 273.$_{3}$; Nidd I 230.$_{13,15}$; 392.$_{19,25,27}$); or an *ārāma* with monks, which nuns are not allowed to enter without asking for permission (Vin IV 306.$_{24-25}$).

182 63 references in the *Vinaya*: 56 of which are in *Mahā-* and *Cullavagga*, six in the *Suttavibhaṅga*, and one in the *Parivāra*. Six *Suttapiṭaka* references: Vv 131.$_{35}$ = Pv 79 [omitted in E^{e}], Nidd I 374.$_{8-9}$; 500.$_{18}$: *pariveṇato pariveṇaṃ gacchati*; 424.$_{13}$: *pariveṇaṃ sajjanto*.

183 In the *Vinaya* a *koṭṭhaka* which can be at the entrance of an *ārāma* or of single buildings (GRÄFE 1974: 58–59) is allowed in the *Cullavagga* (Vin II 121.$_{5,6,8,11}$ = 142.$_{5,6,7}$ = 153.$_{29,31,34}$; 154.$_{13,14,15}$; 159.$_{4,16,17}$); and mentioned several times in stereotype lists in *Culla-* and *Mahāvagga* (Vin I 49.$_{4,5}$ = 52 = 61 [abbreviated]; 139.$_{35}$ = 140 = 141 = 142 [abbreviated] = II 210.$_{1,2}$ = 219.$_{27,28}$, etc.; I 291.$_{33}$). A passage in the introductory story of Sgh 8 has a parallel in the *Cullavagga* (Vin III 161.$_{11,24,27,32}$ = Vin II 77.$_{32}$; 78.$_{7,10,14}$). In the *Suttapiṭaka* there are seven references only in younger texts (Th 59.$_{6}$ = Ap 58.$_{30}$; 347.$_{16}$; 521.$_{9}$; 539.$_{17}$; J VI 66.$_{9}$; Nidd I 11.$_{4}$ (*koṭṭhavatthu*); 248.$_{5}$ (*koṭṭhakavatthu*).

184 Allowed Vin II 153.$_{8-9}$ for meals; used also for assemblies (Vin I 125.$_{16}$; 163.$_{27}$; III 70.$_{10-11}$ [introductory story of Pār 3]), and sometimes as a place for sleeping (Vin IV 15.$_{28-31}$ [introductory story to Pāc 5]; IV 42.$_{9}$; 45 [abbreviated; casuistries to Pāc 15, 17]), and in stereotype formulations (Vin I 49.$_{5,6}$; 52.$_{22}$ [abbreviated]; 61 [abbreviated]; 139.$_{35}$; 140–142 [abbreviated]; II 159.$_{18}$; 208.$_{5}$; 210.$_{3}$; 219.$_{28,29}$; 226.$_{6-7}$; 231 [abbreviated]). In the *Suttapiṭaka* there is the story about the monk Udena who tells a supporter to have an *upaṭṭhānasālā* built in Pāṭaliputta for the Saṅgha instead of a *vihāra* for him (M II 163.$_{13-28}$, see above, n. 78). Further, the *upaṭṭhānasāla* is mentioned in the *Suttapiṭaka* as the place to which the Buddha goes (M III 88.$_{25-26}$; 190.$_{3}$; S II 280.$_{5}$; A II 51.$_{14}$; 197.$_{1}$; III 195.$_{10}$; 298.$_{27}$; IV 359.$_{2}$; V 128.$_{22}$) where bhikkhus assemble (D II 76.$_{14-15,18,24}$; 119.$_{16}$; M III 88.$_{19}$; 89.$_{2}$; 118.$_{13}$; 119 [abbreviated]; S V 321.$_{14}$; A V 89.$_{2,10-11}$; 128.$_{11,26-27}$; Ud 11.$_{1,9}$); where Dhamma lectures are given (M III 190.$_{5,9}$; A II 51.$_{23}$; IV 358.$_{24}$); as a place for dwelling (Nidd I 226.$_{25}$; 463.$_{21}$; Nidd II B^{e} 274) ; as a place one leaves (Nidd I 67.$_{16}$; 476.$_{26}$; II B^{e} 297); or, one goes from *upaṭṭhānasālā* to *upaṭṭhānasālā* (Nidd I 374.$_{15}$; Nidd II B^{e} 286). Finally, a well-built *upaṭṭhānasālā* is given for the *bhikkhusaṅgha* (Ap I 317.$_{20,26}$).

185 Like a *vihāra* it could have a substructure, be entered by stairs and provided with a door, etc. (Vin II 154.$_{2-10}$). It is mentioned in the *Khandhaka* sections of the *Vinayapiṭaka*, but not in the *Suttapiṭaka*, except for in the late *Apadānas* (Ap I 39.$_{3}$; 215.$_{9,14}$). Alternatively, it is called *agyāgāra* (Vin I 25.$_{28}$) according to GRÄFE 1974: 56. For *agyāgāra* there are several references also in the large *Suttanikāyas* (see CPD s.v. *agyāgāra*).

186 Appears only in enumerations of buildings (Vin I 139.$_{36}$; 140.$_{20}$; 141–142 [abbreviated]; II 159.$_{18}$). Does not appear in the *Suttapiṭaka*. Possibly identical with "the space for allowable things" (*kappiyabhūmi*, Vin I 239.$_{8,13,15,16,18,20-21,27,3133,38}$; 240.$_{1-2}$), i.e. a place for storing food, which also does not appear in the *Suttapiṭaka*.

things), *vaccakuṭis*[187] ("toilets"), *caṅkamas*[188] ("ambulatories"), *caṅkamanasālās* ("halls for ambulatories"), *udapānas*[189] ("wells"), *udapānasālās*[190] ("well houses"), *jantāgharas*[191] ("heated rooms/bathrooms"?), *jantāgharasālās* ("heated room/bathroom halls"), *pokkharaṇīs* ("lotus ponds"), and *maṇḍapas*[192] ("pavilions").[193] Absent from this list are the storage house (*bhaṇḍāgāra*) and the refectory (*bhattagga*, GRÄFE 1974: 56). It can be assumed that this list, which we encounter in several variations in the *Khandhakas* of the *Vinaya*, belongs

187 Not mentioned in the *Suttapiṭaka.*

188 An ambulatory, originally a walkway on the earth was raised and provided with a railing and finally with a hall to protect those walking there from heat and cold (Vin II 119.$_{37}$–120.$_{12}$). It is mentioned several times in the *Vinaya*- and the *Suttapiṭaka.*

189 Wells are allowed in the *Cullavagga* (Vin II 122.$_{9,10,11}$), and they are mentioned in stereotype lists (Vin I 139.$_{37}$; 140.$_{21,33}$–142.$_{7}$ [passages strongly abbreviated]; II 159.$_{19}$). There are a larger number in the *Suttapiṭaka*, also in older texts (S I 33.$_{19}$; II 118.$_{4}$; Ud 78.$_{10,15,17,22,25,26,32}$; 79.$_{5}$; etc.). See also GRÄFE 1974: 57.

190 Allowed Vin II 122.$_{20-21,22}$, and mentioned in stereotype lists in *Mahā*- and *Cullavagga* (Vin I 139.$_{38}$; 140.$_{21,33}$–142.$_{7}$ [passages strongly abbreviated]); II 159.$_{20}$). Not mentioned in the *Suttapiṭaka.* See also CPD s.v. *udapāna, sālā*; GRÄFE 1974: 57.

191 The *jantāghara* and *jantāgharasālā* are mainly mentioned in the *Khandhakas*. In the *Suttvibhaṅga* they appear in younger strata, in the *vinītavatthu* section of Pār 2 (Vin III 58.$_{25}$) and Sgh 1 (Vin III 116.$_{11}$; 117.$_{27,28,30}$ [abbreviated]) and in the introductory story and non-offence-clause of Pāc 56 (Vin IV 116.$_{4,26}$). Only one reference is found in the older strata of the *Suttapiṭaka* where it is contained in a stereotype text (M III 126.$_{28}$), and a few in younger texts (Ap 39.$_{3}$; Nidd I 228.$_{7}$; 229.$_{1,2,7}$ ≠ 390.$_{26}$; 391.$_{21,22,25-26}$). For details concerning their construction, see GRÄFE 1974: 60–61.

192 In the *Suttapiṭaka* mentioned only in the younger texts. Many times in the *Apadāna* (Ap 88.$_{20}$; 306.$_{11,19,21}$; 333.$_{3}$; etc.) and several times in stereotype lists in the *Niddesa* (Nidd I 67.$_{17}$; 226.$_{25}$; 463.$_{22}$; etc.). In the *Vinaya* monks are allowed to store lodgings at the foot of a tree or in a *maṇḍapa* during the eight months outside the rains (Vin IV 40.$_{1}$, in a section subsequent to Pāc 14); the *maṇḍapa* is mentioned in the casuistries of Pāc 15–17 (Vin IV 42.$_{10,12}$; 43.$_{29}$; 45.$_{16,19}$ [abbreviated]), and in the old commentary to Pāc 31 (Vin IV 71.$_{2}$); there are further references in *Mahā*- and *Cullavagga* (Vin I 125.$_{16}$; 163.$_{27}$; 284.$_{15}$; II 159.$_{21}$; 162.$_{36}$; 163.$_{8}$; 208.$_{5}$) often in enumerations of building lists (Vin I 140–142). In addition, a *kaṭhinamaṇḍapa* is allowed (Vin II 117.$_{14}$) and a *pānīyamaṇḍapa* (Vin II 153.$_{23}$) both not mentioned elsewhere, as synonyms for °*sālā*.

193 Vin II 159.$_{16-21}$. For a comparison with archaeological finds in the North and Northwest of India, see ALBERY 2020: 512–513. A shorter list is transmitted in Vin I 49.$_{3-8}$= 52.$_{19-24}$ (abbreviated) (*pariveṇa, koṭṭhaka, upaṭṭhānasālā, aggisālā, vaccakuṭi*), a longer one, probably created from various shorter ones, enumerating buildings built by a lay-follower for the saṅgha, some bhikkhus, one bhikkhu, etc., Vin I 139.$_{27}$–140.$_{22}$ (*vihāra, aḍḍhayoga, pāsāda, hammiya, guhā, pariveṇa, koṭṭhaka, upaṭṭhānasālā, aggisālā, kappiyakuṭi, vaccakuṭi, caṅkama, caṅkamasālā, udapāna, udapānasālā, jantāghara, jantāgharasālā, pokkharaṇī, maṇḍapa, ārāma, ārāmavatthu*), Vin I 140.$_{27-35}$ (built by a layman for himself: *nivesana, sayanighara, udosita, aṭṭa, māḷa, āpaṇa, āpaṇasālā, pāsāda, hammiya, guhā, pariveṇa, koṭṭhaka, upaṭṭhānasālā, aggisālā, rasavatī, caṅkama, caṅkamasālā, udapāna, udapānasālā, pokkharaṇī, maṇḍapa, ārāma, ārāmavatthu*).

to the younger portions of the monastic law code. Several of the buildings listed do not come up in the *Suttapiṭaka* at all, or if they are mentioned then only in the younger texts, especially the *Niddesa* and *Apadāna*. Only some of the buildings enumerated such as the "meeting-hall" (*upaṭṭhānasāla*) or wells (*udapāna*) appear also several times in the *Suttapiṭaka*, and there not only in the younger textual strata. When female laywomen are said to have entered the *ārāma* to walk from *vihāra* to *vihāra*,[194] this clearly shows that *vihāras* were smaller units within an *ārāma*. In the nuns' *Pātimokkha*, rule Pācittiya 51 which prohibits them to knowingly enter an *ārāma* with monks in it without asking for permission, the old word commentary in the *Vinaya* explains "an *ārāma* with monks in it" by "where monks live at the foot of a tree".[195] This suggests that dwelling at the foot of a tree was still a possible way of living in an *ārāma*, which again implies that there were not necessarily *vihāras* built yet. In the context of that same rule, we are informed that the monks after having left their residence (*āvāsa*), returned to it, and that the nuns entered the *ārāma* where these monks dwelled (Vin IV 306.$_{28-32}$). Since on the one hand nuns are not allowed to spend the rains in an *āvāsa* where there are no monks,[196] and on the other hand are not allowed to enter the *ārāma* without the monks' permission, the *āvāsa* obviously is the larger unit comprising the monks' *ārāma* and the nuns' living quarters.

The word *saṅghārāma*, "the community's *ārāma*",[197] used as a term for Buddhist monasteries in epigraphical sources,[198] appears twice in the monastic law code, where it stands for the area inhabited by a Saṅgha.[199] A few times

194 Vin I 216.$_{34-35}$; III 39.$_{1}$; 120.$_{11-16}$, etc. Laypeople visited these places to look at the beautiful *vihāras*, but also to listen to dhamma talks. When the dhamma is told, the monks regularly each go to their *vihāras* (Vin IV 15.$_{28}$)

195 Vin IV 307.$_{27-28}$: *sabhikkhuko nāma ārāmo yattha bhikkhū rukkhamūle pi vasanti*. See also Roth 1997: 11–12.

196 Vin IV 52.$_{19-20}$; 313.$_{14-15}$: *yā pana bhikkhuni abhikkhuke āvāse vassaṃ vaseyya, pācittiyan ti.*

197 In his translation of the *Apadāna* Walters (2022: 66–68 with n. 418, 991) translates *saṅghārāma* as "monastic ashram", and *ārāma* as well as *assama* as "ashram". He explains that he uses "the Anglicized 'ashram' to translate both *ārāma* and *assama*", which however sometimes on metrical grounds he also translates as "hermitage" while trying to "reserve the more technical 'monastery' for *vihāra*" (Walters 2022: 66 n. 418). Nevertheless he occasionally also translates *saṅghārāma* as "monastery" (Walters 2022: 682 [vv. 4416–4417]).

198 See above, n. 11, 161.

199 Vin I 84.$_{19,22}$. The two references belong to the rule which prohibits monks to bar "the entire community's *ārāma*" (*sabba saṅghārāma*) for novices as a punishment for their bad behaviour.

it appears in mostly younger canonical texts of the *Suttapiṭaka*,[200] and not too often in later texts.[201]

Monks are never identified by their affiliation with a certain *ārāma*. The term *ārāmika*, literally "belonging to an *ārāma*", rather is used for non-monastics including slaves working for the Saṅgha (*ārāmā*).[202] These *ārāmikas* do

200 Nidd I 374.$_{6-7}$ = 500.$_{15-16}$ = II B^e 286 (*antosaṅghārāme*, v.l. *anto pi saṅghā°*); Th 59.$_6$ [v. 558] = Ap I 58.$_{30}$ [v. 15] *saṅghārāmassa koṭṭhake*, "at the gateway to the community's *ārāma*"; Th 59.$_9$ [v. 559] = Ap I 59.$_2$ [v. 16]: *saṃghārāmaṃ pavesayi*, "he led me into the community's *ārāma*"; Thī 174.$_3$ [v. 518] = Ap II 512.$_6$ [v. 1]: *bhagavati Koṇāgamane saṅghārāmamhi navanivesamhi*; Ap I 38.$_{7-28}$ [v. 21]: *Sobhanaṃ nāma ārāmaṃ nagarassa puratthato, kiṇitvā* (v.l. *katvā*) *satasahassena, saṅghārāmaṃ amāpayiṃ*. "Having bought the park (*ārāma*) called Sobhana to the east of the city for a hundred thousand, I built the order's *ārāma*"; Ap I 39.$_{1-2}$ [v. 22]: *kūṭāgāre ca pāsāde maṇḍape hammiye guhā, caṅkame sukate katvā saṅghārāmaṃ amāpayiṃ*. "I built that community's *ārāma* by constructing gabled cells, mansions, pavilions, flat-roofed mansions, caves, and well-made walkways." Ap I 39.$_{9,26,28}$ [vv. 26, 34–35]; 40.$_{2,4,8}$ [vv. 36–37, 39]; 59.$_2$ [v. 16]; 63.$_5$ [v. 2]; 75.$_{12}$ [v. 15], etc.; Bv 59.$_{20}$ [v. 10]; Mil 88.$_{19}$: *uṭṭhāyāsanā saṅghārāmaṃ agamāsi*, this is a typical case where in canonical texts we would have found *vihāraṃ* instead of *saṅghārāmaṃ*. Mil 88.$_{24-25}$: *saṅghārāmagatassa* (v.l. *saṅghārāmaṃ gatassa*) *etad ahosi*.

201 Sv I 309.$_{10-15}$: ***kūṭāgārasālāyan*** *ti tasmiṃ vanasaṇḍe saṅghārāmaṃ patiṭṭhapesuṃ. tattha kaṇṇikaṃ yojetvā thambhānaṃ upari kūṭāgāsālāsaṅkhepena devavimānasadisaṃ pāsādaṃ akaṃsu. taṃ upādāya sakalo pi saṅghārāmo 'kūṭāgārasālā' ti paññāyitta. Bhagavā taṃ Vesāliṃ upanissāya tasmiṃ saṅghārāme viharati.* Spk II 256.$_{23}$: *sakalaṃ saṅghārāmaṃ anuvicaranto*; 256.$_{25}$: *saṅghārāme ...°bhaṇḍāni paṭisameti*; Dhp-a II 74.$_{11-12,14-15}$: *Citto ... Ambāṭakavaṇṇaṃ nāma attano uyyānaṃ saṅghārāmaṃ kattukāmo therassa hatthaṃ udakaṃ pātetvā niyyādesi, ... mahāseṭṭhī uyyāne mahāvihāraṃ kāretvā sabbadisāhi āgatānaṃ bhikkhūnaṃ vivaṭadvāro ahosi ...* "Now Citta, ... desiring to make his own pleasure-garden Ambāṭaka Grove a place of residence for the Order, poured water into the right hand of the Elder and made the grove over to the Order. ... The great treasurer caused a splendid monastery to be erected in the grove, and thereafter the door stood open to monks who came from all [four] quarters" (based on Dhp-a transl. II 144). Th-a II 101.$_{23}$ = Bv-a 213.$_{23}$: *saṅghārāmaṃ amāpayiṃ*; Th-a II 101.$_{23}$: *saṅghārāmaṃ sumāpitaṃ* (Quotations from the *Apadāna*). The word *saṅghārāma* is also used only a few times in the *Vinaya* commentary, and there the idea that it is a flower or tree orchard stands in the foreground (Sp II 381,$_{17-20}$: *saṅghassa ambādīsu pana saṅghārāme jātaṃ vā hotu, ānetvā dinnaṃ vā pañcamāsakaṃ vā atirekamāsakaṃ vā agghanakaṃ avarantassa pārājikaṃ*. "But for [him who is] stealing [something] among the Saṅgha's mangos, etc., worth five Māsakas or more than a Māsaka, whether it is grown in the Saṅgha's orchard or brought [and] given, there is an offence entailing defeat; Sp III 627.$_{34}$–628.$_2$: *saṅghārāme pi phalaparicchedena vā rukkhaparicchedena vā katikā kātabbā ...* "Even with regard to a community's orchard an agreement by the limitation of fruit or by the limitation of trees is to be made: ... ." For a discussion of this term, see also ROTH 1997: 12–16.

202 KIEFFER-PÜLZ 2007: 10–22; see also VON HINÜBER 2017: 1486–1492. YAMAGIWA 2002: 363–385 compares the usage of *ārāmika* in various Buddhist schools.

not yet play a major role in the canonical texts, and are only mentioned in the *Vinaya*, and in a few passages of the *Suttapiṭaka*.[203]

In addition to the Buddhist *ārāmas* of the rich donors, in the *Suttapiṭaka* *ārāmas* of non-Buddhist religious mendicants are mentioned, namely "an *ārāma* of religious mendicants of other sects" (*aññatitthiyānaṃ paribbājakānām ārāmo*[204]), or "an *ārāma* of *paribbājakas*" (*paribbājakārāma*).[205]

But there is also mention of the *ārāma* of Saccaka Nigaṇṭhaputta (M I 236.$_{26}$), – later a follower of the Buddha – which is said to be his own (*sake ārāme*, M I 236.$_{22}$) , or of the brahmin Pokkharasādi's own *ārāma* (D I 106.$_{25}$).

Owners of *ārāmas* mentioned in the monastic law code in connection with theft (Vin III 50.$_{6,8}$) are mentioned as *ārāmasāmika* in the *Aṭṭhakathā* layer (Sp II 338.$_{17}$, 339.$_{13}$). It is to be assumed that their position is very similar to that of a *vihārasāmi(ka)*.[206]

2.3 Āvāsa

In connection with the gift of *vihāras* and *ārāmas/uyyānas* the recipient is mostly mentioned as "the Buddhist community of the four quarters" or the "Buddhist community of the four quarters, present and to come",[207] or "the Buddhist community of the four quarters headed by the Buddha.[208] But the rules transmitted in the monastic law code which regulate the communal life of the Saṅgha, do not deal with the Saṅgha that comprises all monks in the world, but with much smaller groups, namely with local communi-

---

203 For the references in the *Suttapiṭaka* (in *Aṅguttara-*, *Majjhimanikāya*, *Buddhavaṃsa*, *Jātaka* and *Apadāna*) see KIEFFER-PÜLZ 2007: 15 n. 44. For a discussion of those in the *Vinaya*, see KIEFFER-PÜLZ 2007: 15–20.

204 M I 84.$_{3-4,5,30,31-32}$; S II 32.$_{33}$–33.$_{1}$; 35.$_{17}$; V 108.$_{6,7}$; 109.$_{6,8}$; 115.$_{16,18-19}$; 117.$_{16,17-18}$; A IV 35.$_{3-4,25,27}$; 37.$_{12}$, etc.

205 *paribbājakārāma*: Vin III 241.$_{3-4}$ (Niss XX); *Sappinikātīre* (v.l. *Sippi°*) *paribbājakārāme* A I 185.$_{30-31,34}$; 187.$_{31}$; II 29.$_{25,29}$; 176.$_{10,14}$; *Udumbarikāya paribbājakārāme* D III 36.$_{5}$; 57.$_{19}$; *Ekapuṇḍarīke/o paribbājakārāme/o* M I 481.$_{16,20,22}$; *Moranivāpa paribbājakārāma* M II 1.$_{5,9,11}$; 29.$_{19,24,26}$; A I 291.$_{21-22}$; V 326.$_{21-22}$; etc. There are also *ārāmas*, where members of different religions have discussions, like the *ārāma* of the Queen Mallikā (*Mallikārāma*), King Pasenadi's wife, which originally was her garden (*uyyāna*) (D I 178.$_{5,12,14-15}$; M II 23,$_{29}$: *samaya-ppavādake tindukācīre ekasālake Mallikāya ārāme*), see also the *Tindukakkhāṇuparibbājakārāma* D III 17.$_{15-16,18}$; 20.$_{3-4}$; 22.$_{8-9}$. See also ROTH 1997: 18; PIERUCCINI 2018: 69.

206 See above, 2.1.4.

207 Vin II 147.$_{25-26, etc.}$, 164.$_{21-22, etc.}$(Jetavana), see above, p. 15.

208 D II 98.$_{3-5}$ ≠ Vin I 233.$_{5-7}$ (*ārāmaṃ/Ambapālivanaṃ*) see above, n. 171; Vin I 39.$_{14-18}$, see above, n. 167; Ap II 512.14–15 [v. 5]: *ārāmaṃ sukataṃ katvā sabbāvayavamaṇḍitaṃ, Buddhapamukhasaṅghassa niyyādetvā pamoditā*. "Having made the *ārāma* well-made, with every part [of it] adorned, delighted we donated [it] to the Saṅgha headed by the Buddha" (based on WALTERS 2022: 992).

ties. The minimum size of a group that can count as a Saṅgha consists of four monks or four nuns (there are no mixed Saṅghas). Such a Saṅgha is capable to carry out most of the legal acts (*kamma*) that arise within a local community. There are also some acts for which five, ten or twenty monastics are required. The monastic law code also explains in detail for each ceremony what to do if there are less than the required number of monks. So, there are directives for carrying out ceremonies by three, two or one. One of the prerequisites for a *kamma* to be legally valid is that it is carried out by a complete (*samagga*) Saṅgha. Even though the determination of a house for the fortnightly observance ceremony (*uposatha*) is described in the *Mahāvagga* of the *Vinaya* (Vin I 107.$_{5-32}$), and even though we read about *vihāras* and *ārāmas*, none of them are mentioned as the space by which the completeness of a Saṅgha is measured. Rather, it is asked whether "complete" refers to all monks on the earth or to all monks of "a single residence" (*ekāvāsa*). And this is answered in the sense that "complete" refers to all the monks within a single residence. Since there was obviously no uniformity regarding the size and shape of an *āvāsa*, it was enacted by the Buddha that monks must agree upon a "boundary" (*sīmā*) that defines its extent.[209] From the maximum measures given for such a *sīmā*, we know that the area of an *āvāsa* could have been quite large. The measure of a *sīmā* may be up to three *yojana*, that is, to between 33 and 39 km. It is not clear whether this refers to the circumference or to the maximum length of one side, but it is obvious in any case that the area enclosed might have been quite large.[210] In the beginning the area enclosed by the *sīmā* and the *āvāsa* were identical. But since its introduction, the boundary (*sīmā*) became the decisive factor for the monastic legal activities of each local community, and thus in the course of time replaced the *āvāsa* in this function. Therefore, the *sīmā* could be determined at will, and could also enclose several *āvāsas*, which is mentioned once in the *Mahāvagga*.[211] The question whether the observance may be performed separately within the different *āvāsas* that were included in the same *sīmā* was one of the points still discussed at the second council (ca. 60 years after the Buddha's *parinibbāna*) under the term *āvāsakappa* (Vin II 294.$_{6}$). This indicates

209 Vin I 106.$_{1-4}$: *atha kho bhikkhūnaṃ etad ahosi: "bhagavata paññattaṃ 'ettāvatā sāmaggī yāvatā ekāvāso' ti. 'kittāvatā nu kho ekāvāso hotī' ti." ... "anujānāmi bhikkhave sīmaṃ sammannituṃ."* "Then it occurred to the monks: 'It is laid down by the Lord that »being all together« (means) as far as one residence. Now, how far does one residence (go)?' ... 'I order, monks, to agree upon a boundary.'"

210 Vin I 106.$_{20-29}$. For the possible meanings of this measure dependent on the form of the *sīmā*, and the resulting sizes of the enclosed areas, see KIEFFER-PÜLZ 1992: 67–69.

211 Vin I 108.$_{26-36}$; see KIEFFER-PÜLZ 1992: 49, 71–72, 126–128.

that at this time *āvāsa* and *sīmā* did not necessarily cover the same area. During subsequent developments, the *āvāsa* became irrelevant for these administrative tasks, and therefore the word *āvāsa* became free to be used in other meanings.[212]

In the entire monastic law code, the central space for the legal communal life is the *āvāsa*.[213] After the introduction of the *sīmā*, additional paragraphs were inserted into the monastic law code, that contained sentences formulating what was said with the term *āvāsa* already, but now under the usage of the term *sīmā*. These sentences were meant to be inserted into the preceding paragraphs, formulated with the term *āvāsa*.[214] Since in the beginning both areas were identical, nothing really changed. That most rules established with respect to the Saṅgha as an acting legal body were created during a period in which the *āvāsa* was the decisive legal space also becomes visible through the fact that the monks who stayed in an *āvāsa* were affiliated with it. This is reflected in the designation *āvāsika*, "[monk] belonging to the residence", for monks who belonged to an *āvāsa*, in contrast to monks who came to this *āvāsa* from elsewhere. The latter were called "guest monks" (*āgantuka*), literally, "arriving" monks. The rights and duties of both parties were mutually different, and as residents the *āvāsikas* had more administrative or other rights concerning their *āvāsa* than the *āgantukas*.[215] If a community in an *āvāsa* was not able to solve a conflict, or had any other problems, its members were urged to ask for help in a community in another *āvāsa*,[216] not in another *vihāra* or *ārāma*.

Āvāsa, according to the Pali Dictionaries refers to the residing, dwelling, as well as to the place where one dwells. In that latter meaning the dictionaries list a variety of words such as "dwelling-place, abode, house, home,

---

212 This can be seen from the commentarial literature, where *āvāsa* is mostly used for a single dwelling. For a more detailed sketch of the development of the *sīmā* in relation to the *āvāsa*, see KIEFFER-PÜLZ 1992: 46–52.

213 For instance, in the chapter on the *uposatha* house (Vin I 106.$_{36}$–108.$_{23}$), and in the chapter on the rains retreat (Vin I 135–156), only the *āvāsa* is spoken of, not a *sīmā*. The *kaṭhina* period is opened in an *āvāsa*, and one of the impediments for ending the *kaṭhina* period is the existence of the *āvāsa-palibodha*, i.e. when a monk still is linked to that *āvāsa*. When a monk has been suspended in a legal act this information has to be proclaimed in residence after residence (*āvāsaparamparā*; Vin II 22.$_{4-6}$).

214 For example, Vin I 132.$_{6-17}$ containing six sentences formulated with the word *sīmā*, which could be inserted in the four preceding paragraphs Vin I 128.$_{34}$–132.$_{5}$; or Vin I 167.$_{14-25}$ containing sentences to be inserted in the paragraphs Vin I 164.$_{29}$–167.$_{13}$.

215 See for instance the regulation concerning the date for the observance (Vin I 132.$_{17ff.}$).

216 For instance, if the monks in one *āvāsa* were not able to solve a legal question (*adhikaraṇa*), they should go to another *āvāsa* with more monks (Vin II 94.$_{8-11}$).

monastery, residence, settlement". All dictionaries stress that the word is used especially for "a place fit for residence of bhikkhus", and some mention a convent or monastery in that connection.[217] According to Upasak (2001: 34) an *āvāsa* is

> "a place fit for residing [sic] the members of the Buddhist Order; viz. a *Vihāra*, an *Aḍḍhayoga*, a *Pāsāda*, a *Hammiya* and a *Guhā*. (Mv. pp. 55, 100; Cv. pp. 68–69, 239). It is the same as *Senāsana*. (*Āvāso nāma vasanatthāya katasenāsanaṃ* – SP Vol. III, p. 1244)."

The connection of *āvāsa* with the five shelters allowed for a dwelling does not have a basis in the canon, where these five buildings are subsumed under the term "shelter" (*leṇa*), not *āvāsa*. There is not a single reference in the entire canonical literature where *āvāsa* is used to describe the lodging (*senāsana*) or dwelling place (*vihāra*) of an individual monk or another human being. The respective passage cited by Upasak is from the *Vinaya* commentary, and thus stems from a period when the function of an *āvāsa* in the administrative life of the Buddhist community had long been taken over by the *sīmā*. In the canonical writings *āvāsa* in the sense of "abode" is used only with respect to the abode of animals, demons, etc., or for describing the body as an abode for diseases.[218] Even these cases show that large areas such as the great ocean or a charnel ground were considered as such abodes. Regarding Buddhist monks, *āvāsa* designates the residence within which monks stayed during the three months of the four months of the rainy season, originally the only period in which Buddhist monastics stayed at one and the same place for a certain length of time. Therefore, the *āvāsa* is also often called "rains residence" (*vassāvāsa*).[219] And if this is a residence within a settlement or includes settlements, it may also be called *gāmakāvā-*

---

217 CHILDERS 1976 s.v. *āvāso*: "residing, dwelling; a dwelling, a residence; a monastery"; CPD s.v. *āvāsa*: "1. living, dwelling, residing; 2. dwelling-place, abode, house, home, residence, settlement; 3. (esp.) a place fit for residence of bhikkhus, convent, monastery, community of monks"; DoP s.v. *āvāsa*: "living sojourn; dwelling-place, inhabited place; residence, esp. a residence or dwelling for bhikkhus"; PED s.v. *āvāsa*: "sojourn, stay, dwelling, living; dwelling-place, residence".

218 The charnel ground, for instance, is mentioned as an abode (*āvāsa*) of non-humans (A III 268.$_{29}$, 269.$_{22}$), or the great ocean as an abode of large beings (Vin II 238.$_{15,20}$; 240.$_{8,13}$; A IV 200.$_{4,9}$; 203.$_{27}$; 204.$_{5,10}$; 206.$_{28}$; 207 (passage abbreviated in E^{e}); Ud 54.$_{15}$; 56.$_{17}$). The body is compared to an abode for every disease (Ap II 467.$_{14}$ [v. 28]).

219 Vin I 137.$_{3,9-11}$; 138.$_{9}$; 153.$_{25,31-32}$; etc.

sa.[220] *Āvāsas* were not institutions with permanent, unvarying residents, but rather spatial units with changing residents, open to newcomers who could become *āvāsikas*, and *āvāsikās* who left for other places at least temporarily. The structural equipment probably varied considerably depending on the number of resident monks, the location of the *āvāsa*, and the support the monks experienced from the lay-followers.

Within an *āvāsa* monks may have lived in *ārāmas*. Nevertheless, the monks who stayed in that *ārāma* were called *āvāsikas*.[221] Even within such an *ārāma* the monks stayed in huts (*kuṭi*) or *vihāras*, at least during the rains retreat, because then they were not allowed to stay in the open, at the foot of a tree, in charnel houses, etc. (Vin I 152.$_{14ff}$.) but rather had to stay in a lodging (*senāsana*) for which the fives shelters mentioned in connection with a *vihāra* were allowed.[222] There certainly existed also *āvāsas* without *ārāmas*.

A sentence repeated again and again in the context of *ārāmas* is that the donors ponder which place is considered ideal for monks to live in. And it is regularly stated that the best place is one not too close to a settlement, but also not too far from it.[223] This has led to the assumption that monks' monasteries are situated outside of settlements, an assumption in fact corroborated by the younger tradition. But in the canonical writings we not only hear of the Buddha and several monks who spent the rains in towns like Rājagaha or Sāvatthi,[224] but there are also several references to "village residences" (*gāmakāvāsa*) in which nuns or monks spent the rains.[225]

220 Concerning nuns, they must live within settlements, that is villages, market towns, and cities. The word *gāma* "village" is often used to cover settlements in general. Accordingly, nuns' residences may be referred to as *gāmakāvāsa* "village residence" (*bhikkhuniyo gāmakāvāse vassaṃ vuṭṭhā*, Vin IV 245.$_{18}$; 313.$_{4,28}$). But there are also monk's *āvāsas* referred to as *gāmakāvāsa* (Vin I 300.$_{13-14,29-30}$; II 170.$_{5}$; IV 306.$_{15}$). Normally *āvāsas* are not described as belonging to someone but see the mention of King Pasenadi of Kosala's rains residence (Vin I 153.$_{25}$; 154.$_{1-2,10}$: *rañño Pasenadissa Kosalassa vassāvāso/ vassāvāsaṃ*) which he also mentions as "our rains residence" (*amhākaṁ vassāvāsaṃ*, Vin I 153.$_{31-32}$).

221 This is obvious when guest monks enter an *ārāma* and do not pay respect to the elder *āvāsika* monks, or when a person enters an *ārāma* and wonders where the *āvāsika* monks had gone to, etc. (Vin II 207.$_{16-19}$; 208.$_{3-4}$).

222 See above, 2.1.5.

223 Vin II 158.$_{26-27.31-32}$; similarly for the lodging (*senāsana*, D II 38.$_{3-6}$; M II 118.$_{20-24}$, etc.), see also ROTH 1997: 1, 33.

224 Though it may be that they stayed in some place nearby understood to belong to these towns.

225 For nuns, see above, n. 220. It is stated for instance that the Buddha (Vin I 79.$_{28-29}$) or monks spent the rains in Rājagaha (Vin I 299.$_{36-37}$; II 285.$_{20-21}$; III 145.$_{1-2}$; M II 185.$_{1}$), the monks of the first Council spent the rains in Rājagaha (Vin II 285ff.), other monks spent

There is, furthermore, one passage stating that monks spent the rains in a village district (*gāmakkhetta*), and that they assembled for the fortnightly observance ceremony (*uposatha*) measuring the completeness of the Saṅgha required for this ceremony by the extension of this village district.[226] This shows that monks of the Pāli tradition spent the rains also in settlements. It further shows that the boundaries of a worldly settlement was taken as the measure for the completeness of the Saṅgha living there. And this, again, hints at a stage in the development of the Buddhist Saṅgha in which the monks did not yet live in a permanent monastery.[227]

A situation similar to that described in the canonical texts seems to be reflected in Asoka's schism edict, where Asoka stated that "[whoever] should split the Saṅgha, whether monk or nun, should be made to wear white clothes and to reside in what is not an *āvāsa*" (*anāvāsasi āvāsayiye*).[228] Asoka refers to an *āvāsa*, not to a monastery, and wants the schismatic monks to live in what is not an *āvāsa*.[229] And connecting these data we can assume that in the middle of the 3rd century BCE and possibly far into the first century BCE the *āvāsa* was the legal unit relevant for Buddhist communities. Schopen's and Bronkhorst's observation that in Asoka's pillar inscription at the Buddha's birthplace, in Lumbini, a donation to the village of Lumbini is recorded, but none to a monastery,[230] fits well into this picture. Both schol-

---

the rains in Sāvatthi, and then went to another *gāmakāvāsa* (Vin I 299.$_{29-30}$: *Sāvatthiyaṃ vassaṃ vuṭṭhā aññataraṃ gāmakāvāsaṃ agamaṃsu*; I 300.$_{13-14}$: *Upanando Sakyaputto Sāvatthiyaṃ vassaṃ vuṭṭho aññataraṃ gāmakāvāsaṃ agamāsi*; similar 300.$_{29-30}$; Vin II 168.$_{2-3}$: *Sāvatthiyaṃ senāsanaṃ gahetvā aññataraṃ gāmakāvāsaṃ agamāsi, tatthapi senāsanaṃ aggahesi.*). *Bhikkhus* in a *gāmakāvāsa* made robes (Vin IV 306.$_{15}$), resident monks in another *gāmākāvāsa* were afflicted (Vin II 170.$_{4-5}$: *aññatarasmiṃ gāmakāvāse āvāsikā bhikkhū upaddutā honti*).

226 M III 10,$_{8-13}$.

227 KIEFFER-PÜLZ 1992: 95 n. 156 assumed that this is a younger stratum in the development of the legal literature; VON HINÜBER 1996: 103–104 (2009: 235–236) in his review considered it to represent an earlier stage, which seems correct.

228 *saṃghaṃ bhākhati bhikkhu vā bhikhuni vā se pi cā odātāni dusāni sanaṃdhāpayitu anāvāsasi āvāsayiye*. Already BECHERT 1982: 63f. hinted at the fact that the language of Asoka in this edict corresponds closely to that in the *Vinayas*. He, however, introduces the concept of *sīmā* (64) into the discussion about that inscription, even though it is not yet mentioned by Asoka. For a new and very interesting approach to this inscription, starting from the vocabulary used with regard to a political Saṅgha, see OLIVELLE 2025: 349–364.

229 This is very similar to the usage of *āvāsa* and *anāvāsa* in the *Vinaya* (Vin I 134.$_{30,32,34}$, etc.).

230 SCHOPEN 1994: 550 [= 2004a: 76–77]; BRONKHORST 2011: 18 n. 25. BRONKHORST (2011: 19) states "The historical evidence does not allow us to determine with precision when buddhist monks and nuns settled down permanently in monasteries." See also

ars interpret this in such a way that it "may mean that Aśoka did not know anything about Buddhist monasteries, which indeed may not yet have existed at that time."[231]

3. The *Aṭṭhakathā* Layer

The second layer of scriptures to be looked at are the so-called *Aṭṭhakathās*. They were written between, roughly, the fourth and tenth centuries CE (referred to as *Aṭṭhakathā* layer). The subsequent commentarial literature is of no interest in the present context.

3.1 Vihāra

According to the *Aṭṭhakathās* the word *vihāra* may still refer to a single building used for various purposes possibly situated in an *ārāma*,[232] among them a dwelling place of a single monk.[233] This is due to the fact that the commentaries often quote words from the canon, where *vihāra* is the dwelling of a single monk.[234] But *vihāra* can also refer to an entire monastery as the same passage shows where it is stressed, that *vihāra* in that context does not refer to the entire *vihāra* (*sakalavihāra*), i.e., to a monastic compound.[235] Whether *vihāra* is used for the dwelling of an individual or for a permanent monastic compound

---

SCHOPEN 1996b: 81–82 [2004a: 219]; 2006b: 316 [= 2014: 277]; 2007: 61. ROTH 1997: 16–17 also refers to the fact that there are no references to an *ārāma*, *saṅghārāma*, *vihāra* (in the sense of a building) or *mahāvihāra* in the Aśoka inscriptions.

231 BRONKHORST 2011: 18.

232 Sp V 1211.$_{22-24}$: ***vihāraṃ vā*** *ti* (Vin I 284.$_{19}$) *yo ārāmamajjhe ... vihāro vā aḍḍhayogo vā hoti, so sammannitabbo.* "**Or a vihāra** means: Which *vihāra* or *aḍḍhayoga* there is in the middle of the *ārāma*, that one is to be agreed upon [as a storeroom]."

233 Sp IV 778.$_{5-6}$: ***vihāro*** *ti* (Vin IV 42.$_{9}$) *antogabbho vā aññaṃ vā sabbaparicchannaṃ guttasenāsanaṃ veditabbaṃ*; Sp VI 1237.$_{9-10}$: ***vihāro*** *nāma yaṃ kiñci pāsādādisenāsanaṃ.* Sv II 584.$_{7}$: ***vihāran*** *ti* (D II 143.$_{20}$) *idha maṇḍalamālo vihāro ti addhippeto*; Mp V 87.$_{6-7}$: ***pañcasataṃ vihāran*** *ti* (A V 347.$_{13}$) *pañcasatagghanikaṃ paṇṇasālaṃ kāresī ti attho*; Sn-a I 276.$_{16-17}$: ***vihāro*** *ti* (ad Sn v. 220) *vasanokāso, so ca bhikkhuno araññe, luddakassa ca gāme.* "Their 'dwelling' is their dwelling place: that of the bhikkhu is in the forest, that of the hunter is in the village." (BODHI 2017: 668).

234 Sp III 574.$_{30-31}$: *ettha ca vihāro ti na sakalavihāro, eko āvāso, ten' evāha "ayyassa vihāraṃ kārāpessāmī" ti* (Vin III 155.$_{29-30}$). "And here *vihāra* is not an entire monastery, [but] a single abode. Only therefore he said: 'I will have a *vihāra* built for the Honorable One.'" Sp IV 778.$_{5-6}$, see above, n. 233; Dhp-a III 414.$_{11}$: *eso te vihāro*; In several cases *vihāra* is explained as *gandhakuṭi*, i.e. as referring to the Buddha's room: Mp III 299.$_{4}$; Th-a II 200.$_{18-19}$: ***vihāran*** *ti gandhakuṭiṃ*; Sv I 252.$_{18}$; Ps III 350.$_{26}$; Mp V 29.$_{9}$: ***vihāro*** *ti gandhakuṭiṃ sandhāya āhaṃsu.* Ud-a 312.$_{3}$: *gandhakuṭi hi idha vihāro ti adhippetā.*

235 See n. 234; for *sakalavihāra*, see also Dhp-a II 140.$_{20}$, 141.$_{3}$; etc.

is often to be deduced from the context.[236] When 1000 dwellings (*āvāsa*) and innumerable monks are mentioned as residents it clearly refers to a permanent monastic compound (see below, n. 242), and the same holds true when we are told that a palace (*pāsāda*) is situated in the middle of a *vihāra*,[237] or that Raṭṭhapāla has built 54,000 *pāsādas* inside a *vihāra*.[238] References to large *vihāras* (*mahā vihāra*) may be used with regard to dwellings as in the canon, but they may also be used for monastic compounds.[239] The decisive factor to define a monastery, in the *Aṭṭhakathā* layer obviously is the monastic boundary (*sīmā*), which in this period mostly encloses the monastery within which a Saṅgha lives, and, therefore, is also called *vihārasīmā*,[240] a term not yet used in canonical literature.

Vihāra as used in the canonical writings is also explained in commentarial layers to refer to the Buddha's shrine room, the *gandhakuṭi*.[241]

As a designation for a dwelling place the word *vihāra* is equated with the word *āvāsa*, meaning now "abode, dwelling". As a designation for a monastic

---

236 When an entire Saṅgha is mentioned that inhabits a *vihāra*, *vihāra* probably refers to a monastery, even though it naturally cannot be excluded that such a Saṅgha consists of only four monastics. Sp III 733.$_{30}$–734.$_{1}$: ***saṅghassa pariṇataṃ aññasaṅghassā** ti* (Vin III 266.$_{15-16}$) *ekasmiṃ vihāre saṅghassa pariṇataṃ aññavihāraṃ uddisitvā "asukasmiṃ nāma vihāre saṅghassa dethā" 'ti pariṇāmeti.* "**[If he apportions something] apportioned to a Saṅgha to another Saṅgha** (means): Having specified another *vihāra*, he apportions [something] apportioned to a Saṅgha in one *vihāra* [saying] 'you should give [it] to the Saṅgha in such and such a *vihāra*'."

237 Sp VI 1239.$_{3}$: *... manussānaṃ vihāramajjhe pāsādo ...* "People have a palace in the middle of a *vihāra*."

238 Ap-a 332.$_{11}$: *vihārabbhantare catupaññāsasahassāni pāsādāni ca aham akārayiṃ.*

239 *Mahāvihāra* in Vv 44.8 is explained in the commentary as referring to the Pubbārāma which Visākhā had built for the Saṅgha close to Sāvatthi (Vv-a 190.$_{13,17}$). The commentary thus equates the *māhāvihāra* of the canon with *ārāma*. Whereas normally two monks were agreed upon as assigners of lodgings (*senāsanaggāhaka*), in a large *vihārā* (*mahante vihāre*) three to four or, following the early Kurundī, eight to sixteen of them should be agreed upon (Sp VI 1229.$_{13-15}$: *mahante pana mahāvihārasadise vihāre tayo cattāro janā sammannitabbā. Kurundiyaṃ pana "aṭṭha pi soḷasa pi jane sammannituṃ vaṭṭatī" ti vuttaṃ*). This presupposes a monastery with higher number of monks dwelling there.

240 A *vihārasīmā* is a monastic boundary that belongs to the category of the "determined boundaries" (*baddhasīmā*) and includes the monastery (*vihāra*). For details, see KIEFFER-PÜLZ 1992: 191–192.

241 Sv I 252.$_{18}$= Ps III 350.$_{25}$ = Mp V 29.$_{9}$: ***vihāro** ti gandhakuṭiṃ sandhāya āhaṃsu.*

compound, *vihāra* is a larger structure, and *āvāsa* describes single dwellings within that *vihāra*.[242] Therefore, we have the equations:[243]

vihāra = *āvāsa* = dwelling place[244]
vihāra = *sakalavihāra* = monastic compound with *āvāsas*, i.e. single dwellings, inside the *vihāra*.

Vihāras are still described as belonging to the Saṅgha, and there certainly existed *vihāras* which the Saṅgha not only possessed, but also owned,[245] that is, for which there existed no private donors who still had some rights and obligations.[246] But in addition, there also existed *saṅghika* and *puggalika vihāras* which were owned by *vihārasāmikas*.[247] This is evident when a *vihārasāmika* complains that his *vihāra* is used only by a single monk (Th-a II 127); or, when a monk who wants to go elsewhere in case there is no other monk in that *vihāra* (of which he normally has to take leave), has to take leave of

242 "But if it is a large *vihāra*, with thousand *āvāsas* and numerous monks, it is difficult to assemble all the monks, how much more to ask [them] in succession." (*sace pana vihāro mahā hoti anekabhikkhusahassāvāso, sabbe bhikkhū sannipātetum pi dukkaraṃ, pageva paṭipāṭiyā āpucchituṃ*, Sp V 1003.$_{6-8}$). "If there is an old *āvāsa* in the middle of a *vihāra* (i.e. monastery), and [if] it suffices for the monks as a place for sitting down, [then] having assembled there the observance is to be carried out. If the old *āvāsa* is dilapidated and crowded, another *āvāsa* that has been erected later, is not crowded, then observance is to be carried out there." (*sace porāṇako āvāso majjhe vihārassa hoti, pahoti c' ettha bhikkhūnaṃ nisajjaṭṭhānaṃ, tattha sannipatitvā uposatho kātabbo. sace porāṇako paridubbalo c' eva sambādho ca, añño pacchā uṭṭhito āvāso asambādho, tattha uposatho kātabbo.* Sp V 1049.$_{15-19}$).

243 I did not see any passage, where *āvāsa* is used for a monastery, and *vihāra* for the dwellings within that monastery.

244 Where we find the term *vihāradānaṃ* in the canon, the commentary uses *āvāsadānaṃ*, see below, n. 263.

245 The texts do not clearly formulate the difference between the ownership of a donor and the fact that the donated *vihāra* becomes the Saṅgha's possession. What we can deduce from the texts is that the Saṅgha has the right to assign such a *saṅghika vihāra* to the monk of their choice, and that the *vihārasāmi* has no right to reject this choice. One the other hand, the *vihārasāmi* is the person responsible for financial questions. He is to be asked when tools, materials or workers are needed for the maintenance of the *saṅghika vihāra*. The Saṅgha only is going to provide means if neither the *vihārasāmi* nor any other sponsor is going to pay for it. For more details, see KIEFFER-PÜLZ 2022.

246 This we can assume from the section dealing with the exchange of real estate between a Saṅgha and people. See VON HINÜBER 2006: 20–21 [= 2009: II 886–887].

247 Although monastics as well as lay people are mentioned as donors of *vihāras* in the monastic law code (see above, n. 148), in the *Aṭṭhakathā* layer only lay people are mentioned as *vihārasāmis* (KIEFFER-PÜLZ 2022). This also is the case in the Mūlasarvāstivāda tradition (SCHOPEN 1996b [= 2004a: 219–259]).

other persons which are mentioned in descending order as follows: a novice, a monastery attendant (*ārāmika*), or the 'owner of the *vihāra*' (*vihārasāmika*), or, in his absence, any family member of the *vihārasāmika*.[248]

Concerning the individual *vihāras*, the options discussed in connection with the canonical texts are valid here too. That means a *vihāra* may be owned by an individual monk because he had built it himself with his own wealth, or it may belong to him (*puggalika vihāra*), but be owned by a lay-follower because the latter had given it to him.[249] But in the *Aṭṭhakathā* an additional way of receiving an individual *vihāra* is described which goes back to one of the early lost Sinhalese commentaries quoted in the *Samantapāsādikā*, namely the *Kurundī*. If a Saṅgha is not capable to maintain all real estates belonging to the Saṅgha there is the possibility to hand over parts of a building or an entire building to a monk who had to care for it. Thereby a *vihāra* became an individual (*puggalika*) *vihāra* for as long as this monk lived. With his death it returned into the property of the Saṅgha.[250] Thus, Saṅgha property which according to the canon must not be transferred and not be distributed, in this case is transferred for a lifetime to an individual monk as a final measure to preserve it.

Finally, in addition to the recipients of donations mentioned in the canon, namely a Saṅgha, an individual or a *cetiya*, in the *Aṭṭhakathā* a *vihāra* ("monastery"), *navakamma* and a *cetiya* are mentioned. A *vihāra* is not only allowed to accept whatever is given to it, but rather the monastics are obliged to accept it. These donations were not bound by the rules formulated in the monastic law code for the Saṅgha and individual monastics, and thus enabled monasteries to accumulate goods, money, real estate, etc. The *vihāra* thus became a representative for the Saṅgha which was not bound by the same rules as the Saṅgha and the monastics. That *navakamma* is also mentioned as a recipient of donations shows the importance that restoration and building work had gained by the time of the *Aṭṭhakathās*. We do not know whether the money for *navakamma* was administrated by the bhikkhu installed as a

---

248 Sp IV 777.$_{15-19}$: ***anāpucchaṃ vā gaccheyyā*** *ti* (Vin IV 41.$_{22}$) *ettha bhikkhumhi sati bhikkhu āpucchitabbo, tasmiṃ asati sāmaṇero, tasmiṃ asati ārāmiko, tasmiṃ pi asati yena vihāro kārito so vihārasāmiko, tassa vā kule yo koci āpucchitabbo*, ... "**[If a monk] should go away without taking leave**: here if there is [another] monk, [that] monk should be taken leave of, if there is no [other monk] a novice [should be taken leave of], if there is no [novice], an *ārāmika*, if there is even no [*ārāmika*], the owner of the *vihāra* by whom the *vihāra* was caused to be built, or anybody in his family should be taken leave of." See KIEFFER-PÜLZ 2022: 191–192.

249 In that case the donor should also be the owner as in the case of the *saṅghika vihāras*.

250 Sp VI 1246.$_{14}$–1247.$_{5}$; VON HINÜBER 2006: 20–21 [= 2009: II 886–887].

navakammika, but this also cannot be excluded. The *cetiya* was mentioned in one younger section of the *Suttavibhaṅga* as a unit to which things could be apportioned, but as an explicit recipient of donations it becomes visible in the *Aṭṭhakathā* layer.[251]

3.2 *Ārāma*

Just as in the canonical writings *ārāma* appears as the word for the gardens (*uyyāna*) of the rich donors given to the Saṅgha.[252] Thus these are *ārāma*s within which *vihāra*s may be built.[253] Similarly to the canonical texts *ārāmas* in addition are mentioned as orchards.[254] There are, however, also equations of *ārāma* and *vihāra*, indicating that both are meant to refer to a Buddhist monastery.[255] *Vihāra* also refers to large monasteries which are given together with *ārāma*s that are specifically planted for those *vihāras*.[256] Different

---

251 For a discussion of this entire complex, see KIEFFER-PÜLZ 2024.

252 Sv II 365.$_{21-23}$ = Ps III 266.$_{11-13}$: *Mallikāya pana Pasenadirañño deviyā uyyānabhūto, so pupphaphalasampanno* (Ps *°sañchanno*) *ārāmo ti katvā* ***Mallikāya ārāmo*** *ti saṅkhaṃ gato.* "That [which] has been the garden of Mallikā, the queen of king Pasenadi, having been made an *ārāma* provided with flowers and fruits, is called **the *ārāma* of Mallikā.**"

253 Ps II 61.$_{14-16}$: ***Nigrodhārāme*** *ti* (M I 91.$_{2}$) *Nigrodho nāma sakko. so … attano ārāme vihāraṃ kāretvā bhagavato niyyātesi.* "**In the Nigrodhārāma**: A Sakka named Nigrodha. Having had a *vihāra* built in his own *ārāma* he dedicated [it] to the Blessed One." Ps II 393.$_{16-21}$: *tayo pi janā attano attano ārāme … bhagavato vasanatthāya vihāre kārāpayiṃsu. … Kukkuṭārāmo … Pāvārikambavano … Ghositārāmo nāma ahosi.* "Three people, each in his own *ārāma* had *vihāra*s erected for the dwelling of the Blessed One; … called Kukkuṭārāma, … the Pāvārika-Ambavana … Ghositārāma."

254 Sp VI 1238.$_{9-31}$, where the exchange of orchards (*ārāma*) of the Saṅgha and of lay-followers is discussed. Vv-a 288.$_{19-20}$: *ārāmapālo ārāmaṃ gantvā ambarukkhamūlesu paṃsuṃ apanetvā …*, "The keeper of the *ārāma* went to the *ārāma*, [and] at the foot of the mango tree he removed some soil …" Vv-a 302.$_{9-11}$: *ārāmarukkhāni cā ārāmabhūte rukkhe, ārāmaṃ katvā tattha rukkhe ropesin ti attho.* "And trees in an *ārāma* means trees that are plants in an *ārāma*, having made an *ārāma*, I had trees planted there, [is] the meaning."

255 Ap-a 332.$_{7-9}$: ***saṅghārāmaṃ*** *buddhappamukhassa bhikkhusaṅghassa vasanatthāya ārāmaṃ vihāraṃ* ***akārayiṃ*** *kāresiṃ.* (passages in bold are quoted from the Ap I 63.$_{5}$ [v. 2]). **I built** (=) I erected (different verb form) **an *ārāma* for the Saṅgha** (=) an *ārāma* for the dwelling of the monks' community headed by the Buddha (=) a *vihāra*." Ps I 146.$_{33}$: ***ārāmagatānan*** *ti* (M I 28.$_{34}$) *vihāre sannipatitānaṃ.* "**Being in the *ārāma*** means assembled in the *vihāra*."

256 Bv-a 168.$_{27-30}$; 169.$_{3-4,7-9}$: … *Jayaseno nāma rājakumāro yojanappamāṇaṃ vihāraṃ kāretvā … ārāmaṃ ropetvā buddhappamukhassa bhikkhusaṅghassa nīyādesi. … puna Uggato rājā … Sunandaṃ* (v.l. *Surindaṃ*) *nāma vihāraṃ kāretvā buddhappamukhassa bhikkhusaṅghassa adāsi. … puna Mekhalānagare dhammagaṇo dhammagaṇārāmaṃ nāma pavarārāmaṃ vihāraṃ* (B^{e} *mahāvihāraṃ*) *kāretvā buddhappamukhassa bhikkhusaṅghassa datvā saha sabbaparikkhārehi dānaṃ adāsi.* "Having had a *vihāra* built a *yojana* in extent and having planted the park … he dedicated it to the Order of monks with the Buddha at the head. Again, the king named Uggata, having had a *vihāra* named Surinda built … gave it to the Order

from the canonical texts where first an *ārāma* was given to the Saṅgha, and then *vihāras* built within it, here *vihāras* are built and *ārāmas* are planted as parks of these *vihāras* simultaneously. *Ārāmas* may also stand for a monastery, and the dwellings within it are referred to as *āvāsas*.[257]

3.3 *Āvāsa*

The "residence" (*āvāsa*), i.e. the decisive unit in the monastic law code,[258] replaced by the monastic boundary (*sīmā*) already there,[259] in this function does no longer play a role in the *Aṭṭhakathā* layer. There it mostly designates a single dwelling, taking over the meaning that *vihāra* had in the *Vinaya*. This becomes visible when the *vihāra* ("dwelling place") built for the monk Channa (Vin III 155.$_{28-30}$) is referred to as "a single abode" (*eko āvāso*) in the commentary.[260] Thus *vihāra* as well as *āvāsa* are understood as referring to a dwelling place.[261] Sometimes *āvāsa* appears without a relation to *vihāra*,

---

of monks with the Buddha at the head. ... Again, having had a (large) *vihāra* built in a glorious park (*ārāma*) named Dhammagaṇa Park in Mekhala city, giving it to the Order of monks with the Buddha at the head, he gave the gift together with all the requisites." (HORNER 1978 [2008]: 243).

257 Vism-nid B^{e} 21: *bahū janā tasmiñ ca ārāme aññāttha ca bahū āvāse katvā tesaṃ denti*. "Many people having built many *āvāsas* in that *ārāma* and elsewhere, give it to them."

258 For references of *āvāsa* in this function, see KIEFFER-PÜLZ 1992: 43 n. 56.

259 Vin I 106.$_{1-4}$ (introduction of the *sīmā* as limitation of an *āvāsa*); for the development of the usage of the *sīmā* in relation to the *āvāsa*, see KIEFFER-PÜLZ 1992: 46–52.

260 Sp III 574.$_{30-31}$ see above, n. 234.

261 Sp V 1049.$_{19-24}$: ***yattha vā pana thero bhikkhu viharatī*** *ti* (Vin I 108.$_{33-34}$) *etthāpi sace therassa vihāro sabbesaṃ pahoti, phāsuko hoti, tattha uposatho kātabbo. sace pana so paccante visamappadese hoti, therassa vattabbaṃ: "bhante, tumhākaṃ vihāro aphāsukadeso, natthi ettha sabbesaṃ okāso, asukasmiṃ nāma āvāse okāso atthi, tattha gantuṃ vaṭṭatī" ti*. "**Or where the elder bhikkhu lives**: here too, if the *vihāra* of the elder is convenient, suffices for all, [then] the observance is to be performed there. But if that [*vihāra*] is at the border, in an uneven area, it should be said to the elder: 'Sir, your *vihāra* is an inconvenient place, there is not space for all; in such an *āvāsa* there is space, it is suitable to go there.'" Dhp II 77.$_{10-16}$: ***āvāsesū*** *ti saṅghikesu ca āvāsesu, yāni vihāramajjhe paṇītāni senāsanāni, tāni attano sandiṭṭhasambhattādīnaṃ bhikkhūnaṃ "tumhe idha vasathā" ti vicārento sayam pi varasenāsanaṃ palibuddhanto, sesānaṃ āgantukabhikkhūnaṃ paccantimāni lāmakasenāsanāni c' eva amanussapariggahitāni ca "tumhe idha vasathā" ti vicārento āvāsesu issariyaṃ icchati*. "**With regard to the āvāsas** ('dwellings'): and regarding the *āvāsas* belonging to the Saṅgha. One distributing the excellent lodgings in the middle of a *vihāra* ('monastery') among the bhikkhus who are his own friends and mates [with the words] 'you shall live here', keeping back an excellent lodging for himself indeed, [and] distributing to the remaining guest monks the adjacent inferior lodgings and those taken possession of by non-humans [with the words] 'you shall live here', [that one] excercises lordship with regard to the *āvāsas* ('dwellings')."

but in the same sense, i.e., as a designation of a dwelling place or a lodging (*senāsana*).[262] In the *Aṭṭhakathās* which quote the verses from the *Vinaya* praising the gift of a *vihāra* (*vihāradāna*) to the saṅgha (see above, 2.1.2), this is preceded by a prose passage in which the "gift of a dwelling" (*āvāsadāna*), is described as yielding great merit.[263] In the *Buddhavaṃsaṭṭhakathā* where it is described how the Buddha, after having accepted the Veḷuvanārāma, expressed his thanks for the donation of *vihāras* (*vihāradānānumodana*), the first verse begins with the advantage of the donation of *āvāsas*.[264]

Āvāsa used in the sense of "residence" in the *Vinaya* is defined by the commentary – completely in accordance with the use of the word *āvāsa* there – as a lodging built for living (*āvāso nāma vasanatthāya katasenāsaṃ*, Sp VI 1167.$_{7–8}$;[265] 1191.7–8). And *anāvāsa*, a non-residence in the *Vinaya*, is explained by the commentary in enumerating places that do not work as dwellings for monks (a *cetiya*, a *bodhi* tree shelter, a shed, etc.; Sp VI 1167.$_{8–10}$), though it certainly does not have this sense in the *Vinaya*. Because of understanding the *āvāsa* to be a dwelling, the person that might build and donate it, in analogy to a *vihāra* is designated as *āvāsasāmika*.[266] *Āvāsa* in the sense of residence may also be equated with *vihāra* in the sense of "monastery".[267]

262 Bv-a 67.$_{7–8}$: ***āvāsaṃ puññakamminan*** *ti āvasanti ettha puññakammino jānāti āvāso*. "**A dwelling-place for doers of merit** means: a dwelling-place in the sense that doers of merit dwelt there." (HORNER 1978 [2008]: 100); Vv-a 113.$_{29}$: *sukhavihārassa āvāso*. "A dwelling for living in happiness" (MASEFIELD 2015: 165); Vv-a 256.$_{9}$: *atth' ettha koci vasanayoggo āvāso?*" "'Is there some dwelling-place suitable [for us] to reside in?'" (MASEFIELD 2015: 393); Sp V 1088.$_{11–15}$: ***senāsanaṃ paññāpesī*** *ti* (Vin I 196.$_{29–30}$) *bhisiṃ vā kaṭasārakaṃ vā paññāpesi, paññāpetvā ca pana Soṇassa ārocesi: "āvuso satthā tayā saddhiṃ ekāvāse vasitukāmo, gandhakuṭiyaṃ yeva te senāsanaṃ paññāttan" ti*. "**He prepared a lodging**: he prepared a cushion or a mat; and having prepared [it] he announced to Soṇa: 'Friend, the Lord wants to stay together with you in a single (= the same) dwelling; your lodging is prepared in the Gandhakuṭi indeed.'" In the commented *Vinaya* passage *ekavihāra* was used for *ekāvāsa*.

263 Ud-a 419.$_{15–16}$: *āvāsadānaṃ nām' etaṃ gahapatayo mahantaṃ puññaṃ*; Ps III 26.$_{1–2}$ = Spk III 50.$_{30–31}$: *āvāsadānaṃ nām' etaṃ mahārāja mahantaṃ (puññaṃ tumhākaṃ)*.

264 Bv-a 21.$_{27}$: *āvāsadānassa pan' ānisaṃsaṃ*.

265 Here the commentary in accordance with most references in the *Aṭṭhakathā* layer explains *āvāsa* in *ekacchanne āvāse* as *senāsana*, though in the *Vinaya āvāse* does not refer to a dwelling place, but to the entire residence within which the respective monk is not allowed to live under one roof (*ekacchanne*) with an integer monk (Vin II 22.29–30).

266 Sp VI 1246.$_{14–16}$: *sace so āvāso jīrati, āvāsasāmikassa vā tassa vaṃse uppannassa vā kassaci kathetabbaṃ "āvāso vo nassati jaggatha etaṃ āvāsan"* ti (KIEFFER-PÜLZ 2022: 195).

267 Sp III 613.$_{27–30}$: ***āvāsikā hontī*** *ti ettha āvāso etesaṃ atthī ti āvāsikā. 'āvāso' ti vihāro vuccati. so yesam āyatto. navakammakaraṇa-purāṇapaṭisaṅkharaṇā-dubhāra-hāratāya te āvāsikā*. "**They are āvāsikās**, in this context the *āvāsa* ('residence') belongs to them [therefore, they are] *āvāsikas*. *Āvāsa* is called *vihāra*. That [*āvāsa* = *vihāra*] belongs to them. Because

4. Conclusions

To sum up, *vihāra* in the canonical texts is essentially used for a variety of small residential buildings made from different materials, inhabited by single monks or smaller groups of monks. They were erected or given by householders or monastics either to a single monk or to the Saṅgha or to the Saṅgha of the four quarters present and to come or, in the youngest strata of the canon, to the Buddha (i.e. as a shrine room). The donors of *vihāras* also had to supply the residents with the necessary requisites. Monks are not identified by their affiliation with a *vihāra*. *Vihāras* given to the Saṅgha are designated as *saṅghika vihāra* ("*vihāras* belonging to the Saṅgha") in the *Vinaya*, but not yet in the *Suttapiṭaka*. Individual *vihāras* are not yet described as *puggalika vihāra* in the entire canon, but only in the *Aṭṭhakathās*.

In the *Aṭṭhakathā* layer *vihāra* still designates single dwellings, especially in passages quoted from the canon, but in addition also designates permanent monastic compounds. Like the *āvāsa* in the canon these monastic compounds could be enclosed by a monastic boundary (*sīmā*). This boundary is then called among other things *vihārasīmā*, "boundary of the monastery", a term that does not yet exist in the canon. Whereas in the canon the Saṅgha, an individual (*puggala*) and, in a younger stratum of the *Vinaya*, a *cetiya* are mentioned as recipients of donations, in the *Aṭṭhakathā*, *navakamma* and a *vihāra* are added to this list. In epigraphical sources, the earliest donations to *vihāras* traced so far date from the first century CE. Unlike with donations to the Saṅgha, a group or an individual for which the rules in the monastic law code had to be observed, in the case of donations to *vihāras* even goods not allowable according to the monastic law code, like money, gold and silver, slaves, etc., must be accepted. Thus, everything could be given to a *vihāra*, and everything had to be accepted. The *vihāra* ("monastery") thus developed into the representative of a local Saṅgha and enabled the latter to accept whatever donors wanted to give. This shows that by the time of the *Aṭṭhakathā*, *vihāras* not only had developed into permanent monastic compounds that served as residences for local Saṅghas, but that they had become important instruments for the legal administration and economic situation of the Buddhist communities.

---

they take over [tasks] hard to bear [such as] carrying through new building work and restoration of old [structures, therefore] they are *āvāsikas*." Sp VI 1166.$_{27}$: ***abhikkhuko āvāso*** *ti* (Vin II 32.$_{23}$) *suññavihāro*. "**A residence without monks**, means: an empty *vihāra* (monastery)".

Ārāma was essentially used as a *pars pro toto* designation for the dwelling of a monks' community, or it described orchards or parks. In the *Aṭṭhakathās* the *ārāma* does not play an essential role.

The *āvāsa* which was the decisive unit for shaping the rules of the Buddhist communities in the canon, was a very large, not uniform area, that could enclose settlements (*gāma*), *ārāmas*, *vihāras* and *kuṭis*. At some time before the redactional closing of the Pāli canon it was defined by a boundary (*sīmā*) which then took over its function. At the time of the canon monks were not affiliated to *vihāras* or *ārāmas*, but to *āvāsas*. The bulk of the rules in the Pāli *Vinaya* are formulated for the *āvāsa*. In the *Aṭṭhakathās* the word *āvāsa* mostly describes a dwelling place, forming a synonym to *vihāra* in this meaning. And, in accordance with that, an owner of a dwelling could also be designated as *āvāsasāmi*.

Though the canon reflects a stage of development when monks used to live in buildings, those buildings seem to have been relatively small standalone buildings, often for one or two monks, or, in the younger textual strata, for groups up to thirty monks. The mention of meeting-halls in the *Sutta-* and *Vinayapiṭaka* shows that also larger rooms for the gathering of monastics were built. This corresponds to the archaeological record in the Western Deccan, were in addition to *vihāras* and worship caves with small *thūpas*, larger caves that could function as assembly halls formed part of what Rees defines as a monastery. This would align well with the sense of *āvāsas* as comprising individual dwellings.

The lists of buildings enumerated in the *Cullavagga* as having been built in an *ārāma* already at the Buddha's lifetime are of a later date, since several of the buildings listed are either not mentioned in the *Suttapiṭaka* at all (*kappiyakuṭi, vaccakuṭi*) or only in younger strata (*koṭṭhaka, aggisālā, jantāghara, maṇḍapa*). *Vihāras* used for specific purposes such as a storeroom (*bhaṇḍāgāra*), an *uposatha* house or a hut for things allowable according to the monastic law (*kappiyakuṭi*) are only mentioned in the *Vinaya* a few times, but again not in the *Suttapiṭaka*. The task of restoration (*navakamma*) of buildings mentioned in the *Khandhaka* section of the *Vinaya*, and the office of a *navakammika* introduced there, are both not traced in the *Suttapiṭaka*. This shows that activities connected with building work, with differentiating buildings according to their function, and with installing monks in offices to supervise restoration work as mentioned in the *Khandhaka* sections of the *Vinaya*, are largely unknown to the older sections of the *Suttavibhaṅga*, and to the *Suttapiṭaka*.

All in all, the Pāli canon reflects a stage in the development of monastic life where the not yet standardized association of monks living in individual *vihāras* within an *āvāsa* stood in the foreground. The rise of permanent monastic complexes and the associated administration are mainly to be traced to the *Khandhaka* section of the *Vinaya*. Thus, if we consider the various chronological strata of the *Vinaya*- and *Suttapiṭaka* it becomes obvious that large parts of these collections originated at a time when permanent monastic abodes were not yet the rule.

Acknowledgments

I thank Taiken Kyuma, Christian Lammerts, Annette Schmiedchen, Walter Slaje and Martin Straube for their suggestions and corrections, and Christian in addition for checking and improving my English. Thanks also go to Gethin Rees and Julia Shaw for providing me with several of their articles.

Abbreviations

The Abbreviations of the Pāli texts follow the abbreviations suggested in Helmer Smith, *A Critical Pāli Dictionary, Epilegomena to Vol. I*, Copenhagen: Ejnar Munksgaard, 1948. https://cpd.uni-koeln.de/intro/. The texts are quoted according to the editions of the Pali Text Society as far as available, for the rest the Burmese Chaṭṭhasaṅgīti Editions are quoted.

BD I–VI	*The Book of the Discipline*, see Bibliography, Horner, BD.
CPD	*A Critical Pali Dictionary*, Vols. 1–3 fasc. 8, begun by V. Trenckner, ed. D. Andersen et al., Copenhagen, Bristol 1924–2012 (Online: https://cpd.uni-koeln.de/search)
CSCD	Chaṭṭhasaṅgīti CDRom, Databank of Pali Texts (Online: https://tipitaka.org/cst4)
DOP	*Dictionary of Pali*, ed. MARGARET CONE, Vols. 1–3. Oxford, Bristol: Pali Text Society, 2001, 2010, 2020. (Online: combined and revised by MARTIN STRAUBE https://gandhari.org/dictionary?section=dop)
Niss	Nissaggiya
NWS	*Kumulatives Nachtragswörterbuch des Sanskrit*, WALTER SLAJE, JÜRGEN HANNEDER, PAUL MOLITOR, JÖRG RITTER (https://nws.uzi.uni-halle.de/search)
Pāc	Pācittiya
Pār	Pārājika
PED	*The Pali Text Society's Pali-English Dictionary*, ed. T. W. Rhys Davids, W Stede. London: Pali Text Society, 1921–1925 (Online: https://gandhari.org/dictionary?section=ptsd)
PW	Otto Böhtlingk, Rudolph Roth, *Sanskrit-Wörterbuch*, 7 Bde., St. Petersburg, 1855–1875.
Sgh	Saṅghādisesa

Bibliography

ALBERY, 2020: HENRY ALBERY, *Buddhism and Society in the Indic North and Northwest. 2nd Century BCE - 3rd Century CE.* PhD diss., University of Munich.

ALI 2003: DAUD ALI, Gardens in Early Indian Court Life, *Studies in History* 19.2, N.S., 221–252.

BECHERT 1982: HEINZ BECHERT, The Importance of Aśoka's so-called schism edict. In: *Indological and Buddhist Studies. Volume in Honour of Professor J. W. de Jong on his Sixtieth Birthday*, edited by L. A. HERCUS, F. B. J. KUIPER, R. RAJAPATIRANA, E. R. SKRZYPCZAK. Canberra: Faculty of Asian Studies, 61–68.

— 1992: The Writing Down of the Tripiṭaka in Pāli, *Wiener Zeitschrift für die Kunde Südasiens* 36, 45–53.

BODHI 2000: Bhikkhu BODHI, *The Connected Discourses of the Buddha. A New Translation of the Saṃyutta Nikāya*, Vol. 1. Oxford: Pali Text Society.

— 2002: ID., *The Middle Length Discourses of the Buddha. A Translation of the Majjhima Nikāya.* Translated from the Pāli by Bhikkhu ÑĀṆAMOLI and Bhikkhu BODHI. Pali Text Society Translation Series, No. 49. Oxford: Pali Text Society. [Original 1995, Revised 2001].

— 2017: ID., *The Suttanipāta. An Ancient Collection of the Buddha's Discourses Together with Its Commentaries. Paramatthajotikā II and excerpts from the Niddesa.* Pali Text Society Translation Series. No. 50. Melksham: Pali Text Society.

BOLLÉE 2015; WILLEM BOLLÉE, *A Cultural Encyclopaedia of the Kathāsaritsāgara in Keywords. Complementary to Norman Penzer's General Index on Charles Tawney's Translation.* Studia Indologica Universitatis Halensis. 8. Halle: Universitätsverlag Halle-Wittenberg.

BRONKHORST 2011: JOHANNES BRONKHORST, *Buddhism in the Shadow of Brahmanism.* Handbook of Oriental Studies. Section Two South Asia. 24. Leiden: Brill.

— 2016a. ID., *Āśramas, agrahāras*, and monasteries. In: *On the Growth and Composition of the Sanskrit Epics and Purāṇas. Relationship to Kāvya. Social and Economic Context. Proceedings of the Fifth Dubrovnik International Conference on the Sanskrit Epics and Purāṇas, August 2008.* Zagreb: Croatian Academy of Sciences and Art, 137–160.

— 2016b. ID., *How the Brahmins Won. From Alexander to the Guptas.* Handbook of Oriental Studies. Section Two South Asia. 30. Leiden: Brill.

CHILDERS: ROBERT CAESAR CHILDERS. *A Dictionary of the Pali Language.* Kyoto: Rinsen Book Company [Original: London 1875].

CLARKE 2015: SHAYNE CLARKE, Vinayas. In: *Brill's Encyclopedia of Buddhism*, Vol. 1, edited by Jonathan A. Silk et al. Leiden: Brill, 60–87.

COUSINS 2012: L. S. COUSINS, The Teachings of the Abhayagiri School. In: *How Theravāda is Theravāda? Exploring Buddhist Identities*, edited by PETER SKILLING et al. Bangkok: Silkworm Books, 67–127.

DEHEJIA 1992: VIDYA DEHEJIA, The Collective and Popular Basis of Early Buddhist Patronage: Sacred Monuments, 100 BC–AD 250. In: *The Powers of Art. Patronage in Indian Culture*, edited by BARBARA STOLER MILLER, Delhi: Oxford University Press, 35–45.

DESHPANDE 1959: M. N. DESHPANDE, The Rock-Cut Caves of Pitalkhora in the Deccan, *Ancient India* 15, 66–93.

DUTT 1962: SUKUMAR DUTT, *Buddhist Monks and Monasteries of India.* London: Allen & Unwin.

FALK 1997: HARRY FALK, The Preamble at Paṅgurāriā. In: *Bauddhavidyāsudhākaraḥ. Studies in Honour of Heinz Bechert on the Occasion of His 65th Birthday*, edited by P. KIEFFER-PÜLZ, J.-U. HARTMANN. Indica et Tibetica, 30. Swisttal-Odendorf: Indica et Tibetica, 107–121.

— 2012: ID., Small Scale Buddhism. In: *Devadattīyam. Johannes Bronkhorst Felicitation Volume*, edited by FRANCOIS VOEGELI, VINCENT ELTSCHINGER, DANIELLE FELLER et al. Bern, Berlin: Peter Lang, 491–517.

FIORUCCI 2023: ANTHONY FIORUCCI, *Guilty Pleasures. Kāma in ancient India and the Pali Vinaya.* PhD diss., University of Uppsala.

FOGELIN 2003: JENS FOGELIN, *Beyond the Monastery Walls: The Archaeology of Early Buddhism in North Coastal Andhra Pradesh, India.* PhD diss., University of Michigan.

— 2015: ID., *An Archaeological History of Indian Buddhism.* Oxford: University Press.

GRÄFE 1974: UDO HEINER GRÄFE, *Systematische Zusammenstellung Kulturgeschichtlicher Informationen aus dem Vinayapitakam der Theravādin.* PhD diss., University of Göttingen.

HALLISEY, 2015: CHARLES HALLISEY, *Therigatha. Poems of the First Buddhist Women.* Cambridge, Mass/London: Murty Classical Library.

HEIRMAN & TORCK 2012: ANNE HEIRMAN and MATHIEU TORCK, *A Pure Mind in a Clean Body: Bodily Care in the Buddhist Monasteries of Ancient India and China.* Gent: Ginko Academia Press.

VON HINÜBER 1995a: OSKAR VON HINÜBER, Buddhist Law According to the Theravāda-Vinaya. A Survey of Theory and Practice, *Journal of the International Association of Buddhist Studies* 18.1, 7–45 [Reprint in: VON HINÜBER 2009, 188–226].

— 1995b: ID., Linguistic Considerations on the Date of the Buddha. In: *When Did the Buddha Live? The Controversy on the Dating of the Historical Buddha*, edited by HEINZ BECHERT. Delhi: Sri Satguru, 185–194. [Reprint in: VON HINÜBER 2009, 479–488].

— 1996: ID., *A Handbook of Pāli Literature.* Indian Philology and South Asian Studies, 2. Berlin: Walter de Gruyter.

— 1999: ID., *Das Pātimokkhasutta — Seine Gestalt und seine Entstehungsgeschichte (Studien zur Literatur des Theravāda-Buddhismus II).* Akademie der Wissenschaften und der Literatur, Mainz. Abhandlungen der geistes- und sozialwissenschaftlichen Klasse, Jg. 1999, Nr. 6.

— 2004: ID.,Vom Bettler zum Millionär. Der buddhistische Mönch und das Geld, *Tibet und Buddhismus*, Oktober, November, Dezember 2004, Heft 71, 23–27.

— 2006: ID., Everyday Life in an Ancient Indian Buddhist Monastery. In: *Annual Report of the International Research Institute for Advanced Buddhology at Soka University for the Academic Year 2005.* Tokyo: The International Research Institute for Advanced Buddhology, Soka University, 3–31. [Reprint in: VON HINÜBER 2009, II 869–897].

— 2009: ID., *Kleine Schriften*, Teil I–II, ed. HARRY FALK and WALTER SLAJE. Glasenapp-Stiftung. 47. Wiesbaden: Harrassowitz Verlag.

— 2017: ID., Indien. In: *Handwörterbuch der Antiken Sklaverei* (HAS), Bd. 2, edited by H. HEINEN. Stuttgart: Franz Steiner Verlag, 1486–1492.

HORNER, BD: ISALINE BLEW HORNER (transl.), *The Book of the Discipline.* 6 Vols. Sacred Books of the Buddhists 10–11, 13–14, 20, 25. London: Luzac & Company, 1938–1966.

HORNER 1969: ID., *Milinda's Questions*, translated from the Pali, 2 Vols. London: Luzac & Company.

— 1978 [2008]: ID., *The Clarifier of the Sweet Meaning (Madhuratthavilāsinī), Commentary on the Chronicle of Buddhas (Buddhavaṃsa) by Buddhadatta Thera.* Oxford: Pali Text Society [Original 1978; reprint 2008].

HUNTINGTON & CHANDRASEKHAR 2000: JOHN C. HUNTINGTON & CHAYA CHANDRASEKHAR, Architecture: Buddhist Monasteries in Southern Asia. In: *Encyclopedia of Monasticism*,

Vol. I: *A–L*, edited by WILLIAM M. JOHNSTON, CLAIRE RENKIN. Chicago: Fitzroy Dearborn Publishers, 55–66.

HU-VON HINÜBER 2018: HAIYAN HU-VON HINÜBER, What to Do if the Owner of a Monastery Is Put in Jail? The Saṅgha's Begging Area according to the Early Vinaya Texts. In: *Saddharmāmṛtam: Festschrift für Jens-Uwe Hartmann zum 65. Geburtstag*, edited by O. VON CRIEGERN, G. MELZER & J. SCHNEIDER. Wien: Arbeitskreis für tibetische und buddhistische Studien Universität Wien, 201–214.

KAJIHARA 2017: MIEKO KAJIHARA, Giving the Bride to the Bridegroom with Water at the Ancient Indian Marriage Ritual, *Studies in Indian Philosophy and Buddhism* 25.3: 1–111.

KARASHIMA 2012: SEISHI KARASHIMA, *Die Abhisamācārikā Dharmāḥ. Verhaltensregeln für buddhistische Mönche der Mahāsāṃghika-Lokottaravādins*, hrsg. unter Mitwirkung von OSKAR VON HINÜBER. Bd. III: *Grammatik, Glossar und Nachträge*. Bibliotheca Philologica et Philosophica Buddhica, XIII, 3. Tokyo: The International Research Institute for Advanced Buddhology Soka University.

KIEFFER-PÜLZ 1992: PETRA KIEFFER-PÜLZ, *Die Sīmā. Vorschriften zur Regelung der buddhistischen Gemeindegrenze in älteren buddhistischen Texten*. Monographien zur indischen Archäologie, Kunst und Philologie, 8. Berlin: Reimer Verlag, 1992.

— 1994: ID., Bemerkungen zu dem Wort *jagatī*. In: *Festschrift Klaus Bruhn zur Vollendung des 65. Lebensjahres* dargebracht von Schülern, Freunden und Kollegen, edited by NALINI BALBIR, JOACHIM K. BAUTZE. Reinbek: Wezler, 339–359.

— 2007: ID., Stretching the Vinaya Rules and Getting Away with it (11th I. B. Horner Lecture, 2005), *Festschrift in honour of the 80th birthday of K. R. Norman in 2005 and the 125th anniversary in 2006 of the founding of the Pali Text Society. Journal of the Pali Text Society* 29, 1–49.

— 2010: ID., [Review to:] JONATHAN SILK, Managing Monks. Administrators and Administration, Oxford 2008. *Indo-Iranian Journal* 53, 71–88.

— 2013: ID., *Verlorene Gaṇṭhipadas zum buddhistischen Ordensrecht. Untersuchungen zu den in der Vajirabuddhiṭīkā zitierten Kommentaren Dhammasiris und Vajirabuddhis*, 3 Vols. Veröffentlichungen der Indologischen Kommission, 1. Wiesbaden: Harrassowitz Verlag.

— 2020–2021: ID., Brief Summary of the Development of Buddhist Monastic Law Codes and Institutions, *Buddhism, Law & Society* 6, 147–184.

— 2022: ID., The Owner of a Residential Building or Monastery (*sāmi[ka]*, *āvāsasāmika*, *vihārasāmi[ka]*) in the Theravāda Tradition. In: *Connecting the Art, Literature, and Religion of South and Central Asia. Studies in Honour of Monika Zin*, edited by INES KONCZAK-NAGEL, SATOMI HIYAMA and ASTRID KLEIN. Delhi: Dev Publishers, 189–198.

— 2024: ID., A note on the *vihāra* as a recipient of donations in earlier Theravāda Buddhism. In: *Annual Report of the International Research Institute for Advanced Buddhology at Soka University for the Academic Year 2023*, Vol. XXVII. Tokyo: The International Research Institute for Advanced Buddhology, Soka University, 29–40.

LAMOTTE, ÉTIENNE. 1988: ÉTIENNE LAMOTTE, *History of Indian Buddhism*, transl. from the French by SARA WEBB-BOIN. Publications de l'Institut Orientaliste de Louvain, 36. Louvain-la-Neuve: Université Catholique de Louvain. Institut Orientaliste 1988 [French Original 1958].

MARSHALL 1951: Sir JOHN MARSHALL, *Taxila. An Illustrated Account of Archaeological Excavations Carried out at Taxila under the Orders of the Government of India between the Years 1913 and 1934. In three Volumes.* Vol. I: *Structural remains*. Cambridge: Cambridge University Press.

MASEFIELD 1980: PETER MASEFIELD, *Elucidation of the Intrinsic Meaning so named The Commentary on the Peta-Stories. (Paramatthadīpanī nāma Petavatthu-aṭṭhakathā) by Dhammapāla*, translated by U BA KYAW, edited and annotated by PETER MASEFIELD. London: Pali Text Society

— 2015: ID., *Elucidation of the Intrinsic Meaning so named The Commentary on the Vimāna Stories. (Paramattha-dīpanī nāma Vimānavatthu-aṭṭhakathā)*, translated by PETER MASEFIELD. Bristol: Pali Text Society.

MITRA 1971: DEBALA MITRA, *Buddhist Monuments*. Calcutta: Sahitya Samsad.

NORMAN 2007: K. R. NORMAN, *The Elders Verses* I: *Theragāthā*. Translated with an introduction and notes. Pali Text Society Translation Series No. 38. Lancaster: Pali Text Society

NORMAN, KIEFFER-PÜLZ, PRUITT 2018: K. R. NORMAN, PETRA KIEFFER-PÜLZ, WILLIAM PRUITT. *Overcoming Doubts (Kaṅkhāvitaraṇī)*, Vol. 1: *The Bhikkhu-Pātimokkha Commentary*, translated [from Pāli into English]. Bristol: The Pali Text Society.

OLIVELLE 2025: PATRICK OLIVELLE, Saṅghabheda: Monastic and Political. In: *Minding the Buddha's Business. Essays in Honor of Gregory Schopen*, ed. DANIEL BOUCHER and SHAYNE CLARKE. 249–364. Studies in Indian and Tibetan Buddhism. New York: Wisdom, 349–364.

PIERUCCINI 2018: CINZIA PIERUCCINI, Travelling Śākyamuni, Groves, Reserves and Orchards. In: *Journeys and Travellers in Indian Literature and Art*, edited by DANUTA STASIK, ANNA TRYNKOWSKA. Warsaw: Elipsa, 62–77.

REES 2010: GETHIN REES, *Buddhism and Donation: Rock-cut Monasteries of the Western Ghats*. PhD diss., Wolfson College, University of Cambridge, Department of Archaeology.

ROTH 1997: GUSTAV ROTH, *Ārāma, Vihāra and Mahāvihāra*. Patna: Bauddha Sanskriti Kendra.

SALOMON 1999: RICHARD SALOMON, *Indian Epigraphy. A Guide to the Study of Inscriptions in Sanskrit, Prakrit, and the Other Indo-Aryan Languages*, New York: Oxford University Press.

SCHOPEN 1985 [1997]: GREGORY SCHOPEN, Two Problems in the History of Indian Buddhism. The Layman/Monk Distinction and the Doctrines of the Transference of Merit, *Studien zur Indologie und Iranistik* 10, 9–47 [Reprint in: SCHOPEN 1997, 23–55].

— 1991 [1997]: ID., Archaeology and Protestant Presuppositions in the Study of Indian Buddhism, *History of Religions* 31, 1–23 [Reprint in: SCHOPEN 1997, 1–22].

— 1994 [2004a]: ID., Doing Business for the Lord: Lending on Interest and Written Loan Contracts in the *Mūlasarvāstivāda-vinaya*, *Journal of the American Oriental Society* 114.4, 527–553 [Reprint in: SCHOPEN 2004a, 45–90].

— 1995 [2004a]: ID., Monastic Law Meets the Real World. A Monk' Continuing right to Inherit Family Property in Classical India, *History of Religions* 35.2, 101–123 [Reprint in: SCHOPEN 2004a, 170–192].

— 1996a [2004a]: ID., What's in a Name: The Religious Function of the Early Donative Inscriptions. In: *Unseen Presence: The Buddha and Sanchi*, edited by V. DEHEJIA. Bombay: Marg Publ., 58–73 [Reprint in: SCHOPEN 2004a, 382–394].

— 1996b [2004a]: ID., The Lay Ownership of Monasteries and the Role of the Monk in Mūlasarvāstivādin Monasticism, *The Journal of the International Association of Buddhist Studies* 10.1, 81–126 [Reprint in: SCHOPEN 2004a, 219–259].

— 1997: ID., *Bones, Stones, and Buddhist Monks. Collected Papers on the Archaeology, Epigraphy and Texts of Monastic Buddhism in India. Studies in the Buddhist Traditions*. Honolulu: University of Hawai'i Press.

— 2000b [2004a]: ID., The Good Monk and His Money in a Buddhist Monasticism of 'the Mahāyāna Period', *The Eastern Buddhist*, n.s. 32.1, 85–105 [Reprint in: SCHOPEN 2004a, 1–18].

— 2000c: ID., Hierarchy and Housing in a Buddhist Monastic Code. A Translation of the Sanskrit Text of the *Śayanāsanavastu* of the *Mūlasarvāstivāda-vinaya*. Part One, *Buddhist Literature* 2, 94–106.

— 2004a: ID., *Buddhist Monks and Business Matters. Still More Papers on Monastic Buddhism in India*. Honolulu: University of Hawai'i Press, 219–259.

— 2004b: ID., Art, Beauty, and the Business of Running a Buddhist Monastery in Early Northwest India, in SCHOPEN 2004a, 19–44.

— 2006a: ID., The Buddhist 'Monastery' and the Indian Garden: Aesthetics, Assimilations, and the Siting of Monastic Establishments, *Journal of the American Oriental Society* 126.4, 487–505.

— 2006b: ID., A well-sanitized shroud. Asceticism and institutional values in the Middle Period of Buddhist monasticism. In: *Between the Empires. Society in India 300 BCE to 400 CE*, edited by PATRICK OLIVELLE. Oxford: Oxford University Press, 315–347 [Reprint in: Schopen 2014, 276–310].

— 2007: ID., Cross-dressing with the dead: asceticism, ambivalence, and institutional values in an Indian monastic code. In: *The Buddhist Dead. Practices, Discourses, Representations*, edited by BRYAN J. CUEVAS and JACQUELINE I. STONE. Studies in East Asian Buddhism. 20. Honolulu: University of Hawai'i Press, 60–104.

— 2008 [2014]: ID., Separate but Equal. Property Rights and the Legal Independence of Buddhist Nuns and Monks in Early North India, *Journal of the American Oriental Society* 128.4, 625–640 [Reprint in: SCHOPEN 2014, 73–94].

— 2014: ID., *Buddhist Nuns, Monks, and Other Worldy Matters. Recent Papers on Monastic Buddhism in India*. Honolulu: University of Hawai'i Press.

SHAW 2009: JULIA SHAW, Stūpas, Monasteries, and Relics in the Landscape. Typological, Spatial, and Temporal Patterns in the Sanchi Area. In: *Buddhist Stupas in South Asia*, edited by JASON HAWKES and AKIRA SHIMADA. Delhi, Oxford: Oxford University Press, 114–145.

— 2011: ID., Monasteries, Monasticism, and Patronage in Ancient India: Mawasa, a Recently Documented Hilltop Buddhist Complex in the Sanchi Area of Madhya Pradesh, *South Asian Studies* 27.2, 111–130.

SLAJE 2022: WALTER SLAJE, *Kaschmir unter den Šāhmīrīden. Śrīvaras Jaina- und Rājataraṅgiṇī, A.D. 1451–1486. Vier zeitgeschichtliche Herrscherviten eines indo-persischen Sultanats*. Studia Indologica Universitatis Halensis. 20. Halle: Universitätsverlag Halle-Wittenberg.

STRONG 1977: JOHN S. STRONG, *Gandhakuṭī*: The Perfumed Chamber of the Buddha, *History of Religions* 16.4, 390–406.

UPĀSAK 2001: C. S. UPĀSAK, *Dictionary of Early Buddhist Monastic Terms (Based on Pali Literature)*. Nālanda: Nava Nalanda Mahavihara, second ed.

WALTERS 2017: JONATHAN WALTERS, *Legends of the Buddhist Saints. Apadānapāli*, translated [from the Pāli]. Whitman College 2017. (http://apadanatranslation.com).

— 2022: ID., *Legends of the Buddhist Saints. Apadānapāli*, translated [from the Pāli]. Published by Jonathan S. Walters and Whitman College 2022. (http://apadanatranslation.com).

YAMAGIWA 2002: NOBUYUKI YAMAGIWA, *Ārāmika* – Gardener or Park Keeper? One of the Marginals around the Buddhist *Saṃgha*. In: *Buddhist and Indian Studies in Honour of Professor Sodo Mori*, edited by the Publication Committee for Buddhist and Indian Studies in Honour of Professor Dr. Sodo Mori. Tokyo: Kokusai Bukkyoto Kyokai, 363–385.

ZUKAS 2023: DAVID ZUKAS, Early Indian Buddhist Monasteries: Bhaja, Bedsa, and Karla from 200 BCE to 700 CE, *International Journal of Buddhist Thought & Culture* 33.1, 61–92.

Vihāra, mahāvihāra, vihāramaṇḍala: The Terminology for Buddhist Monasteries and Nunneries in Indian Epigraphical Sources from Late Antiquity to the Early Medieval Period

Annette Schmiedchen[1]

1. Introduction

It is a well-known fact that the name of the present Indian state of Bihar is derived from the Sanskrit (and Prākrit) term for 'monastery', *vihāra*. If someone looks up the word *vihāra* in the digital *Nachtragswörterbuch des Sanskrit* (NWS) by the Indology Department of Martin-Luther-Universität Halle-Wittenberg, then he/she comes across, *inter alia*, the German explanation 'buddhistisches oder Jaina-Kloster' from OTTO VON BÖHTLINGK,[2] and the English translation 'Buddhist or Jaina monastery'[3]. This paper will focus on the epigraphic use of the term, which is also referred to in the respective entry in the NWS.[4]

1 The research for this contribution was carried out as part of the project "The Domestication of 'Hindu' Asceticism and the Religious Making of South and Southeast Asia" (DHARMA), funded from 2019 to 2026 by the European Research Council (ERC) under the European Union's Horizon 2020 research and innovation programme (grant agreement no. 809994). I would like to thank Max Deeg, Ryosuke Furui, Petra Kieffer-Pülz, Taiken Kyuma, and Vincent Tournier for their numerous suggestions on an earlier, still much shorter, draft of this paper.

2 See BÖHTLINGK (1879–89, vol. 6: 141): "*vihāra* m. n. ... 7) *ein buddhistisches* oder Jaina-*Kloster, ein solches Heiligthum*". See also the respective entry on https://nws.uzi.uni-halle.de/.

3 See SIRCAR (1966: 371): "*vihāra* ... a Buddhist or Jain monastery or temple or convent".

4 For the term *mahāvihāra*, see also DURT & FORTE 1983, esp. 679–681 of this entry on Daiji.

DOI: 10.13173/9783447124249.057

Attestations for the use of the term *vihāra* in inscriptions related to Jainism are mainly confined to Bengal and the Gupta period.[5] In the context of Buddhism, the term *vihāra* appears in numerous non-epigraphic texts composed in Sanskrit, Prākrit, and Pāli, as well as in various types of inscriptions from several regions and different times. In secondary literature, the term 'vihāra'[6] has been applied to the archaeological remains of Buddhist monastic edifices, too. However, such labels and identifications are often rather problematic, unless corroborated by written sources.

As already mentioned, this article will focus on the epigraphic use of these terms, and more specifically on the occurrence of the expressions *mahāvihāra* and *vihāramaṇḍala* in contrast to the 'simple' word *vihāra* in inscriptions dating from late antiquity to the early medieval period, as these were the centuries when those derivations were employed. Relevant phrases are attested in copper-plate and stone inscriptions, as well as on seals or sealings, denoting

1. Buddhist monastic edifices in an original/narrower sense, namely, residential buildings of monastic orders,
2. Buddhist monastic institutions in a later/broader sense, and
3. a combination of both, as the distinction is not always clear.

In epigraphic boundary descriptions and on seals/sealings, the terms *vihāra* and *mahāvihāra* are used in phrases expressing a monastery's rights over land or its ownership of other objects. However, most frequently these inscriptional terms do occur when a specific monastery received a grant, donation, or endowment. A *vihāra* could be mentioned

1. as the residence of a Buddhist monastic order receiving a donation,
2. as the direct recipient of a grant, or
3. as the institution to which other religious edifices or structures like *stūpas*, etc. were attached.

In epigraphic eulogies and panegyrics, kings and rulers were often lauded in a general way as builders of *vihāras* and other religious edifices or infrastructure. Besides, there are also inscriptions that record and praise the erection of specific monastic buildings. In the course of time, when reno-

5 The attestations come from three copper plates, namely, the Jagadishpur plate, dated Gupta era 128, the Paharpur plate, dated Gupta era 159, and a grant of land to three Jaina monasteries at ancient Śiṣīpuñja, Madhyamasṛgālikā and Grāmakūṭagohālī, dated Gupta era 198; see GRIFFITHS 2018: 35–39, 45–50.

6 I will not italicise these terms if used by archaeologists without epigraphic corroboration.

vating older structures might have become a relevant factor, the term *vihāra* began to appear in the stipulations of the purposes of endowments of land and villages stating that the income from these assets was also to be used for the maintenance of the edifices.

Based on inscriptions from various Indian regions, but with no claim of comprehensiveness, this paper attempts to investigate potential structural differences between monasteries called *vihāra*, *mahāvihāra*, or *vihāramaṇḍala*. Additional foundations and endowments (German: 'Zustiftung') had the potential to change the character of the already existing monastic institutions. 'Ordinary' monasteries (*vihāra*) could be turned, through the addition of further architectural and organisational units (*vihāra* or *vihārikā*, 'small monastery'[7]), into 'great monasteries' (*mahāvihāra*) or into whole 'monastic complexes' (*vihāramaṇḍala*). But there is also evidence for the fact that some *mahāvihāras* were called 'great monastery' right from the time of their erection or inauguration; and in a number of cases, no structural differences are discernible, or, at best, differences in size or 'importance' between monasteries denoted as *vihāra* or as *mahāvihāra*.

2. Āndhradeśa, 3rd Century

The terms *vihāra* and *mahāvihāra* are used in several 3rd-century epigraphs of the Ikṣvāku rulers from Āndhradeśa in Southeast India.[8] Especially at the multi-site Buddhist monastic centre of Nagarjunakonda (now an island in present-day Palnadu District of Andhra Pradesh ; see Figure 1), the ancient Vijayapurī or capital of the Ikṣvāku dynasty, attestations of the two expressions have been found in Prākrit inscriptions engraved on pillars or on other artefacts.

Two pillar inscriptions from site 1 at Nagarjunakonda, dating from the rule of Vīrapurisadatta (reigned c. 240/50–265/75 CE; EIAD 10 & 21), mention a *mahāvihāra*. EIAD 10 belongs to a series of epigraphs inscribed on the extant remains of 18 *āyaka* pillars recovered from the west, south, east, and north sides of the great stūpa.[9] These texts, issued on the very same day in the 6th regnal year, are closely related to each other (BAUMS et al. 2016: 379). In the words of TOURNIER & SHIMADA (forthcoming: 18), these inscriptions

7 A *vihārikā* may have also existed as an independent structure; see, e.g., BOSMA 2018: 95.

8 For early attestations of the term *vihāra*, see TOURNIER 2021–22: 5, fn. 11; GRIFFITHS & TOURNIER, EIAD 3, line 2 = http://hisoma.huma-num.fr/exist/apps/EIAD/works/EIAD0003.xml.

9 Non-italicised terms indicate archaeologists' use without any direct epigraphic attestation.

bear testimony to the fact that the great stūpa "was built with the support of an impressive group of eight female aristocrats." The collective donative effort was led by Cāntisirī, the paternal aunt of King Vīrapurisadatta. But the use of the term *mahāvihāra* is attested only in one epigraph of this series, in EIAD 10, in which the genitive form *mahāvihārasa* is applied to describe the *mahācetiya* (Sanskrit *mahācaitya*), the stūpa site where this pillar was erected, as belonging to the 'great monastery'.[10]

EIAD 21, on the other hand, is one inscription in a series of fragments of at least six pillars found at the columned hall of site 1. Two of the epigraphs, including EIAD 21, are dated to the 15th regnal year of King Vīrapurisadatta. They seem to record the erection of a stone structure, most probably a *maṁtava* (Sanskrit *maṇḍapa*) or pavilion, 'together with' or 'enclosed by four houses' (*sa-cātusāla; cātusāla-parigahita*), by the same royal lady Cāntisirī for the school of the Aparamahāvinaseliyas. These monastic structures are described to have been located "at the base of the great shrine" (*mahācetiya-pādamūle*), or, according to EIAD 21 even more specifically, "in the great monastery, at the base of the great shrine" (*mahāvihāre mahācetiya-pādamūle*).[11]

EIAD 28, dated to the 18th year of the reign of Vīrapurisadatta, appears to commemorate the same act of the erection of a *maṁtava* with a *cātusāla* by Cāntisirī, now being also described as mother-in-law of the king. The inscription is engraved on floor slabs which were discovered in the apsidal temple of site 1. The *mahāvihāra* is not mentioned as point of reference; the landmarks here are first – and newly – the *cetiyaghāra*, a shrine hall being identified with the apsidal temple, the epigraph's findspot, and secondly, again the base of the *mahācetiya*.[12]

In a commentary on EIAD 21, GRIFFITHS & TOURNIER explain the Prākrit term *cātusāla* thus: "This word seems to denote a building with rows of cells on all sides. For a ground plan indicating the referent of this gift, see SARKAR 1960: pl. LXVIII."[13] The monastic residence at Nagarjunakonda's site 1, however, has, although being quadrangular in shape, only three residen-

10 See GRIFFITHS & TOURNIER, EIAD 10, line 5: *mahāvihārasa mahācetiya-* = http://hisoma.huma-num.fr/exist/apps/EIAD/works/EIAD0010.xml.

11 For this attestation of the term *cātusāla*, see GRIFFITHS & TOURNIER, EIAD 21, line 6: *sa-cātu[sāla]* = http://hisoma.huma-num.fr/exist/apps/EIAD/works/EIAD0021.xml.

12 For the reference to the apsidal temple, see GRIFFITHS & TOURNIER, EIAD 28, line 1: *cetiyaghar⟨e⟩* = http://hisoma.huma-num.fr/exist/apps/EIAD/works/EIAD0028.xml. For the great stūpa, see EIAD 28, line 3: *ma⟨⟨hā⟩⟩cetiyapādam[ū]le*. See also BAUMS et al. 2016: 386 and fn. 83.

13 See EIAD 21. For the same ground-plan, see also SARKAR 1966: pl. XIII.

tial wings, with no cells along the entrance side. The Sanskrit equivalent *catuḥśāla* is known as designation for a common Indian house type, i.e., an "edifice with four wings arranged around an open courtyard" (OTTER 2010: 231). Art historians have assumed that the development of the 'quadrangular or courtyard monastery' in Buddhist architecture was inspired by this traditional house type (PLAESCHKE ²1974: 29–31). Some of the most ancient archaeological remains of this form in Buddhist architecture dating from c. 100 CE have been found in South Asia's northwest, in the Gandhāra region. An adaptation of this type of residence is also traceable in the cave architecture at the western coast. In course of time, inward-facing cells arranged around a rectangular courtyard became the most prominent form of monastic dwellings in India (recently COPPLESTONE 2024: 25). This type of living space is also well-attested in Nagarjunakonda's excavated remains, not only at site 1.[14] But it is known from the commentarial literature on the Pāli *vinaya* as well as from archaeology that cells built in a single row with a veranda in front were typical for Āndhra (KIEFFER-PÜLZ 1993: 191–194; FOGELIN 2006: 85–90; TOURNIER & SHIMADA forthcoming: 8–9).

The sequence of the epigraphically recorded building activity at site 1 is particularly revealing with regard to the question what the term *mahāvihāra* might have meant at Nagarjunakonda where several structural phases can be distinguished archaeologically. EIAD 10 commemorates the first step which was probably completed in the 6th year of King Vīrapurisadatta, the erection of the *mahācetiya*, the great stūpa, assigning this structure already to the *mahāvihāra*, although residential quarters seem not to have existed yet at the site. According to EIAD 21, the erection of the residential quarters, consisting of a pavilion or pillared hall (*maṁtava*) which was surrounded by a four-house structure (*cātusāla*) "in the *mahāvihāra*, at the base of the great shrine", presumably seems to have followed in the 15th regnal year of Vīrapurisadatta. The third phase of this building programme is attested in EIAD 28 from the 18th regnal year of the same king. While this inscription apparently mentions the erection of the residential quarters again, it also refers to the *cetiyaghara* for the first time. The latter fact taken together with the findspot, the apsidal temple, makes a chronological link between the erection of this shrine hall and the date of EIAD 28 plausible.

TOURNIER & SHIMADA (forthcoming: 16) call the *mahācetiya* or great stūpa of site 1 with its diameter of 27.5 metres and its typically Āndhra four car-

14 Four-winged structures were located at sites 5, 24, 32A, 38, 43, 106; three-winged structures at sites 1, 2, 3, 4, 9. For a map, see http://hisoma.huma-num.fr/exist/apps/EIAD/gis.html.

dinal āyaka platforms with originally five pillars each "the most imposing Buddhist monument near the capital Vijayapurī". To the east of the great stūpa, so-to-say *mahācetiya-pādamūle*, the residential quarters were situated, with the entrance towards the west and consisting of a pillared stone pavilion in the courtyard and surrounding wings with altogether 25–29 cells. At the western wall of the residential building, between its entrance and southwest corner, the *cetiyaghara* was located, with its apsis directed south. Site 1 was a typically Āndhra composite structure of a large free-standing main stūpa, an enshrined secondary stūpa, and a quadrangular living space.

But the question remains what the term *mahāvihāra* exactly denotes in EIAD 10 and 21.[15] It seems very likely that this expression was meant to refer not only to the dwelling space, but rather to the whole monastic complex of site 1. It is also possible that the use of this term already at a time when the monastic compound was still in the making alludes to the fact that there must have been a detailed planning for this architectural endeavour. The reason for designating this site as a *mahāvihāra*, and not only as a *vihāra*, might have been the intended (and later actual) size of the whole monastic complex, also underlined by the fact that the *mahācetiya* or the main stūpa of site 1 was – as already mentioned – "the most imposing" structure at Nagarjunakonda.

A series of three pillar epigraphs from site 5 at Nagarjunakonda, dated to year 2 of the reign of King Ehavala-Cāntamūla (reigned c. 265/75–290/300 CE; EIAD 44–46), records that the king's mother, the queen of Vīrapurisadatta, had established a *vihāra*, which is once explicitly labelled *devī-vihāra* (EIAD 45), and which is in all the three inscriptions specified as a monastery dedicated to the teachers of the Bahuśrutīya school.[16] Archaeology reveals that site 5 comprised of a great stūpa (*mahācetiya* in Āndhra taxonomy), two apsidal halls with stūpas (*cetiyaghara*), a pillared hall (*maṁtava*) surrounded by four wings (*cātusāla*), with four times seven, altogether 28, cells, and some other structures.[17]

---

15 At Nagarjunakonda, the term *mahāvihāra* is also attested in EIAD 20, line 3; EIAD 61, line 2. For a detailed discussion of these two inscriptions, see KIEFFER-PÜLZ forthcoming.

16 EIAD 44 is known to have been discovered at the pillared hall. See also GRIFFITHS & TOURNIER, EIAD 44, line 8 = http://hisoma.huma-num.fr/exist/apps/EIAD/works/EIAD0044.xml; EIAD 45, lines 10–12 = http://hisoma.huma-num.fr/exist/apps/EIAD/works/EIAD0045.xml; EIAD 46, line 7 = http://hisoma.huma-num.fr/exist/apps/EIAD/works/EIAD0046.xml.

17 For typical Āndhra monastic compounds and epigraphical taxonomy, see SARKAR 1966: 90–94; TOURNIER 2021–22: 23 and fn. 64; TOURNIER & SHIMADA forthcoming: 8; KIM 2024: 11–12.

In terms of extent, the residential structure of site 5 is comparable to that of site 1: The measurements of the two *maṁtavas* and both *cātusālas* as well as the total numbers of cells are almost the same.[18] Only with regard to the dimensions of their respective *mahācetiya*, size may have been a distinguishing feature between a *vihāra* and a *mahāvihāra* in early Āndhradeśa. The composite structure of *vihāras* and *mahāvihāras* seems to have been equally similar. The compound character of site 5 is not directly reflected in the extant epigraphs. It can be assumed, however, that the term *vihāra* likewise referred to the whole monastic complex, including its substructures, all the more as it is explicitly stated that the *vihāra* was 'equipped with everything' (*sava-jāta-niyuta*).[19]

Other inscriptions from Nagarjunakonda also allude to the fact that the term *vihāra* (as well as *mahāvihāra*) was used with a superordinate connotation, beyond any purely residential meaning. EIAD 20, for instance, records, *inter alia*, the erection of one *cetiyaghara* **in the** *vihāra* on Siripavvata, of another *cetiyaghara* **in the** Kulaha-*vihāra*, of a *bodhirukha-pāsāda* **in the** Sīhaḷa-*vihāra*, etc.[20]

Not only several stone inscriptions, but also the oldest extant copper-plate charter discovered in India, the Patagandigudem plates of the Ikṣvāku king Ehavala-Cāntamūla, contains the term *mahāvihāra* twice. The findspot of this Buddhist endowment record issued from a royal military camp at Dhaññakaḍa (Dhānyakaṭaka) is reported to be the hamlet Patagandigudem near the village of Kallacheruvu (in Kamavarapukota Mandal of present-day Eluru District, see Figure 1). The charter (EIAD 55), composed in Prākrit, except for the introductory formula in Epigraphic Hybrid Sanskrit, mentions that the king had founded a *cātusāla* at the western gate of the *mahāvihāra* in a locality called Pithuṇḍa.[21] It also records that Ehavala-Cāntamūla granted

---

18 The number of cells for site 1 is given as "at least twentyfive" by SARKAR (1960: 83; 1966: 93), as 27 (three times nine) by KRISHNAMURTHY (2006: 164), and as 29 (nine plus nine plus eleven) by RAMACHANDRAN (1953: 26–27 and fig. 4). The number of cells for site 5 is given as 28; see SARCAR 1960: 83; 1966: 93. The size of the individual cells was different at sites 1 and 5.

19 See EIAD 44, line 8; EIAD 45, line 11; EIAD 46, line 6. A similar term like *sava-jāta-niyuta*, namely, *sava-niyuta*, is also attested in other contexts; see EIAD 20, line 2 (related to a *cetiyaghara*); EIAD 24, line 10; EIAD 28, line 2 (both related to a *maṁtava*); EIAD 31, line 6; EIAD 32, line 6; EIAD 33, line 6 (all three related to five āyaka pillars).

20 See http://hisoma.huma-num.fr/exist/apps/EIAD/works/EIAD0020.xml.

21 For recent editions, see FALK 1999–2000: 276, lines 5–6; GRIFFITHS & TOURNIER, EIAD 55, lines 5–6: *ettha pithuṁḍe ... mahāvihārasa avaraddāre cātusāle amhehi kāritaṁ* = http://hisoma.huma-num.fr/exist/apps/EIAD/works/EIAD0055.xml.

two plots of agricultural land (32 *nivartana* and 64 *nivartana*) for repairs and for the sustenance of the monks of the school of the Aparamahāvinaseliyas who would be coming to and who were residing in the *cātusāla*.[22] The first donated plot, in my understanding of the text, is described as having been located "north of the *mahāvihāra* in Pithuṇḍa [and also north] of the city [of Pithuṇḍa]", near a *mahācetiya* and at the path to a [neighbouring] village.[23] The second plot was also situated to the north of Pithuṇḍa. Finally, the king declared these plots to be the usufruct of the monks of the *cātusāla*.[24]

As ancient Pithuṇḍa is still an unidentified place, the structure of the *mahāvihāra* at this locality unfortunately cannot be verified on the basis of archaeological data. From the epigraphical evidence, however, it seems to be relatively clear that this 'great monastery' must have been – like the one at site 1 of Nagarjunakonda – a composite structure, with the *cātusāla* founded by King Ehavala-Cāntamūla being just one constituent of it. It is also remarkable that the royal endowment was specifically bestowed upon the monks of this living space and not upon the *mahāvihāra* as a whole.

3. Gujarat, 3rd–5th Centuries

In West Indian Gujarat, at Intwa, northeast of Junagadh (see Figure 1), the remains of an early brick monastic site were excavated by G. V. Acharya in 1949. The only inscribed object found there was a baked clay sealing, the Sanskrit legend of which was read by CHHABRA (1949–50: 175) as: *mahārā-ja-rudrasena-vihāre bhikṣu-saṁghasya*, which can be translated as "belonging

22 See EIAD 55, lines 6–18.

23 See EIAD 55, lines 13–15: *pithuṇḍe mahāvihārasa nagarassa uttaradisāye mahāsetīye mahā-celakasa eṭṭhassa k[ū]latthapaddaggāmapatthe* ... FALK's (1999 – 2000: 279) reading is more or less the same, and he renders the crucial portion of this passage as: "At Pithuṇḍa, north of the Great Monastery (and) of the town (Dhānyakaḍa)". GRIFFITHS & TOURNIER, EIAD 55, translate: "to the Great Monastery in Pithuṇḍa ... in the northern direction of the town", thus understanding the first genitive as reference to the recipient of the endowment. I rather follow FALK in taking *mahāvihārassa* as also depending on *uttaradisāye*, although an 'and' (*ca*) has to bis substituted then. A genitive or dative object to go with the verbal form is not necessarily required in this construction, as there are many endowment records which do not directly specify the donee, but only indirectly mention the beneficiary in the stipulation on the purposes of the grant, which are in this case the (potential) repairs of the *cātusāla* and the sustenance of the monks there. In my opinion, this plot was situated north of the *mahāvihāra*, which was located in Pithuṇḍa, and also north of Pithuṇḍa town, not Dhānyakaḍa, as assumed by FALK (see above).

24 See EIAD 55, line 19: *cātusālassa halo bhikhubhogaṁ kātūṇa*.

to the order of monks in the monastery of King Rudrasena".[25] The use of the locative *vihāre* indicates that the *bhikṣusaṁgha* resided in Rudrasena's monastery. The fact that the residential building was called after a ruler named Rudrasena might mean that the *vihāra* was established in his name, but it is even more likely that King Rudrasena himself was the founder. On the basis of palaeographic considerations, Chhabra tentatively identified this *mahārāja* with the Western Kṣatrapa ruler Rudrasena I (reigned c. 200–220 CE). During the excavations at Intva, a rectangular structure measuring 17.4 x 19.8 metres, i.e., c. 350 square metres, was dug out, with probably 24 cells (3 x 3 metres each), grouped along the four sides of an inner courtyard.[26]

The Buddhist site of Devnimori in north Gujarat (Aravalli District, Bhiloda Taluk ; see Figure 1), some 400 km away from Junagadh, spreads over 4 square kilometres and consists of the so-called *mahāstūpa*, four smaller stūpas, a caitya, and at least two residential structures.[27] The most important discovery at the *mahāstūpa* of the Devnimori site was a reliquary casket in chlorite schist with two epigraphs. One of them is a Sanskrit donative epigraph dated to the year 127 of the Kathika era[28] and the reign of another ruler named Rudrasena (TOURNIER 2023: 409, v. 2). If the otherwise unknown Kathika era is equated with the Kalacuri-Cedi era of 248 CE, then the date would be c. 375 CE and the ruler could have been King Rudrasena III (reigned c. 350–380 CE) of the Western Kṣatrapa dynasty. The inscription records the erection of the *mahāstūpa* by two monks (*śākyabhikṣu*)[29] "in the vicinity of the *mahāvihāra*" (ibid.: 409, v. 3), and the donation of the reliquary, to be deposited in the *mahāstūpa*, by another monk (ibid.: 409–410, v. 5). When the phrase *mahāvihārāśraye* is taken literally and rendered as '**in the vicinity of the great monastery**', then the *mahāstūpa* and the *mahāvihāra* can be understood as two separate entities, namely, the 'great relic shrine' and the 'main residential quarters'. But TOURNIER (ibid.: 409, fn. 17) has noted that *āśraya* could have been "used here with a semi-expletive meaning".

25 SCHOPEN (1996: 82) has remarked: "Without yet being able to say what the genitive or possessive implies, this should probably be rendered: 'of the Community of Monks in the Monastery of the Great King Rudrasena,' or '... in the Great King Rudrasena's Monastery'." See also ALBERY 2020: 286, 300, 804.

26 See MAJMUDAR 1960: 91; SOMPURA 1969: 15 and fig. 10; VERMA MISHRA & RAY 2017: 29.

27 These residential structures were called 'vihāra' by the excavators; see MEHTA & CHOWDHARY 1966: 33-66; CHOWDHARY 2010: 43-76. See also SOMPURA 1969: 25–26; SANKALIA 1987: 137.

28 According to TOURNIER (2023: 404f, fn. 6), a dating to the late 4th / early 5th century is secure.

29 For a discussion of the implications of the term *śākyabhikṣu*, see TOURNIER 2023: 411.

Therefore, *mahāvihārāśraye* might simply stand for *mahāvihāre*, in which case the *mahāstūpa* would be defined as being located **'in the great monastery'**, parallel to EIAD 21 already discussed above, where the *mahācetiya* of site 1 at Nagarjunakonda was also described in a similar way.

On the basis of the inscription, the excavators assumed that the *mahāstūpa* was erected around 375 CE. They also identified the epigraphically attested *mahāvihāra* with the archaeological remains of monastery no. 1 at Devnimori. This residential structure is located near the *mahāstūpa*, towards its southwest, a caitya hall being located in between. The measurements of the (once one-storey) residential building are roughly 38 x 41 metres, i.e., c. 1,550 square metres, with 30 cells grouped around an inner courtyard (MEHTA & CHOWDHARY 1966: 35ff.). The large central cell on the southern side, opposite the entrance in the north, was probably used as a 'shrine room', i.e., for the Buddha worship. The excavators, in a kind of understatement, call these monastic remains "a small brick structure" (ibid.: 45). But compared with the *cātusāla* buildings of sites 1 and 5 from Nagarjunakonda, monastery no. 1 at Devnimori does not at all seem to be a small structure. Based on their identification of the *mahāvihāra* of the inscription with monastery no. 1, the excavators have come to the following conclusion (ibid.: 29):

> If the Mahastupa was planned and constructed as noted above in the third quarter of the fourth century A.D., the Mahavihara should precede it as can be seen from the inscription. But how many years before the construction of the Stupa, the vihara was constructed is a moot point. Stratigraphically, the earliest phase of the vihara and the stupa are on the natural black earth, so the stratigraphy does not help to find out the time gap. Here it seems that the first Buddhist settlement might have begun by establishing a large vihara. ...

The entire argument seems to rest on the fact that the inscription recording the erection of the *mahāstūpa* at Devnimori already mentions a *mahāvihāra* as point of reference. Archaeology neither seems to support nor contradict this claim. However, if we, again compare this situation with the evidence from site 1 at Nagarjunakonda, where one of the epigraphs documenting the erection of the great stūpa (*mahācetiya*) also talks about the *mahāvihāra*, although this inscription clearly predates the foundation records of the residential structures by some nine years, then it seems plausible that the term *mahāvihāra* in the donative record from Devnimori not only referred to the dwelling space or monastery no. 1, but rather to the whole monastic complex of the site.

4. Central India, 5th Century

Two 5th-century private Sanskrit inscriptions from Sanchi in Central Indian Madhya Pradesh (see Figure 1), engraved on railings of the large stūpa no. 1, also use the term *mahāvihāra*. These epigraphs, dated to the year 93 [of the Gupta era] (412/13 CE; FLEET 1888: 29–34; BHANDARKAR 1981: 247–252) and the year 131 [of the Gupta era] (450/51 CE; FLEET 1888: 260–262), record that certain private donors gifted some *dīnāra* coins as *akṣaya-nīvī*, 'perpetual deposit'.[30] The endowment of the year 131 was made "for the honourable Buddhist order of the four directions in the great monastery at Kākanādaboṭa" (*kākanādaboṭa-śrī-mahāvihāre cātur-ddiśāyāryya-saṁghāya*).[31] The Buddhist site at Sanchi had definitely a composite character. But on the basis of the extant epigraphic and archaeological material, it cannot be decided whether the term *kākanādaboṭa-śrī-mahāvihāra* referred to a single large structure at Sanchi or to the site's compound-like layout as such. FLEET (1888: 31), in his edition of this inscription in volume 3 of the series *Corpus Inscriptionum Indicarum*, opined: "The Kākanādaboṭa convent is, of course, the Great Stūpa itself." BHANDARKAR (1981: 248–249), the author of the revised edition of volume 3 of *Corpus Inscriptionum Indicarum*, has rightly rejected this interpretation:

> But a *vihāra*, which is a place of residence for monks, is always distinguished in Buddhist literature from a *thūpa* or *stūpa*, which is an object of worship. The remains of many monasteries were exhumed by John Marshall during his excavations at Sāñchī. But none of them is earlier than the seventh century A. D. In some places, however, he lighted upon traces of older monasteries on which the latter ones were erected. Anyhow the *Mahāvihāra* referred to in this record has not been identified.

The study by JULIA SHAW (2013: 21, 84, 90–91, 136) on the 'archaeologies' of the Sanchi Hill and the surrounding areas has shown that some of the monastic constructions, namely, the type of the 'platformed monastery', actually predate the courtyard style and date from the pre-Gupta period. But we still have to admit that the remains of none of the monastic structures at Sanchi can be safely attributed to the Gupta period. However, as the two inscriptions do not refer to the foundation of residential buildings in the Gupta period, and as the toponym Kākanāva/Kākanādaboṭa is used in very early epigraphs in the

30 For *akṣayanīvī*, see SCHOPEN 1994: 532–535; STRAUCH 2021: 199, 203; MARTINI 2022: 144–169.

31 See FLEET 1888: 261, lines 2–3. The phrase in the inscription of the year 93 is slightly different: *kākanādaboṭa-śrī-mahāvihāre ... cātur-ddigabhyāgatāya śramaṇa-puṅgavāvasathāyāryya-saṅghāya*; see FLEET 1888: 31, lines 1–2.

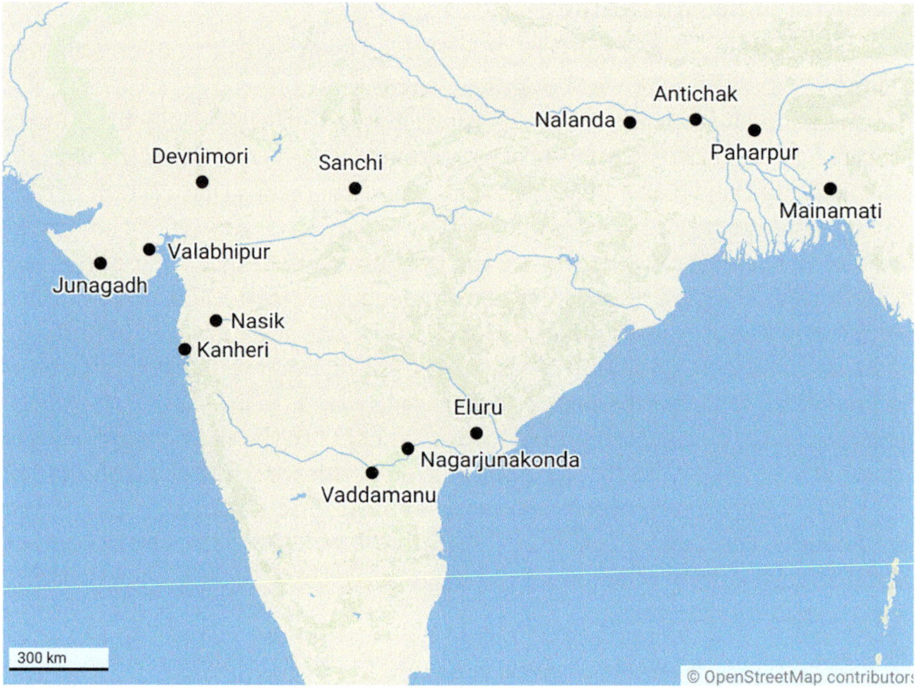

Figure 1: Map of the relevant sites for this study, created with Datawrapper.

Sanchi area, the 5th-century endowments could well have benefitted a much older monastery.[32] Moreover, in line with the argument put forward in the discussions on the use of the term *mahāvihāra* at Nagarjunakonda's site 1 and at Devnimori, it is also possible that this expression referred to a larger monastic compound at Sanchi, including its so-called great stūpa as well as residential structures.

5. Āndhradeśa, 5th/6th Centuries

For more attestations of the terms *vihāra* and *mahāvihāra*, it is useful to return to Āndhradeśa. In some 5th/6th-century Sanskrit copper-plate charters of the Viṣṇukuṇḍin kings and their subordinates, both expressions appear side by side. In the first set of Tummalagudem copper plates (EIAD 174),

32 I owe this clarification to a comment by Vincent Tournier on an earlier draft of this paper.

which presents King Govindavarman I (reigned c. 422–462 CE) as the main donor,[33] this Viṣṇukuṇḍin ruler is described as

> ... [one] who has adorned all directions by repairing and by newly erecting many temples (*devāyatana*), monasteries (*vihāra*), meeting halls (*sabhā*), water dispensaries, tanks, wells, and pleasure-groves (*ārāma*) ...[34]

In charters issued by his successors, King Govindavarman I is associated with the erection of numerous great monasteries (*°aneka-mahāvihāra-pratiṣṭhāpana°*) (EIAD 175[35] and EIAD 180[36]) and characterised as

> ... [one] who had adorned the whole Deccan with crown jewels of wonderful *stūpas* and *vihāras*.[37]

The actual Buddhist monasteries endowed with landed property by the charters of the Viṣṇukuṇḍin kings and their subordinate ruler Pr̥thivīśrīmūla are almost exclusively classified as *mahāvihāra*. Only in EIAD 174, the beneficiary is called "monastery of the chief queen" (*°agramahiṣyā[ḥ] paramamahādevyā vihāra-*).[38] In EIAD 175 of Viṣṇukuṇḍin Vikramendravarman II

33 The date of EIAD 174 is still debated; see TOURNIER (2018: 27–28, fn. 16): "... the identity of Govindavarman featuring as the main donor in EIAD 174 [has] not been definitively settled. I tentatively follow here the interpretation of Sankaranarayanan, according to which the issuer of the grant was Govindavarman I, grandfather of Vikramendravarman I, who was himself the grandfather of Vikramendravarman II (r. ca. 555–572), the issuer of the second Tummalagudem grant (EIAD 175)." For palaeographic and other reasons, it is "possible that EIAD 174 was produced as a ... copy of a lost or damaged original grant by Govindavarman I ...".

34 For the Sanskrit text, see GRIFFITHS & TOURNIER, EIAD 174, lines 8–9 = http://hisoma.huma-num.fr/exist/apps/EIAD/works/EIAD0174.xml?&odd=teipublisher.odd. The inscription has *°pratisaṁskārapūrvvakaraṇa°*, but the EIAD editors opine in their apparatus that "[i]t seems necessary to follow here the silent emendation of SANKARANARAYANAN 1974, reading *°pratisaṁskārāpūrvvakaraṇa°*. The EIAD editors have translated *apūrva-karaṇa* as 'building anew'; for a discussion of this term, see also TOURNIER 2018: 28–29, fn. 19. I am grateful to Eli Franco for a private communication on the proper English rendering of *apūrva*.

35 For the Sanskrit text, see GRIFFITHS & TOURNIER, EIAD 175, line 5 = http://hisoma.huma-num.fr/exist/apps/EIAD/works/EIAD0175.xml?&odd=teipublisher.odd.

36 See TOURNIER 2018: 33; see also GRIFFITHS & TOURNIER, EIAD 180, line 6 = http://hisoma.huma-num.fr/exist/apps/EIAD/works/EIAD0180.xml?&odd=teipublisher.odd.

37 See EIAD 175, lines 25–26: *°adbhuta-stūpa-vihāra-cūḍāmaṇibhir alaṁkr̥ta-sakala-dakṣiṇāpatha.*

38 See EIAD 174, lines 21–22. As already mentioned above (fn. 33), EIAD 174 was probably a 6th-century copy based on a much earlier grant. The difficulty of the dating is also illustrated by the fact that EIAD 173, an inscription "engraved on a boulder found in Caitanyapuri in the outskirts of Hyderabad, is likely to stem from the period of Viṣṇukuṇḍin rule, since it refers to a Govindarājavihāra, bearing the name of the first

(reigned c. 555–572 CE), dated to the year 488 of the Śaka era (566 CE), which is a second set of copper plates found at Tummalagudem (in Ramannapet Mandal of present-day Yadadri Bhuvanagiri District in Telangana), discovered near the findspot of the first set (EIAD 174),[39] the same monastery is labelled *paramabhaṭṭārikā-mahāvihāra*.[40]

EIAD 180, the Patagandigudem plates of the regnal year 26 of Viṣṇukuṇḍin Mādhavavarman II (reigned c. 462–502 CE), refers to a *mahāvihāra* which was the recipient of two villages in the Veṅgī district, granted by Mādhavavarman's son Vikramendravarman I, the governor of Trikaliṅga and Veṅgī.[41] The monastery is described as "Trilokyāśrayarāja-*mahāvihāra*, established by us in Asanapura".[42] Thus EIAD 180 provides evidence for an endowment by the Viṣṇukuṇḍin prince Vikramendravarman I (who later reigned c. 502–527 CE) to a *mahāvihāra* which he had founded himself and which was, as has been shown by TOURNIER (2018: 43), probably named after him, using the sobriquet 'Trilokyāśraya'. The 'great monastery' is also referred to in the description of a monk: Saṅghadāsa, who was made responsible (*uddiśya*) for the grant, is labelled a resident of the monastery (*mahāvihāra-vāsin*) and a Tāmraparṇīya.[43]

---

important figure in this dynasty. ... It is however not a royal inscription, for it records the gift of a monk named Saṅghadeva. It is also the only inscription of this corpus to be in Middle Indo-Aryan" (TOURNIER 2018: 23, fn. 3). On its date, the EIAD editors (GRIFFITHS & TOURNIER, EIAD 173) state: "Attributable to the latter half of the 4th century CE on palaeographic grounds", which is much earlier than the usual dates calculated for the reign of Govindavarman I, i.e., c. 422–462 CE; see TOURNIER 2018: 26.

39 See above, fn. 33. EIAD 174 is attributed to Govindavarman I, and EIAD 175 was issued by his great-great-grandson Vikramendravarman II. EIAD 174 may have been produced as a copy of an earlier original during the reign of the latter king; see TOURNIER 2018: 27–28, fn. 16.

40 See EIAD 175, line 30.

41 See EIAD 180, lines 14–16. For the first set of copper plates from Patagandigudem, see above and EIAD 55.

42 See EIAD 180, lines 28–32: *asanapure 'smat-pratiṣṭhāpita-trilokāśraya-rāja-mahāvihārāya ... mayā dattav*, which literally means "[the two villages] were given by me to the Trilokāśraya-rāja-*mahāvihāra* established by us in Asanapura". TOURNIER (2018: 40), in his discussion of the donative portion of EIAD 180, translates as follows: "[These gifts, made] ... are for the royal *mahāvihāra* named Trilokāśraya established by me, at Asanapura." But I think that it is also possible to render this expression as "great monastery of the prince Trilokāśraya".

43 See also EIAD 180, line 23. For a discussion of the evidence related to the history of this specific *nikāya*, see TOURNIER 2018. For his arguments against the interpretation that the use of the term *mahāvihāra-vāsin* would establish a connection with the Sinhalese Mahāvihāra tradition, the Great Monastery *par excellence* at Anurādhapura in Sri Lanka, see ibid.: 53.

In four charters of King Pṛthivīśrīmūla (reigned c. 510–566 CE) favouring four different *mahāvihāras*, a particular monk assigned as the person in charge of the grant(s) and/or the local order of monks is described as 'residing in the great monastery' (*mahāvihāra-vāsin*).[44] Three of the 'great monasteries' had been founded by Pṛthivīśrīmūla and his son, respectively.[45] Two of the four *mahāvihāras* were situated at a place called Guṇapāśapura.[46] Two of the four 'great monasteries' belonged to the Aparaśaila school,[47] one to the Tāmraparṇīyas.[48] Three of the charters (EIAD 187–189) have been found together at the same place, a rock shelter at Kondavidu Fort (in today's Palnadu District), but the records do not reveal any internal connection between each other.

Only one of these 'great monasteries' has been successfully identified with a known archaeological site: "the Vardhamāni-*mahāvihāra* founded by Śrī-Mahāmeghavāhana" mentioned in EIAD 187.[49] As has been convincingly shown by TOURNIER (2021–22: 8–13), Vardhamāni can be relatively safely identified with Vaddamanu (in present-day Guntur District; see Figure 1), an important Buddhist sanctuary, situated some 35 km northeast of Kondavindu Fort, the findspot of the plates.

6. Konkan and Western Ghats, 3rd–9th Centuries

There were, of course, many more Buddhist monastic sites of a composite type in ancient India: first and foremost, the famous rock-cut architectural remains at places like Ajanta, Ellora, Kanheri, Nasik, etc. in western Maharashtra, which were started to be built well before the 3rd century CE. Although archaeologists and art historians call the residential quarters at these Buddhist sites very often 'vihāra', the extant Prākrit stone epigraphs in the caves regularly use a different terminology, namely, the expression *leṇa* (Sanskrit *layana*). PIA BRANCACCIO (2011: 55 & fn. 66) has summarised her observations on this evidence as follows:

44 See EIAD 186, lines 21 & 22; EIAD 187, line 11; EIAD 188, lines 14–15; EIAD 189, line 15.

45 See EIAD 186, line 22; EIAD 188, line 14; EIAD 189, line 14.

46 See EIAD 186, line 22; EIAD 189, line 14.

47 See EIAD 188, line 19; EIAD 189, line 18; see also TOURNIER 2018: 47 & 66. For the identification of Guṇapāśapura with Nagaram Island in the East Godavari District, see ibid.: 47, fn. 76.

48 See EIAD 186, line 34. See also above, on EIAD 180.

49 See EIAD 187, lines 10–11: *śrī-mahāmeghavāhana-pratiṣṭhāpita-varddhamāni-mahāvihāra°*.

> Inscriptions from several caves demonstrate that monks still cherished the ideal of Buddhist forest asceticism and that they referred to their rock-cut residences as *leṇas* (caves) and not *vihāras*.

Indeed, early epigraphic attestations of the term *vihāra* are relatively rare in the region of the Western Ghats. An illustrative example are the inscriptions in cave 10 of Nasik (see Figure 1), which once was a living space consisting of a hall of 13.1 by 13.7 metres with three surrounding wings of together 16 cells, which jointly make up for a size of approximately 360 square metres.[50] Uṣavadāta, the son-in-law of the Western Kṣatrapa ruler Nahāpana, who most probably ruled in the mid-first century CE, referred to these residential quarters as "my cave" (*mama leṇa-*) in an epigraph composed in Epigraphical Hybrid Sanskrit (EHS).[51] In a similar way, Nasik's cave 3, another living space of a similar size, which had been founded by the ruling Sātavāhana king's grandmother is called *devi-leṇa*, "queen's cave", in a Prākrit inscription.[52] Another EHS epigraph by Uṣavadata in cave 10 is the earliest known dated epigraphic attestation of the term *akṣaya-nīvī* (here in the form *akṣayanivi*).[53] This inscription records the deposition of a certain amount of money with two guilds, the interest of which was to be used for the benefit of the monks residing in this very cave.[54]

In a mid-3rd-century EHS epigraph from the reign of the Ābhīra king Īśvaradāsa engraved in cave 10 at Nasik, the term *vihāra* appears to be used for the first time at this site. This is an endowment record of a Śaka woman saying that she had deposited an *akṣaya-nīvī* (here *akṣayanivī*) with certain guilds for the benefit of the monks residing in the Triraśmiparvata-*vihāra*.[55] It does not arise from the text whether the term *vihāra* refers here only to cave 10 or rather to the whole monastic complex of the Triraśmi Mountain,

---

50 For the description and a plan of this cave, which is called 'cave VIII' there, see FERGUSSON & BURGESS 1880: 270 & pl. XIX, bottom.

51 For this inscription, see SENART 1905–06: 78–81, no. 10. For *mama leṇe* in this epigraph, see ibid.: 78, line 4. For the classification as EHS, see DAMSTEEGT 1978: 229–230.

52 For the description and a plan of cave 3, see FERGUSSON & BURGESS 1880: 267–268 & pl. XIX, top. For the inscription, see SENART 1905–06: 65–71, no. 3. For *devi-leṇa°*, see ibid.: 65, line 12.

53 See above, fn. 30. For a discussion of this inscription, see also FALK 2008: 143–145; VISVANATHAN 2018: 519.

54 See SENART 1905–06: 82–85, no. 12. For *akṣayanivi* in this epigraph, see ibid.: 82, line 1.

55 See SENART 1905–06: 88–89, no. 15; MIRASHI 1955: 1–4, no 1. The inscription is dated to the year 9 of an unspecified era. Mirashi identifies this year as one referring to the Kalacuri-Cedi era of 248 CE, and has, thus, included this epigraph in *Corpus Inscriptionum Indicarum* 4.1. Although the exact interpretation of this date is doubtful, the general chronological classification as a third-century document seems to be correct.

which consisted of some 20 caves, built already in the Sātavāhana-Kṣatrapa period.

Although with more than 100 caves much larger in size,[56] the situation at Kanheri near Mumbai (see Figure 1) is in many respects comparable to that of Nasik. The Kanheri caves were established under the Sātavāhana dynasty and flourished during their rule from the 1st to the 3rd centuries, as recorded in numerous Prākrit stone inscriptions from the site. The earliest epigraphic attestation of the term *mahāvihāra* is preserved in a late-5th-century Sanskrit copper-plate inscription referring to the rule of the Traikūṭaka dynasty of north Konkan and recording the donation of a *caitya* by a person named Buddharuci hailing from the Sindh region (*sindhu-viṣaya*).[57] This single copper plate was discovered (together with another plate) in a votive stūpa in front of Kanheri's cave 3, the so-called great caitya hall of the site (BRANCACCIO 2022: 73). The *caitya* whose erection is dated in the year 245 of an unspecified era identified by MIRASHI (1955: 30) as the Kalacuri-Cedi era of 248 CE, and which is said to be located in the Kr̥ṣṇagiri-*mahāvihāra*, i.e., "in the great monastery at the Black Mountain"[58] (present-day Kanheri), was very likely the votive stūpa in which the plate has been found. It is also probable that the term *mahāvihāra* does, again, not merely refer to some residential quarters, but rather to the whole monastic complex at 5th-century Kr̥ṣṇagiri.

The next attestations of the term *mahāvihāra* at Kanheri date from the second half of the 9th century, i.e., from the latest phase of Buddhist occupation. Three Sanskrit stone inscriptions from caves 11 and 12, barely legible and also otherwise problematic, are known to have been commissioned during the reign of the Rāṣṭrakūṭa ruler Amoghavarṣa I and his Śilāhāra subordinate Kapardin II. One of the epigraphs, dated Śaka era 775 (853 CE), is engraved on the architrave of cave 11, the largest non-caitya-structure at Kanheri, which is usually referred to as 'Darbar Cave'.[59] It records the execution of some construction "in this Śrī-Kr̥ṣṇagiri-*mahārāja-mahāvihāra*" on behalf of a Buddhist (*paramasauga-*

56 Kanheri was the largest and longest occupied Buddhist cave site in Western India, with the highest number of inscriptions; see EFURD 2018: 393. BRANCACCIO 2022: 73.

57 See MIRASHI 1955: 29–32, no. 10.

58 See ibid.: 31, line 1: *kr̥ṣṇagiri-mahāvihāre*.

59 Different systems exist for the numbering of the Kanheri caves; see REVIRE 2016: 164, fn. 138. I am following the current system of the Archaeological Survey of India. For the description and a plan of the 'Darbar Cave', see FERGUSSON & BURGESS 1880: 353–355 & pl. LIV, where this cave has the number 10.

ta) from Bengal (*gauḍa-viṣaya*), and his grant of a perpetual deposit (*akṣainīvi* for *akṣayanīvī*) of a 100 *drammas*, *inter alia*, for the clothing of the monks.[60]

The other two epigraphs are engraved on the architrave of cave 12, which is a much smaller architectural excavation just opposite cave 11.[61] The text whose date has been tentatively read as Śaka [765] (843 CE) reports on the *akṣainīvi* of 160 *drammas* by another donor for several specified purposes, "after having made obeisance to the monastic order at Śrī-Kr̥ṣṇagiri".[62] The term *mahāvihāra* is not attested in this inscription, but the perpetual endowment was to be used, *inter alia*, for repairs "here, at this very *vihāra*".[63] The other epigraph from cave 12, dated *Śaka* 799 (877 CE), resembles that from cave 11 in recording the execution of some excavation and the endowment of a 100 *drammas*, while it features another donor.[64] The term *mahāvihāra* appears here in a phrase stipulating that the money had been "handed over in the Śrīmat-Kr̥ṣṇagiri-*mahāvihāra* to/for the honourable community of monks staying there".[65]

Cave 11 was described by Fergusson & Burgess (1880: 353) as follows:

> It is not a Vihāra in the ordinary sense of the term, though it has some cells, but a Dharmaśālā or place of assembly ...

And Pia Brancaccio (2022: 80)[66] adds that it was

> not a residential cave but rather a large, rectangular plain hall with two long low-cut benches likely used by monks to study, recite and copy ... It is an unusual type of cave in western Deccan, comparable only to the multi-storied Cave 5 at Ellora, thus likely a contemporary excavation.

---

60 See Kielhorn 1884: 134–135, no. 15; Mirashi 1977: 3–6, no. 2; Gokhale 1991: 66–71, no. 21. See especially line 4 of the text: *°asmiṁ kr̥ṣṇagiri-mahārāja-mahāvihāre*.

61 For the descriptions and a plan of cave 12, see Fergusson & Burgess 1880: 355 & pl. LIV, where this cave has the number 78. These two authors (ibid.: 355, fn. 5) also comment on the numbering: "No. 78 in Dr. Bhau Dāji's numeration, which is an unfortunately awkward one, no system having been followed, but as numbers are painted on the caves, and have been used by Messrs. West and others, it does not seem desirable to change them now."

62 See Kielhorn 1884: 136–137, no. 43B; Mirashi 1977: 1–3, no. 1; Gokhale 1991: 71–72, no. 22. See especially line 3 of the text: *śrī-kr̥ṣṇagirau śrīmad-ārya-saṁghaṁ praṇamya*.

63 See the previous fn. and line 4 of the text: *ihāsminn eva vihāre*. But the reading of this line is very uncertain; see Mirashi 1977: 2, fn. 7.

64 See Kielhorn 1884: 135–136, no. 43A; Mirashi 1977: 6–8, no. 3; Gokhale 1991: 72–73, no. 23.

65 See the previous fn. and lines 2–3 of the text: (*śrī*)*mat-kr̥ṣṇagiri*-(*mahāvi*)*hāre ... bhikṣūṇāṁ tatrasthārya-saṁghasya drammāṇāṁ śatam ekaṁ dattvā*.

66 Brancaccio (2022: 80, line 7 and fn. 9) has mixed up the numbering of caves 11 and 12 here.

Cave 12 at Kanheri, is described by FERGUSSON & BURGESS (1880: 355; pl. LIV) as

> a small cave with two pillars and two half ones in the verandah ... Inside is a small hall with a rough cell at the back, containing only an image of Buddha on the back wall.

The inscription of Śaka [765] apparently recorded an endowment of altogether 200 *drammas*, the interest of which was to be used not only for the worship of the Buddha, for necessary repairs, and for the monks' clothing, but also for manuscripts (*pustakārtham*).[67] As the latter donative purpose is a rarely attested one, the eagerness to interpret this as evidence for the existence of a library at Kanheri is understandable.[68] One should, however, be reminded that this epigraph is not engraved at the large hall-like cave 11, but at the small shrine-like cave 12. Both, the inscription of Śaka 775, engraved at cave 11, and that of Śaka 799, also engraved at cave 12, refer to the excavation of certain structures (°*veśmikā*), but it is unclear which architectural expansions are meant by this term.[69]

As caves 11 and 12 are no (or at least no typical) monastic dwellings, the attestations of the word *mahāvihāra* in the 9th-century epigraphs appear to confirm the notion gained from the 5th-century inscription of Kanheri's cave-5 area that the term 'great monastery' designated the entire monastic complex. The question is why the expression used in Śaka 775 was *mahārāja-mahāvihāra*,

---

67 I am following here MIRASHI's (1977: 1–3, no. 1) interpretation of the (badly preserved) text, assuming that the perpetual deposit consisted of 40 *drammas* + 40 *drammas* + 120 *drammas*. The (annual) interest from this deposit is given as 20 *drammas* (for worship) + 3 *drammas* (for repairs) + 5 *drammas* (for robes) + 1 *dramma* (for manuscripts), i.e., a total of 27 *drammas*, which corresponds to an annual interest rate of 14.5 % and a monthly rate of roughly 1.2 %; see SCHMIEDCHEN 2014: 261–262. BRANCACCIO (2022: 79) seems to have misunderstood the financial details, and hence her conclusion (ibid.: 80) that the "monetary gift for books significantly surpasses the amount designated for repairs at the *vihāra*" appears to be also untenable.

68 See, for instance, BRANCACCIO 2022: 77 & 80.

69 The term was read by KIELHORN (1884: 134, no. 15, line 4; 136, no. 43A, line 3) as *kol(h) i-veśmikā*, and by MIRASHI (1977: 5, no. 2, line 4; 7, no. 3, line 3) as *koli-veśmikā*. KIELHORN (1884: 134) translated *upaśama-koli-veśmikā* in Śaka 775 as "hall-mansions (suitable) for meditation". The study on Kanheri by BRANCACCIO (2022: 79) contains, *inter alia*, also this information: "A poorly legible inscription from Cave 11 that still remains unpublished (personal communication by Nicolas Morrissey) offers a further attestation to this late phase of prosperity and growth of the cave monastery. It relates the donation of two separate endowments for the repair and expansion of a *vihāra* overseen by a *navakarmika* at the *Kṛṣṇagiri mahāvihāra*."

literally, "a great monastery of a great king".[70] This phrasing could allude to the collective memory that the monastic site at Kanheri had been a royal endeavour in its initial stage, or it could be the result of the perception that a *mahāvihāra* must have been a royal foundation *per se*.[71]

In terms of architectural structure, PIA BRANCACCIO (2022: 74–75) stated:

> Remarkably, the Kṛṣṇagiri *mahāvihāra* did not include caves designed to function as large communal monastic dwellings of the type seen at Ajanta, with a square court-[yard – AS] and rows of cells opening on three sides. Instead, at Kanheri one finds a great number of smaller and independent rock-cut units scattered on the hill, typically consisting of one cell opening onto a room and preceded by a porch … . Such small structures were undoubtedly more conducive to the cultivation of individual ascetic goals rather than to practice of cenobitic monasticism.

7. Gujarat, 5th–8th Centuries

A new term, i.e., *vihāramaṇḍala*, is attested in the copper-plate charters of the Maitraka dynasty of Valabhī (present-day Valabhipur; see Figure 1), whose kings ruled in parts of Gujarat, mainly in the Kathiawar region, from the 5th to the 8th centuries. The epigraphic corpus of the Maitrakas shares the lack of supporting archaeological evidence with the more or less contemporary corpus of the Viṣṇukuṇḍin dynasty from Āndhradeśa discussed above. But the dense and rich Maitraka corpus itself offers some clues regarding potential structural differences of institutions labelled *vihāramaṇḍala* in contrast to 'simple' *vihāras*. More than 110 Sanskrit epigraphs of this royal line are known, all of them copper-plate charters recording royal grants of villages and land to religious donees. The majority of the Maitraka grants, i.e., seventy per cent of the known corpus, record endowments to Brahmins; and in one quarter, grants to Buddhist institutions are registered, which is a relatively large share compared with other Indian regions in the early medieval period. More than half of the 26 Buddhist endowment records extant, dating from the 6th and 7th centuries, were found in and around the Maitraka capital Valabhī, which Yijing describes as one of the two major centres of

70 KIELHORN (1884: 135, fn. 12) remarked on his translation: "… I omit the word *mahārāja* before *mahāvihāre*", without substantiating his decision, maybe regarding this as a scribal error.

71 It is perhaps noteworthy in this context that none of the rulers mentioned as having reigned when the inscription was commissioned in the 9th century is labelled *mahārāja*. Rāṣṭrakūṭa Amoghavarṣa and his predecessor bore the imperial title *mahārājādhiraja*, whereas Śilāhāra Kapardin and his predecessor are classed as *mahāsāmanta-śekhara*.

Buddhist learning in India, the other being Nālandā in Bihar (TAKAKUSU 1896: 177; LI 2000: 149).

The most famous monastic establishment in the city of Valabhī seems to have been the Ḍuḍḍā-*vihāra*, a monastery (for monks) founded by (*kārita*)[72] and named after the niece (*bhāgineyī*) of the Maitraka ruler Dhruvasena I. In one of Dhruvasena's endowments, Ḍuḍḍā is portrayed as *paramopāsikā*, 'excellent [Buddhist] laywoman' (SCHMIEDCHEN 2013: 108). Later, she was also called *rājñī*, 'princess'. The Ḍuḍḍā-*vihāra* is described as being located on the city territory of Valabhī. This Buddhist institution, referred to in twelve charters,[73] was called *mahāvihāra*, 'great monastery', in one inscription (INSMaitraka00025, 566 CE). And it was termed *vihāramaṇḍala*, 'monastic complex', in at least two other copper-plate charters (INSMaitraka00060, 629 CE; INSMaitraka00085, 662 CE). There might be more attestations of the term *vihāramaṇḍala*, as some of the relevant charters are fragmentary, with lacunae in the pertinent passages.

At least six other structures belonged to the Ḍuḍḍā-*vihāra* complex[74]: *vihāras* founded by the monks Buddhadāsa, Vimalagupta, and Sthiramati, by the trader Kakkamākila, and by one Gohaka, as well as a Tārā temple erected by the chief secretary (*divirapati*) Skandabhaṭa II. The relation between the Ḍuḍḍā-*vihāra* and its subsidiary structures is described in general terms like °*abhyantara*, 'within'.[75] Other expressions used are °*antargata*, 'included in',[76] °*prāveśya*, 'belonging to',[77] and °*parikalpita*, 'attached to'.[78]

For many of the relevant copper-plate charters, it cannot be verified when the monasteries which were favoured by particular royal donations had been originally erected. Only if the founders of these institutions were somehow directly connected with the donor kings, can we deduce that not too much time had elapsed between the inauguration of the monastery and a later endowment for it. This holds true for the foundations by the princess Ḍuḍḍā, the niece of Dhruvasena I, as well as by the *divirapati* Skandabhaṭa II, who acted as chief secretary under the kings Dhruvasena II and Dharasena IV (SCHMIEDCHEN 2018: 38).

72 For *kārita*, I am using the equivalents 'founded', 'established', 'erected' as quasi-synonyms.

73 For INSMaitraka00019–00020, 00024–00025, 00039, 00044, 00060, 00078, 00082, 00085, 00091, and 00096, see SCHMIEDCHEN, https://dharmalekha.info/texts/INSMaitraka00019, etc.

74 For further details see SCHMIEDCHEN 2021: 9; 2021–22: 68–69.

75 See SCHMIEDCHEN, https://dharmalekha.info/texts/INSMaitraka00039, line 22.

76 See SCHMIEDCHEN, https://dharmalekha.info/texts/INSMaitraka00060, line 35; and see also https://dharmalekha.info/texts/INSMaitraka00085, lines 21–22.

77 See SCHMIEDCHEN, https://dharmalekha.info/texts/INSMaitraka00085, line 22.

78 See SCHMIEDCHEN, https://dharmalekha.info/texts/INSMaitraka00091, line 52.

INSMaitraka00019 of Dhruvasena I, Ḍuḍḍā's uncle, dated 534 CE, is the first known endowment for the Ḍuḍḍā-*vihāra* itself. Already rather early, other edifices must have been attached to the Ḍuḍḍā-*vihāra*: INSMaitraka00020 of the same ruler, dated 536 CE, mentions a *vihāra* (or a *vihāra-kuṭī*)[79] founded by the learned Buddhist monk Buddhadāsa as apparently being attached to the Ḍuḍḍā monastery. Due to the fragmentary character of the charter, the way in which the affiliation of the monk's foundation with the Ḍuḍḍā-*vihāra* was actually described is not clear. But it can be deduced that Buddhadāsa must have erected a whole *vihāra*, not merely a *vihāra-kuṭī*, because the text refers to the "order of monks residing in the two monasteries", namely, the Ḍuḍḍā-*vihāra* and the Buddhadāsa-*vihāra*. The relevant passage reads:

> ... *(valabhī-tala-sva-bhāgineyī-ḍuḍḍā-kārita-[++++++++++])cāryya-bha(da)nta-buddhadā(sa)-kārita-vihāra-kuṭ(y)āṁ pratiṣṭ[h]āpita-bhagavat(āṁ samya)[k-saṁbuddhānāṁ] (buddhānā)m· gandha-dhūpa-puṣpa-dīpa-tailopayogi vihārasya ca (khaṇḍa-sphuṭita-patita-)[vi](śīr)ṇṇa-pratisaṁskāraṇārtthaṁ catur-ddiśābhyāgatobhaya-(vihāra-)prati(vāsi)-bhikṣu-saṅghasya (ca pi)ṇḍapāta-śayanāsana-g(l)āna-pra(tya)ya-bhaiṣajya-pariṣkāropayo(gā)rtthaṁ* ...[80]

The grant was made for three purposes:

1. for the worship of the Buddha [images] installed in the sanctum of the *vihāra* erected by Buddhadāsa,
2. for the necessary repairs of the *vihāra*, and
3. for the subsistence "of the order [singular!] of monks residing in the two *vihāra*s".

This is remarkable in terms of organisation. The foundation by Buddhadāsa was affiliated to the Ḍuḍḍā-*vihāra*, and, if taken literally, the last phrase indicates that the monks living in these two *vihāra*s constituted one single *bhikṣusaṅgha*.

In INSMaitraka00025 of king Guhasena, dated 566 CE, the Ḍuḍḍā-*vihāra* is called a 'great monastery'; this copper-plate charter records an endowment for the order of monks "in the great Ḍuḍḍā monastery founded by the honourable Ḍuḍḍā on the city territory of Valabhī" (*valabhī-tala-sanni-*

79 For a discussion of the potential meaning(s) of the term *vihāra-kuṭi*, see several contributions to *Buddhism, Law & Society* 7 (2021–22), referred to in SCHMIEDCHEN, GRIFFITHS & FURUI 2021–22: XVI–XVII.

80 See SCHMIEDCHEN, https://dharmalekha.info/texts/INSMaitraka00020, lines 17–21. The phrase *buddhadāsa-kārita-vihāra-kuṭyāṁ* might perhaps stand for *buddhadāsa-kārita-vihārasya gandhakuṭyāṁ*; see SCHOPEN 1990: 185–186.

viṣṭa-ḍuḍḍā-pāda-kārita-ḍuḍḍā-mahāvihāre),[81] and hence not a grant to any subordinate structure.

In INSMaitraka00039 of Dharasena II, dated 589 CE, the grantee was a *vihāra* established by a trader (*vāṇija-kakkamākila-kārita-vihāra*) and depicted as being situated "within the Ḍuḍḍā-*vihāra*" (*ḍuḍḍā-vihārasyābhyantare*).[82]

Furthermore, in INSMaitraka00060 of Dhruvasena II, dated 629 CE, a *vihāra* erected by a person named Gohaka (*gohaka-kārita-vihāra*) is described as being "included in the monastic complex founded by princess Ḍuḍḍā on the city territory of Valabhī" (*valabhī-sva-tala-sanniviṣṭa-rājñī-ḍuḍḍā-kārita-vihāramaṇḍalāntargata*).[83] The wording of the inscription indicates that the endowment was given "to the noble order of monks residing in the *vihāra* erected by Gohaka" (*gohaka-kārita-vihāra-nivāsy-āryya-bhikṣu-saṅghāya*), and that this monastic community seems to have been organisationally independent from, albeit formally affiliated to, the complex which had grown around the monastery founded by Ḍuḍḍā.

In INSMaitraka00085 of king Śīlāditya III, dated 662 CE, the expression *ḍuḍḍā-vihāramaṇḍala* is used to describe the affiliation of two monasteries to this 'monastic complex'. Due to the fragmentary state of the charter, the relation between the two *vihāra*s founded by the two monks is not clear. Line 21 refers to an object "erected by the monk Vimalagupta in the *vihāra* founded by the monk Sthiramati, which was included in the *vihāramaṇḍala* [named after] Ḍuḍḍā".[84] Here it seems as if two levels of subsidiary structures had existed, i.e., the *vihāra* erected by the monk Vimalagupta might have been a substructure of the *vihāra* established by Sthiramati. Line 22, on the other hand, directly links the structure erected by Vimalagupta, most probably a *vihāra*, with the Ḍuḍḍā-*vihāramaṇḍala*, without an apparent intermediate level.[85] H. G. SHASTRI (2000: 221) has rightly observed that perhaps both the monasteries founded by the two monks had an equal position as grantees.[86]

81 See SCHMIEDCHEN, https://dharmalekha.info/texts/INSMaitraka00025, line 8.

82 See SCHMIEDCHEN, https://dharmalekha.info/texts/INSMaitraka00039, line 22.

83 See SCHMIEDCHEN, https://dharmalekha.info/texts/INSMaitraka00060, line 35.

84 See https://dharmalekha.info/texts/INSMaitraka00085. Unfortunately, the readings of this charter could not be checked due to the lack of any estampage. The edition has been taken from DISKALKAR 1925: 39, line 21: ... *ḍuḍḍā-vihāra*(*maṇḍalāntarggatā*)-*cāryya-bhikṣu-sthiramati-kārita-vihāre ācāryya-bhikṣu-vimalagupta-kāri*(*ta*)...

85 See https://dharmalekha.info/texts/INSMaitraka00085, on the basis of DISKALKAR 1925: 39, line 22: *ḍuḍḍā-vihāramaṇḍala-*(*praveśya-*)*kukkurāṇaka-grāma-niviṣṭācāryya-bhikṣu-vimalagupta-kārita-*(*vihāre*) ...

86 The *vihāra* erected by Vimalagupta is likewise mentioned as the donee of the endowment recorded in INSMaitraka00091 (https://dharmalekha.info/texts/INSMaitraka00091),

Figure 2: Map of the findspots of Maitraka grants for Buddhist monasteries; © Peter Palm, Berlin.

But even in the 7th century, when we have clear evidence for the composite structure of the monastic complex named after Ḍuḍḍā, the explicit reference to the *vihāramaṇḍala* only occurred when the beneficiary of the endowment was plainly a subsidiary structure, not when the recip-

line 52, and as being "attached to the Ḍuḍḍā-*vihāra*[*maṇḍala*]". INSMaitraka00038 refers to the Śrī-Bappapādīya-*vihāra* as also being founded by a monk named Sthiramati.

ient was the principal monastery, i.e., the Ḍuḍḍā-*vihāra* itself, as, e.g., in INSMaitraka00096.

A particular constellation is recorded in INSMaitraka00078, a mid-7th-century copper-plate charter by Dharasena IV in favour of a Tārā temple erected by his chief secretary Skandabhaṭa II in the village of Kāṇasīhānaka. The connection of this subsidiary structure of a specific, non-*vihāra*, type, with the Ḍuḍḍā-*vihāra* is also expressed in a distinct way:

> for the superintendents (*vārika*) in charge, residing in the Śrī-Tārā temple, appointed by and bound to the noble order of monks of the Ḍuḍḍā monastery in Valabhī (*valabhy-abhyantara-ḍuḍḍā-vihāraryya-bhikṣu-saṅgha-nirūpita-tat-pradita-pratijāgari-śrī-tārāpura-nivāsi-vārikānāṁ*).[87]

Elsewhere in the text, the subsidiary structure is called *devakula*.[88] Its administrators-in-charge are referred to as *vārika*.[89] The charter describes these 'temple managers' as residing in the Śrī-Tārapura and as having been appointed by the *bhikṣusaṅgha* of the Ḍuḍḍā-*vihāra*. This group of *vārikas* is mentioned in two contexts in INSMaitraka00078:

1. in the description of the purposes of the endowment as those whose subsistence should be provided by the grant;[90] and
2. in the stipulation saying that no hindrance should be made while the recipients of the grant were enjoying it.[91]

In the inventory of the objectives which this endowment should serve, the following five purposes are listed:

1. the subsistence of the *vārikas* or administrators (mentioned above);

87 Read from digital photographs received from the CSMVS, Mumbai. See SCHMIEDCHEN, https://dharmalekha.info/texts/INSMaitraka00078, lines 42–43 and 47–48.

88 See ibid., line 41.

89 For discussions of the term *vārika*, see SCHOPEN 1990: 193–194; SILK 2008: 101–125; KIEFFER-PÜLZ 2010: 79–84; VON HINÜBER 2012: 373–389.

90 See SCHMIEDCHEN, https://dharmalekha.info/texts/INSMaitraka00078, lines 42–43. This is a typical stipulation regarding provisions related to food, clothing, furniture, and medicine, normally used for the local *saṅgha* of a *vihāra*: *valabhy-abhyantara-ḍuḍḍā-vihāraryya-bhikṣu-saṅgha-ni(rū)pita-tatp(r)adita-pratijāgari-(śrī-)tārāpura-(n)ivāsi-(vārikāṇāṁ) cīvara-piṇḍapāta-śayanāsana-glāna-bhaiṣajyādy-artha(ṁ)*.

91 See ibid., lines 47–48: *valabhy-abhyantara-ḍuḍḍā-vihāraryya-bhikṣusaṅgha-nirūpita-tatpradita(pratijāgari-)[śrī-tārāpura-]ni(vā)si-(vā)rikā(ṇāṁ) ... na (kai)ś ci(d) vyāsedhe varttitavyam* ...

2. the worship of the Tārā [image(s)] installed in the Tārāpura founded by *divirapati* Skandabhaṭa in the village of Kāṇasīhānaka;[92]
3. the necessary repairs of the *devakula* (namely, the Tārāpura);[93]
4. the sustenance of the servants (*pādamūla*);[94] and
5. the charitable feeding (*sa[t]tra*) of beggars, strangers, etc.[95]

The examples cited show that during the 6th and 7th centuries, several subsidiary structures were gradually attached to the *vihāra* which had been founded by the Maitraka princess Ḍuḍḍā around the second quarter of the 6th century. This continuous process of foundations fostered by monks, officials, traders, and others created a monastic complex (*vihāramaṇḍala*) around the Ḍuḍḍā monastery as the principal institution. The kings of the Maitraka dynasty supported the Ḍuḍḍā-*vihāra* and its subsidiary units through several individual endowments of villages (and land).

The expression *vihāramaṇḍala* seems to have been used only when a subsidiary *vihāra* received a grant, in order to provide its 'coordinates' in a composite structure. The term *vihāramaṇḍala* was apparently not used when the principal monastery itself obtained a village (or land). Hence, the royal donors did obviously not regard the whole 'monastic complex' as one legal entity. This patronage pattern indicates that the institutions founded by other donors and affiliated to the Ḍuḍḍā monastery were regarded as economically independent structures.

In terms of monastic organisation, the degree of independence of the subsidiary units is not so clear. Normally, the order of monks residing in the *vihāra* directly favoured by an endowment would be the donee and/or beneficiary. But in the case of the (early) grant for the *vihāra* founded by Buddhadāsa (INSMaitraka00020), it seems as if the monks living in the Ḍuḍḍā-*vihāra* and those in the affiliated Buddhadāsa-*vihāra* formed one single *saṅgha* (see above). Perhaps this very practice was only followed in the early period. However, the system appears to have been similar when the institution affiliated to the Ḍuḍḍā monastery was of a clearly non-*vihāra* type, as in the case of the Tārā temple (INSMaitraka00078): the superintendents

92 See ibid., lines 40–41: *kāṇasīhānaka-grāme divirapati-(śrī-)skandabhaṭa-kā(r)i(t)a-(śrī-)[tā]rāpura-pratiṣṭhita-tārādevī-pādebhya(ḥ pū)jā-snapana-gandha-puṣpa-dhūpa-dīpa-tailādy-arttha(ṁ).*

93 See ibid., lines 41–42: *devakulasya ca khaṇḍa-sphuṭita-prati(saṁ)skara(ṇāya).*

94 See ibid., line 42: *(p)ādamūla-prajīvanāya ca.*

95 See ibid., line 44: *karppaṭika-vaideśy-(ād)īnāṁ satropayogārtthaṁ.*

of this shrine had been obviously chosen by the *bhikṣusaṅgha* of the Ḍuḍḍā-*vihāra*, and perhaps also belonged to this order of monks.[96]

Not much can be said about the architectural form of this complex called Ḍuḍḍā-*vihāramaṇḍala*, because practically no archaeological remains of any monastic structures have been excavated at Valabhipur so far, probably because this is still an inhabited site. But some indications are contained in the epigraphs as well. It is evident from the Maitraka copper plates that the Ḍuḍḍa-*vihāra* itself had been erected on the city territory of Valabhī. The location was perhaps rather "to the east of the inner part of Valabhī".[97] Furthermore, it can be assumed that some, if not most, of the subsidiary *vihāras* were located in the vicinity of the Ḍuḍḍā-*vihāra*, and thus also on the city territory of Valabhī. But this definitely does not hold true for all of them. In at least two cases, these institutions were situated in (or perhaps in the vicinity of) villages explicitly mentioned by name.

The *vihāra* established by the monk Vimalagupta is said to have been located in Kukkurāṇakagrāma (INSMaitraka00085, INSMaitraka00091).[98] And also the Tārā temple erected by the chief secretary Skandabhaṭa is described as having been built in a rural area, in Kāṇasīhānakagrāma (INSMaitraka00078).[99] However, the location of these villages has not been identified yet. Even the provenance of the relevant charters is only known for INSMaitraka00085, which is reported to have been found at the ruins in the northwest of Valabhipur in 1900 (together with ten other records of the Maitraka kings).[100] A Tārā shrine (*gandhakuṭī*) founded by *divirapati* Skandabhaṭa II in the village Kāṇasīhānaka is also mentioned in INSMaitraka00079, which is a fragmentary charter discovered together with INSMaitraka00078. In the preserved text of INSMaitraka00079, the Ḍuḍḍā-*vihāramaṇḍala* is not mentioned. But it is likely that the Tārāpura / *devakula* of INSMaitraka00078 and the *gandhakuṭī* of Tārā in INSMaitraka00079 were one and the same institution. INSMaitraka00079 contains the information

96 See above and fn. 90.

97 See SCHMIEDCHEN, https://dharmalekha.info/texts/INSMaitraka00091, line 51: *śrī-valabhy-ābhyantarikā-pūrvva-niviṣṭa-ḍuḍḍā-vihāra*[+++]. For a convincing attempt to localise monastic structures in ancient Valabhī through the use of remote sensing data, see PRADEEP & RAJANI 2025.

98 See ibid, line 52; see also, https://dharmalekha.info/texts/INSMaitraka00085, on the basis of DISKALKAR 1925: 39, line 22.

99 See SCHMIEDCHEN, https://dharmalekha.info/texts/INSMaitraka00078, line 40.

100 For seven of these copper-plate charters, namely, INSMaitraka00023, 00042, 00046–00047, 00055, 00082, and 00096, see https://dharmalekha.info/texts/INSMaitraka00023, etc.

that the village of Kāṇasīhānaka was situated in Surāṣṭra,[101] which is the ancient name for the Kathiawar peninsula. However, the geographical limits of Surāṣṭra vis-à-vis the Valabhī region are by far not clear, although we know that the Chinese Buddhist pilgrim Xuanzang, who visited this area in the 7th century, made a plain distinction between Valabhī and the Surāṣṭra region in his report. Xuanzang described Surāṣṭra as dependent on Valabhī;[102] and for him, Surāṣṭra seems to have been the rest of Kathiawar. In the Maitraka corpus of copper-plate charters, the place name 'Surāṣṭra' appears only from the second half of the 6th century onwards more frequently and then mostly in references to the localisation of the land or villages granted to several religious beneficiaries. Surāṣṭra also included, for instance, the ancient district of Hastavapra, present-day Hathab, some 60 km to the southeast of ancient Valabhī (see Figure 2).[103]

Xuanzang did not mention the existence of nunneries for any places he visited in India. But although the majority of *vihāra*s attested in the epigraphic corpus of the Maitrakas were monasteries for monks, there are also some inscriptional references to apparently economically independent nunneries in Valabhī; and it is noteworthy that the term used for such convents was also *vihāra*.[104] Two of these *vihāras* for *bhikṣuṇī*s attested in three Maitraka charters, which were found together during excavations undertaken near the Ghora-Dana tank at Valabhipur in 1930,[105] are significant with regard to the structural phenomenon of *vihāramaṇḍala*s: The first of them is the Yakṣaśūra-*vihāra*, a nunnery in the capital (INSMaitraka00048, INSMaitraka00050). The second is another convent, which had been founded by a lady with the name Pūrṇabhaṭṭā. She is portrayed as a 'daughter of [good] family' (*kulaputrikā*) and the mother of

101 Only the second plate of the originally two-plate charter is preserved; see SCHMIEDCHEN, https://dharmalekha.info/texts/INSMaitraka00079, line 7: ... (*surāṣṭreṣu kāṇasīhānaka-grāme*).

102 LI 1996: 298–303; DEEG 2012: 151.

103 The provenance of many Maitraka records is not exactly known. Supposed that the known findspots of the Maitraka copper plates could give any clue, then most of the charters referring to villages in Surāṣṭra have been found in the Bhavnagar District, to which also Valabhipur belongs. Others come from the Botad, Amreli, Rajkot, Junagadh, and Gir Somnath Districts.

104 For *varṣaka*, 'retreat house', as a standard term for 'nunnery' in the *Mūlasarvāstivādavinaya*, see SCHOPEN 2000: 154, fn. III.12. Also SCHOPEN 2009: 361: "... in a minority of cases the residence of nuns, like the residence of monks, even in this literature is referred to by the term *vihāra*, But the term *varṣaka* or its Tibetan translation occurs hundreds of times in this *Vinaya* ...".

105 GADRE 1934: 74–85, 88–91. The current name is Ghoda Daman; see PRADEEP & RAJANI 2025: 1769.

the subordinate ruler (*sāmanta*) Kakkuka (INSMaitraka00068). This second nunnery is described as being attached to the Yakṣaśūra-*vihāramaṇḍala*,[106] which indicates that complex monastic structures did not only exist in the environment of *bhikṣu-vihāras*, but also in that of *bhikṣuṇī-vihāras*. Nothing is known about Yakṣaśūra, except for his name. It is only once explicitly said that he was the founder of the monastery named after him. The terminology of the three title-deeds for nunneries is similar to that encountered in endowments for monks. However, INSMaitraka00048 commissioned by Śīlāditya I and dated 606 CE, is particularly interesting. This is the confirmation of a previous grant through a reissue, because the original charter had been lost:

> The Nirguḍaka village ..., which has been earlier and [still] is being enjoyed, its charter being lost, having so considered [and] enquired, has been confirmed [by me] ... as a religious grant like before (*mayā ... ni(r)gguḍaka-grāmaḥ pūrvva-bhukta-bhujyamā[na]ka(ḥ) pranaṣṭa-ś(āsanaka) iti-kṛ(t)v(ān)vi(ṣ)ya ... dharmma-(dā)yatayā pūrvvavat samanujñāta(ḥ)*).[107]

This passage testifies that the original charter (*śāsana*) had gone missing (*pranaṣṭa*) and that the king had to 'enquire', without mentioning any documentary evidence for this enquiry. The reason for the loss is also referred to in the new record, which stipulates that the respective village was to be used, *inter alia*:

> for the subsistence of the ... order of nuns ... which is now, as this nunnery is not existing anymore, living in the Yakṣaśūra nunnery (... *(vala)...(ta)... (bhikṣuṇī)-saṁghasy(e)dānī[ṁ] (t)ad-vihāra-sthānābhāvād yakṣaśūra-vihāre prativasa(taś)*).[108]

No structural differences are evident between a *vihāramaṇḍala* for monks and one for nuns. In the Maitraka corpus, *bhikṣu-vihāras* and *bhikṣuṇī-vihāras* are described in the very same way; their subsidiary structures received own grants and were economically independent. In the stipulations regarding the purposes of royal Buddhist grants, there is only one difference discernible. This might have had consequences for the architectural structure of *vihāras* for monks vs. nunneries. From the 7th century onwards, Maitraka grants for male monastic communities should serve, *inter alia*, an objective which is so far not attested in endowments to *bhikṣuṇīs*. The gifts were to be used also: 'for the living of the soles of the feet' (*pādamūla-prajīvanāya*), i.e., for the sustenance of the monastic servants. Hence, the Ḍuḍḍā-*vihāramaṇḍala*

106 See SCHMIEDCHEN, https://dharmalekha.info/texts/INSMaitraka00068, lines 33–34.
107 See SCHMIEDCHEN, https://dharmalekha.info/texts/INSMaitraka00048, lines 21–27.
108 See ibid., lines 21–22.

(for monks) most probably had to accommodate such people,[109] while the Yakṣaśūra-*vihāramaṇḍala* (for nuns) apparently did not have to provide residential quarters for this kind of servants.[110]

8. Bihar and Bengal, 6th–10th Centuries

There is at least one more area for which we get abundant epigraphic evidence of the composite character of Buddhist monasteries: the Bihar-Bengal region in the eastern part of the subcontinent.[111] The inscriptional data for these monastic compounds, although not labelled *vihāramaṇḍala*, is more diverse in East India than in the sources from Gujarat, in terms of geographical spread as well as chronological range. Furthermore, the epigraphic attestations from Bihar and Bengal have the advantage of being partly corroborated by archaeological data and also more specifically by the records of the Chinese pilgrims Xuanzang and Yijing, who visited some of these places in the 7th century.

The first relevant inscription is the 6th-century Jayarampur copper plate of the time of Gopacandra (INSBengalCharters00076), which appears to be contemporary to the early grants of the Maitrakas, and also lacks supportive archaeological evidence. The text records the addition of a subsidiary *vihāra* to the Bodhipadraka-*mahāvihāra* as one of the purposes of the land transfer attested:

> for the construction of a monastery at the great monastery in Bodhipadraka (*°vodhipadraka-mahāvihāre vihāra-karaṇāya*).[112]

However, at the end of the description of the transfer, it is explicitly stated that the village was given to the *bhikṣusaṅgha* at Bodhipadraka,[113] which implies the following conclusion by Ryosuke Furui (2021–22: 112–113):

---

109 For the relevant attestations in INSMaitraka00060, 00078–00079, 00082, 00091, and 00096, see Schmiedchen, https://dharmalekha.info/texts/INSMaitraka00078, etc.

110 See Schmiedchen 2021–22: 80. In the Maitraka corpus, the stipulation referring to *pādamūla* is attested in a number of Buddhist and non-Buddhist institutional endowments: to *vihāras* of male Buddhist monastic communities, to Tārā shrines, and to temples of Hindu deities, like Śiva, the Sun-god, a local goddess, etc. For the relevant evidence on the term *pādamūla* in the Bhaumakara epigraphical corpus from Odisha, see Schmiedchen. fortcoming: 9.

111 Apart from the Indian states of Bihar and West Bengal, this region also includes parts of present-day Bangladesh.

112 See Furui & Bricout, https://dharmalekha.info/texts/INSBengalCharters00076, line 18.

113 See ibid., lines 29–30: *śrī-vodhipadra(kīya)-[++]mahāyānika-[+]bhi(kṣu-)saṁghāya pratipāditaḥ.*

> The construction of a *vihāra* at Bodhipadrakamahāvihāra, one of the purposes stated in the inscription, suggests that a *mahāvihāra* was an institution which could contain more than one *vihāra* within its compound. It should be noted at the same time that the donation was made for the entire *saṁgha* of the Bodhipadrakamahāvihāra and that the religious practices and provision for monks were organized at the *mahāvihāra*, not at each constituent *vihāra*.

This evidence perhaps coincides with the case described in INSMaitraka00020 for Gujarat.[114] With regard to the Jayarampur copper plate, FURUI (ibid: 113) has stated:

> This makes a stark contrast with *mahāvihāras* in the later period, when each *vihāra* and even sub-structures ... had their own *saṁgha* ...

The *mahāvihāras* of the later period in Bihar and Bengal show similar features as the 'regular' *vihāramaṇḍalas* of the Maitraka kingdom. The Nālandā-*mahāvihāra* in Bihar and the Somapura-*mahāvihāra* at present-day Paharpur in Bangladesh are the most prominent examples of such composite structures from Eastern India (see Figure 1). Both monastic complexes are unanimously called *mahāvihāra* in sealing inscriptions, though the excavated archaeological remains differ remarkably in terms of structure.

The site of Nālandā, the *mahāvihāra* par excellence in secondary literature, consisted of a number of individual buildings situated in close proximity to each other (see Figures 3 and 4). The individual buildings were apparently founded by different donors, but we possess specific epigraphic data only for very few of them. Xuanzang, who visited this place in the 7th century, confirmed its composite structure and mentioned one common enclosure for all the monasteries.[115] MAX DEEG makes the following observation on the terminology used by Xuanzang and the slightly later Yijing, who both resided and studied at Nālandā for several years:

> In context of the "title" or status of the monastery it is striking that Xuanzang ... does not call Nālandā *mahāvihāra* (*dasi* ...) but Nalantuo-sengjialan ..., Nālandā-saṅghārāma. This may indicate that at the time of his visit the monastery had not yet received the status of a "great monastery" (*mahāvihāra*). Yijing's anthology of *dharma*-searching monks is the only Chinese source which uses the full-fledged title Shili-Nalantuo-mohepiheluo ..., Śrī-Nālandā-mahāvihāra ...[116]

114 See above and fn. 80.

115 See LI 1996: 250. See also the translation of this passage by DEEG 2018: 116–117.

116 DEEG 2018: 106–107. See his translation of T.2066.5b.17ff. in appendix 4a (ibid.: 123–127).

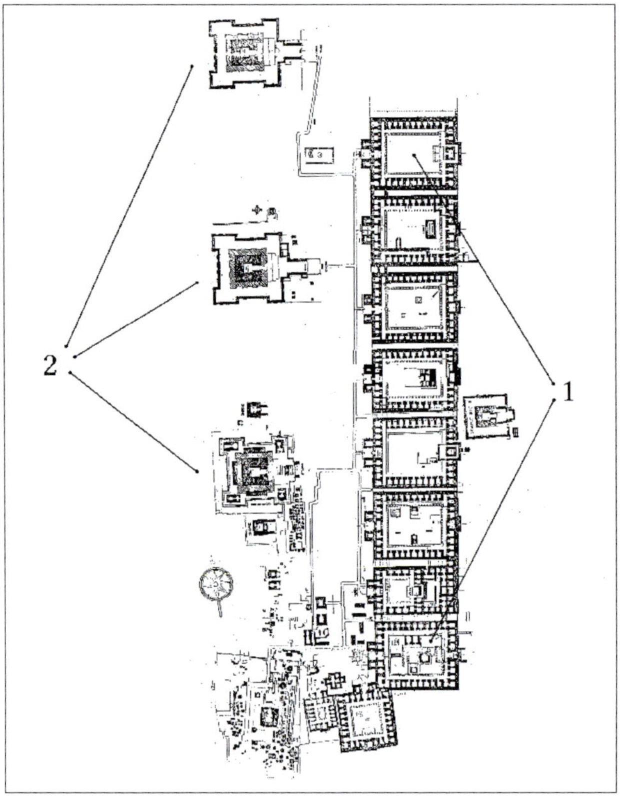

Figure 3: Layout of the Buddhist monastic complex of Nālandā.

Figure 4: Ruins of the Buddhist monastic complex of Nālandā.

In fact, the designation *mahāvihāra* for this monastic compound is best attested in numerous clay sealings found during archaeological excavations at Nālandā.[117] Although sealing inscriptions are usually short, they are a major source for the reconstruction of the monastic administration at Nālandā. Whereas "only Nālandā has yielded such a large number of seals and sealings containing valuable information" (KARUNATILLAKA 1980: 58), a serious problem is posed by the uncertain chronology of much of the material. On the basis of palaeographical considerations, it has been assumed that the large majority of the sealings does not seem to be significantly older than the 8th century, despite some remarkable exceptions. The relevant sealing inscriptions correspond to Yijing's wording (DEEG 2018: 107) and frequently read as in the following two examples:

> of the order of venerable monks belonging to the Śrī-Nālandā-*mahāvihāra* (*śrī-nālandā-mahāvihārīyārya-bhikṣu-saṅghasya*);[118]
> of the order of venerable monks from the four directions at the Śrī-Nālandā-*mahāvihāra* (*śrī-nālandā-mahāvihāre cāturddiśārya-bhikṣu-saṅghasya*).[119]

There are, however, sealings in which the Buddhist order of monks is neither specified as 'belonging to the great monastery' (*mahāvihārīya*) of Nālandā, nor as residing 'in the great monastery' (*mahāvihāre*), but the sealing inscription merely refers to 'Śrī-Nālandā'.[120]

The same focus on the name 'Nālandā' without any further terminological specification is also discernible in some stone epigraphs and copper-plate charters. The 8th-century stone inscription of a king named Yaśovarmadeva, which was found in the débris of the so-called monastery no. 1 describes, *inter alia*, Nālandā as "mocking, as it were, all the cities of the kings",[121] and as "containing a row of monasteries" (°*vihārāvalī*).[122] The ar-

117 Some 690 sealings, not all of them mentioning Nālandā or its *mahāvihāra*, have been discovered at the so-called monastery no. 9 alone, "in one chamber which must have been the record room of the establishment in that area" (SASTRI 1942: 36). See also KARUNATILLAKA 1980: 66.

118 See SASTRI 1942: 36, 39–40; MITRA 1971: 268, no. 70. See also the discussion in DEEG 2018: 106.

119 See SASTRI 1942: 39, 41, 43–44. For other examples of *śrī-nālandā-mahāvihāra*°, see ibid.: 37. For a dozen of similar sealings from the archeaological site of Telhara, some 35 km to the west of Nālandā, referring to the Śrī-Prathamaśivapura-*mahāvihāra* situated there, see SANYAL & BOSE 2024: 226–229. For a number of sealings referring to the Śrī-Ratnagiri-*mahāvihāra* from Ratnagiri in Orissa, see Mitra 1971: 226.

120 See ibid.: 37–40.

121 See ibid: 79 (The stone inscription of the reign of Yaśovarmadeva), lines 5–6, stanza 4: … *bhū-bhujāṁ nālandā hasatīva sarvva-nāgarīḥ* …

122 See ibid: 79, lines 6–7, stanza 5.

chaeological evidence coincides with this description, as – with the exception of nos. 1A and 1B – all residential quarters (monasteries nos. 1, 4, 6–11) were arranged in a string aligned from south to north, with their entrances facing westwards (e.g. RAJANI 2016: 2; see Figure 3).

A similarly important attestation for this practice is to be found in the 9th-century stone inscription of the reign of the Pāla king Devapāla from Ghosravan, a Buddhist site, which is located some 15 km to the east of the monastic complex of Nālandā and interpreted by archaeologists as one of its extensions (REVIRE 2016: 254). This inscription "records the career of a monk from Nagarahāra in Afghanistan who became the abbot of the Nālandā monastery" (SALOMON 2018: 20).[123] Nālandā is also described with an allusion to a multitude of monasteries (*śrīmad-vihāra-parihāra*),[124] although the visualisation might be different from Yaśovarmadeva's. Whereas Nālandā is again left without any marker of 'monastic status', the site where the monk Vīradeva had received his ordination, the Kaniṣka monastery, probably identical with the famous erstwhile Buddhist institution near present-day Peshawar, is labelled *mahāvihāra*.[125]

One of the most famous instances is attested in the Nālandā copper-plate inscription of Devapāla, INSBengalCharters00104. This endowment record, dated in the Pāla king's 35th regnal year, refers to the commissioning of a *vihāra* 'at Śrī-Nālandā', without any clear reference to the status of this monastic site, by the ruler of Suvarṇadvīpa (Sumatra). This plate was discovered in 1921 by HIRANANDA SASTRI (1923–24: 310) in the débris of monastery no. 1 as well. However, it is doubtful whether this statement can be actually related to the foundation of monastery no. 1, because this structure might be much older than the 9th century. In his inscription, King Devapāla informs a large number of people potentially concerned, *inter alia*, about the following:

> We have been notified by king Śrī-Bālaputradeva, the ruler of Suvarṇadvīpa, through the mouth of a messenger as follows: "A *vihāra* was established by me at Śrī-Nālandā".[126]

123 For the 'vita' of the monk Vīradeva, see also DATTA 2019: 171–174; FURUI 2020: 151.

124 See KIELHORN 1888: 310, lines 12–13, stanza 11: *nālandayā ... śrīmad-vihāra-parihāra-vibhūsitāṅghyā ...*, which has been translated by the editor (ibid.: 311) as "... by Nālandā ... decorated by a ring of famous *vihāras* ...". For the rendering of *parihāra* as 'ring', see ibid.: 311, fn. 33.

125 See KIELHORN 1888: 310, line 7, verse 6b: *śrīmat-kaniṣkam upagamya mahāvihāram*.

126 See FURUI & GRIFFITHS, https://dharmalekha.info/texts/INSBengalCharters00104, lines 37–38: *suvarṇṇadvīpādhipa-mahārāja-śrī-vālaputradevena dūtaka-mukhena vayam vijñāpitāḥ yathā mayā śrī-nālandāyām vihāraḥ kāritas*. The translation is mine.

The main purpose of the charter, however, is Devapāla's endowment of five villages for the benefit of this newly established *vihāra* at Nālandā.[127] The reports of the Chinese pilgrims also contain information on the landed property of the entire monastic site of Nālandā. Huili, Xuanzang's biographer, states:

> Out of admiration the kings gave more than one hundred settlements [as fiefs] in order to [supply] full support, [each] settlement [consisting of] two hundred households, daily supplying polished non-glutinous rice [and] several hundred *dan* of ghee and milk.[128]

Some decades later, Yijing reports of 200 villages:

> [From T.2066.5b.17ff.:] The *saṅgha* in the monastery [consists] of three thousand five hundred [monks]; there are two hundred and one villages belonging to the monastery which were given, with their population, by successive generations of rulers as eternal offerings [to the monastery].[129]
> [From T.2125.214a3ff.:] Even though the number of monks exceeds [just] three thousand [the monastery] is enfiefed with over two hundred villages which were all donated by rulers of successive generations [so that it will] flourish continuously ...[130]

In contrast to Nālandā, only a single, although extremely large, structure has been excavated at Paharpur (see Figure 1). Several inscriptions on sealings have been found, which call this monastic building or the whole complex the *mahāvihāra* of King Dharmapāla (DIKSHIT 1938: 20), after the Pāla ruler who reigned from the end of the 8th to the beginning of the 9th century and was the father of King Devapāla. The phrasing of those sealing inscriptions is similarly construed as in their Nālandā counterparts (see above):

> of the order of venerable monks belonging to the Śrī-Dharmapāladeva-*mahāvihāra* at Somapura (*śrī-somapure śrī-dharmapāladeva-mahāvihārīyārya-bhikṣu-saṅghasya*).[131]

RYOSUKE FURUI's (2011) edition of the Indian Museum copper-plate charter of Dharmapāla has revealed that we have to assume a composite character also for

127 FURUI & GRIFFITHS, https://dharmalekha.info/texts/INSBengalCharters00104, lines 32–42.
128 This is the translation by DEEG (2018: 121, appendix 2). For another one, see LI 1995: 95.
129 This is the translation by DEEG (2018: 127, appendix 4a).
130 This is the translation by DEEG (2018: 129, appendix 4b).
131 See DISKSHIT 1938: 90 and plate LIXh. See also SANDERSON 2009: 90; COPPLESTONE 2024: 1–2.

the monastic complex at Somapura, very much as for Nālandā. This title-deed records that a subordinate ruler named Bhadraṇāga wanted to grant land in favour of three Buddhist institutions founded by him and his wife. Two of these institutions, a *gandhakuṭī*, 'perfume chamber' or shrine room, and a *vihārikā*, a small monastery, are described as being located in the Somapura-*mahāvihāra*.[132]

The excavated monastic structure at Paharpur, with its size of ca. 280 by 280 metres, i.e., 78,400 square metres, and its 177 cells, is not only "one of the biggest single-unit Buddhist monasteries in South Asia ... organised around a square courtyard with an entrance from the north" (BREUIL & GILL 2007: 129), but is also one prominent example of a unique monastic building type known from Bengal and characterised by a large temple of a 'cruciform' or so-called 'pañcaratha' plan in the centre of the courtyard. Hence, unlike Nālandā, where a row of temples is arranged in parallel to the monastic buildings on their west, the monumental structure at Paharpur is of a composite nature in itself, a 'temple-monastery' (COPPLESTONE 2024: 14–18) to the highest possible degree.

A very similar structure has been excavated some 200 km to the east of ancient Nālandā, at Antichak in Bihar (see Figure 1), a site exceeding even Paharpur in size (350 by 350 metres; 208 cells) and tentatively being identified with Vikramaśīla-*mahāvihāra*, known from literature, but not convincingly verified yet by extant sealings or inscriptions (SANYAL 2018a). Several monastic structures at Mainamati/Lalmai in Bangladesh (see Figure 1), some 300 km to the southeast of Paharpur, also follow this plan, although on a somewhat smaller scale, namely, the so-called Ananda Vihar (195 by 195 metres), the Bhoja Vihar (175 by 175 metres; 122 cells), and the Salban Vihar (167.6 by 167.6 metres; 115 cells) (BHUIYAN 2018: 268, 270).

In addition to fresh interpretations of the complexity of the monumental monastic structure at Paharpur, with a large, centrally-integrated, 'stūpa-temple' (COPPLESTONE 2024: III), SEN, RAHMAN & AHSAN (2014: 50) argue that recent archaeological research has modified the picture of 'a single-unit monastery', particularly criticising the monument-centrism of the traditional approach. They also stress the need to include survey archaeology and geo-archaeological investigations to a larger extent, concluding that "the *mahavihara* not only constituted the several structures that are exposed and visible now, but also had other associated structures and habitation nearby." Furthermore, from the wording of the Indian Museum

132 For a revised edition, see FURUI, https://dharmalekha.info/texts/INSBengalCharters00099.

copper-plate charter of Dharmapāla itself, FURUI (2011: 151) has concluded that "each facility [within the *mahāvihāra* – AS] had its *saṁgha* with its own source of subsistence".[133]

9. Conclusions

Among archaeologists and art historians, it is common practice, grounded on *vinaya* textual use, to call a building a 'vihāra', if it has been identified as a monastic residence on the basis of its architectural structure. Conversely, when the terms *vihāra* and *mahāvihāra* are attested in inscriptions, attempts are made to identify them with the archaeological remains of excavated residential quarters. However, the epigraphic evidence frequently contradicts such a narrow interpretation of the term *mahāvihāra*, and at times even for the term *vihāra*.

Some of the earliest epigraphic attestations of the term *mahāvihāra* are to be found in several 3rd-century Prākrit stone inscriptions from the multi-site Buddhist monastic centre of Nagarjunakonda in Āndhradeśa. The individual sites were composite structures of a large free-standing main stūpa, one or more enshrined secondary stūpa(s), and living spaces of different shapes. At site 1 of Nagarjunakonda, such a compound, not only its dwelling space, was referred to as *mahāvihāra*. In a similar way, the term *vihāra* was used with a superordinate connotation, beyond any purely residential meaning, at other sites of Nagarjunakonda. The reason for designating site 1 as a *mahāvihāra* in contrast to a *vihāra* might have been the planned and later actual size of the whole complex, underlined by the fact that its main stūpa was "the most imposing" structure at Nagarjunakonda. Thus, with regard to the dimensions of their respective *mahācetiya*, size may have been a distinguishing feature between a *vihāra* and a *mahāvihāra* in early Āndhradeśa.

Similar conclusions regarding the composite structure of a *mahāvihāra* and a more than merely residential meaning of this expression might also hold true for the Buddhist structures at Devnimori in the 4th/5th centuries, the monastic compound around the great stūpa of Sanchi in the 5th century, as well as the Buddhist cave complex at Kanheri in the 5th and 9th centuries.

---

133 For further details on the *mahāvihāras* of Bengal, I would like to refer to the extensive work of my Japanese colleague Ryosuke Furui, the latest publication being FURUI 2021–22. For a discussion of the early medieval material from Eastern India, see also GHOSH 2022.

The term *mahāvihāra* is also attested in several copper-plate charters, beginning with the oldest extant specimen of this type of inscription discovered in India, the Patagandigudem plates of the 3rd-century Ikṣvāku king Ehavala-Cāntamūla. As inscribed copper plates are often, unlike most stone epigraphs, discovered outside any architectural context, this kind of inscriptional evidence for *vihāras* or *mahāvihāras* is less frequently corroborated by archaeological data, a fact which considerably complicates the interpretation of the structures.

The Buddhist monastic establishments endowed with the income from villages by the royal copper-plate charters of the 5th/6th-century Viṣṇukuṇḍin kings and their subordinate ruler Pr̥thivīśrīmūla are almost exclusively classified as *mahāvihāra*, and some of the monks are described as *mahāvihāra-vāsin*. Several of these institutions in Āndhradeśa had been founded by kings, queens, and subordinate rulers. However, only one of these *mahāvihāras* has been successfully identified with a known archaeological site.

The almost complete lack of corroborative archaeological evidence is also highly relevant for the 6th/7th-century Buddhist copper-plate charters of the Maitraka dynasty from Gujarat. But this dense and rich epigraphic corpus of the kings of Valabhī itself offers some clues regarding the structure of the monastic institutions which benefitted from these royal endowments. The term *mahāvihāra* is only attested in one extant Maitraka charter. But the designation *vihāramaṇḍala* was used for two apparently large monastic complexes situated in the Maitraka capital Valabhī: one for monks and another one for nuns, with several economically independent *vihāras* belonging to each of the compounds. The 'mother monastery' of the *vihāramaṇḍala* for *bhikṣus* had been founded by the Maitraka princess Ḍuḍḍā, whereas the principal institution of the *bhikṣuṇī-vihāramaṇḍala* had been commissioned by a donor named Yakṣaśūra, about whose social status nothing is known. However, most *vihāras* mentioned in the Maitraka corpus were non-royal foundations. A continuous building process fostered by officials, traders, monks, and others created the two monastic complexes. The expression *vihāramaṇḍala* was used only when a subsidiary *vihāra* received a grant, and not when the principal monastery itself obtained a village or land. Not all the epigraphically attested *vihāras* of the Maitraka kingdom were affiliated to a *vihāramaṇḍala*. And whereas all the known nunneries were located in Valabhī, *bhikṣu-vihāras* were also situated in other towns and villages.

East India, especially Bihar and Bengal (including parts of present-day Bangladesh) is the area most frequently associated in secondary literature with the existence of *mahāvihāras* during the early medieval period. The evidence for the composite character of Buddhist monasteries stretches across a rather large region, and spans a very long period, at least from the 6th to the 12th centuries. The source material is rather diverse, containing epigraphic data from copper plates, stone, and clay sealings, archaeological data from numerous excavations, and specific literary data, from the records of the 7th-century Chinese pilgrims Xuanzang and Yijing, from manuscript colophons, and from the list of *mahāvihāras* in the *History of Buddhism* by the much later Tibetan monk Tārānātha who probably lived around 1600. While several *mahāvihāras* in Bihar and Bengal known from literature have been successfully identified with excavated archaeological remains on the basis of sealings and longer inscriptions, like the famous 'great monastery' of Nālandā as well as the Somapura-*mahāvihāra* with the site of present-day Paharpur, others have not or at least still not convincingly.

It is however striking that some of the most famous 'great monasteries' of Bihar and Bengal are not always labelled *mahāvihāra* in the sources. Xuanzang calls Nālandā a *sengjialan* (*saṅghārāma*), and Yijing, the only Chinese author who uses the title 'Shili-Nalantuo-mohepiheluo' (Śrī-Nālandā-*mahāvihāra*) in some of his work, is also not consistent. Due to this evidence, MAX DEEG (2018: 106) assumes that at the time of Xuanzang's visit "the monastery had not yet received the status of a 'great monastery'."[134] It is also remarkable that, apart from sealings, several post-7th-century inscriptions from the site do not refer to this Buddhist establishment as a *mahāvihāra*, but merely as 'Nālandā'. This could perhaps also indicate that due to the high reputation of this Buddhist establishment any other signifier was not deemed to be required. In what is the latest known epigraph from the site, the Nālandā stone inscription of the monk Vipulaśrīmitra, dated on palaeographic grounds to the 12th century, not even the toponym 'Nālandā' does occur. This text contains two direct mentions of Somapura (*śrīmat-somapure*) without any reference to its status of a *mahāvihāra*.[135]

Whereas the *mahāvihāras* at Somapura and Vikramaśīla were regarded as royal foundations of the early Pāla rulers, there is evidence for the establishment of a *mahāvihāra* by a subordinate from the 11th century (FURUI

---

134 In the 7th century, Xuanzang reports on altogether six monasteries (*saṅghārāma*), all foundations by kings, some of which may be identified with the late Guptas. According to the excavators, the oldest monastic buildings, i.e., nos. 1, 1A, and 1B in the south of the site, were probably erected in the 6th century. The oldest layers of the residential structures 4–7 are datable to a period before the 9th century, and nos. 8–11 are altogether younger.

135 MAJUMDAR 1931–32: 98–99, lines 2–3 and 8–10, stanzas 2 and 8.

2013: 115). In one of the 9th-century Kanheri inscriptions, the caves at ancient Kr̥ṣṇagiri are designated as *mahārāja-mahāvihāra*, "a great monastery of a great king". This phrasing could allude to the collective memory that this monastic compound had been a royal endeavour in its initial stage, or it could be the result of the perception that a *mahāvihāra* must have been a royal foundation *per se*.

This observation brings us back to the initial query what characterised a *mahāvihāra* or a *vihāramaṇḍala* in comparison to an 'ordinary' *vihāra* according to epigraphic evidence. The term *vihāramaṇḍala* is so far only attested in the Maitraka corpus,[136] and although there is almost a complete lack of corroborating archaeological evidence, it becomes clear from the copper-plate charters that *vihāramaṇḍala*s in 6th/7th-century Gujarat must have been complex monastic compounds for monks or nuns consisting of several *vihāra*s and partly also including separate shrine or temple structures, which could also be located outside the capital city of Valabhī.

The use of the term *mahāvihāra* was more widespread in terms of geographical scope and chronological range, which raises doubts that a 'great monastery' in 3rd-century Āndhradeśa was the same as in 11th-century Bengal. According to a passage from the *Mūlasarvāstivādavinaya* translated by Yijing, a *dasi* or *mahāvihāra* was 'great' in two respects: donations and form/size (Deeg 2018: 107). For a Chinese monk, a *mahāvihāra* might have had "(semi-)official status ... through royal patronage" (ibid.). But it is rather uncertain whether this really applies as a general rule to Buddhist monasteries in ancient and early medieval India, although a number of *mahāvihāra*s seem to have been royal foundations, for instance, under the Ikṣvākus and the Pālas. However, a certain degree of planned complexity may have been a common feature of all *mahāvihāras*.

The economic and organisational structure in the 8th/9th-century *mahāvihāras* in Bengal and Bihar shows similarities with that of the 6th/7th-century *vihāramaṇḍala*s in Gujarat. In this context, it is striking that a recent study by Pradeep & Rajani (2025) on ancient Valabhī, using remote sensing data, has resulted, *inter alia*, in Digital Elevation Models which reveal a large, dense cluster of high elevation in the southeastern part of the settlement of present-day Valabhipur (the so-called mound M) and a "series of fragmented mounds aligned in a linear pattern" (the so-called mounds M1–M6) in the northwestern part. In terms of shape, scale, and cardinal orientation, Pradeep

136 But see the Āndhradeśa attestation for *vihāramaṇḍale* in Sankaranarayanan 1967–68: 32, line 12.

& RAJANI (ibid.: 1777) see remarkable resemblances of their mounds M1–M6 at Valabhipur with the row of monasteries excavated at the site of ancient Nālandā, and also between mound M at Valabhipur and the monastic sites at Paharpur (Somapura) and Antichak (Vikramaśīla). This notable observation discloses one way forward for future research, using new methods in the field of archaeology.

Bibliography

ALBERY 2020: HENRY ALBERY, *Buddhism and Society in the Indic North and Northwest. 2nd Century BCE - 3rd Century CE*. PhD diss, University of Munich 2020.

BAUMS et al. 2016: STEFAN BAUMS, ARLO GRIFFITHS, INGO STRAUCH & VINCENT TOURNIER, Early Inscriptions of Āndhradeśa: Results of Fieldwork in January and February 2016. *Bulletin de l'École française d'Extrême-Orient* 102 (2016): 355–398.

BHANDARKAR 1981: DEVADATTA RAMAKRISHNA BHANDARKAR, *Inscriptions of the Early Gupta Kings*. [Corpus Inscriptionum Indicarum. 3, revised edition]. Ed. by BAHADURCHAND CHHABRA & GOVIND SWAMIRAO GAI. New Delhi 1981.

BHUIYAN 2018: MOKAMMAL H. BHUIYAN, Mainamati. In: *History of Bangladesh: Early Bengal in Regional Perspectives (up to c. 1200 CE)*, vol. 1: *Archaeology, Political History, Polity*. Ed. by ABDUL MOMIN CHOWDHURY & RANABIR CHAKRAVARTI. Dhaka 2018: 263–280.

BÖHTLINGK 1879–89: OTTO BÖHTLINGK, *Sanskrit-Wörterbuch in kürzerer Fassung*. Petersburg 1879–89.

BOSMA 2018: NATASJA BOSMA, *Dakṣiṇa Kosala: A Rich Centre of Early Śaivism*. Groningen 2018.

BRANCACCIO 2011: PIA BRANCACCIO, *The Buddhist Caves at Aurangabad: Transformation in Art and Religion*. Leiden & Boston 2011.

— 2022: ID., Views from the Black Mountain: The Rock-Cut Mahāvihāra at Kānheri/Kṛṣṇagiri in Konkan. In: *On the Regional Development of Early Buddhist Monasteries in South Asia* [RINDAS Series of Working Papers. 3]. Ed. by NICOLAS MORRISSEY, AKIRA SHIMADA & ABHISHEK AMAR SINGH. Kyoto 2022: 73–88.

BREUIL & GILL 2007: JEAN-YVES BREUIL & SANDRINE GILL, New Research on Paharpur Buddhist Monastery (North Bengal). In: *The Temple in South Asia*. Ed. by Adam Hardy. London 2007: 129–140.

CHHABRA 1949–50: BAHADURCHAND CHHABRA, Intwa Clay Sealing. *Epigraphia Indica* 28 (1949–50): 174–175.

CHOWDHARY 2010: SOORYAKANT NARSINH CHOWDHARY, *Devnimori: Buddhist Monuments*. Baroda 2010.

COPPLESTONE 2024: LOUIS COPPLESTONE, *Monasteries, Mountains, and Maṇḍalas: Buddhist Architecture and Imagination in Medieval Eastern India*. PhD diss, Harvard University, Cambridge (Massachusetts) 2020.

DAMSTEEGT 1978: THEO DAMSTEEGT, *Epigraphical Hybrid Sanskrit: Its Rise, Spread, Characteristics and Relationship to Buddhist Hybrid Sanskrit*. Leiden 1978.

DATTA 2019: SANJUKTA DATTA, Building for the Buddha: Patrons in the Pala Kingdom. *Studies in History* 35.2: 162–177.

DEEG 2012: MAX DEEG, Sthavira, Thera and '*Sthaviravāda' in Chinese Buddhist Sources. In: *How Theravāda Is Theravāda? Exploring Buddhist Identities*. Ed. by PETER SKILLING et al. Chiang Mai 2012: 129–162.

— 2018: ID., Setting the Records Straight. In: *Records, Recoveries, Remnants and Inter-Asian Interconnections: Decoding Cultural Heritage*. Ed. by ANJANA SHARMA. Singapore 2018: 105–140.

— 2022: ID., Between Normativity and Material Emptiness: Indian Buddhist Monasteries and the Chinese Buddhist Travelogues. In: *On the Regional Development of Early Buddhist Monasteries in South Asia* [RINDAS Series of Working Papers. 3]. Ed. by NICOLAS MORRISSEY, AKIRA SHIMADA & ABHISHEK AMAR SINGH. Kyoto 2022: 89–130.

DIKSHIT 1938: KASHINATH NARAYAN DIKSHIT, *Excavations at Paharpur, Bengal* [Memoirs of the Archaeological Survey of India. 55]. Delhi 1938.

DISKALKAR 1925: DATTATRAYA BALKRISHNA DISKALKAR, Some Unpublished Copper-Plates of the Rulers of Valabhī: No. X. - Second plate of a grant of Siladitya III: [Gupta-] Samvat 343. *Journal of the Bombay Branch of the Royal Asiatic Society*, N.S., 1 (1925): 37-40.

DURT & FORTE 1983: HUBERT DURT & ANTONINO FORTE, Daiji. In: *Hōbōgirin. Dictionnaire encyclopédique du bouddhisme d'après les sources chinoises et japonaises*, volume 6: Da–Daijizaiten. Ed. by PAUL DEMIÈVIELLE & JACQUES GERNET. Paris & Tokyo 1983: 679–711.

EFURD 2018: DAVID EFURD, Buddhist Sites of Western India in the Aftermath of the Sātavāhana-Kṣaharāta War: Dynastic Geographies and Patterns of Patronage, Renewal, and Abandonment. *Journal of the International Association of Buddhist Studies* 41 (2018): 359-420.

FALK 1999–2000: HARRY FALK, The Pātagaṇḍigūḍem Copper-Plate Grant of the Ikṣvāku King Ehavala Cāntamūla. *Silk Road Art and Archaeology* 6 (1999–2000): 275–283.

— 2008: ID., Money Can Buy Me Heaven. Religious Donations in Late and Post-Kushan India. *Archäologische Mitteilungen aus Iran und Turfan* 40 (2008): 137–148.

FERGUSSON & BURGESS 1880: JAMES FERGUSSON & JAMES BURGESS, *The Cave Temples of India*. London 1880.

FLEET 1888: JOHN FAITHFULL FLEET, *Inscriptions of the Early Gupta Kings and Their Successors* [Corpus Inscriptionum Indicarum. 3]. Calcutta 1888.

FOGELIN 2006: LARS FOGELIN, *Archaeology of Early Buddhism*. Lanham et al. 2006.

FURUI 2011: RYOSUKE FURUI, Indian Museum Copper Plate Inscription of Dharmapala, Year 26: Tentative Reading and Study. *South Asian Studies* 27.2 (2011): 145–156.

— 2013: ID., Chaprakot Stone Inscription of the Time of Gopāla IV, Year 9. In: *Centenary Commemorative Volume (1913-2013): Bangladesh National Museum*. Ed. by ALAMGIR MUHAMMAD SERAJUDDIN et al. Dhaka 2013: 110–117.

— 2020: ID., *Land and Society in Early South Asia: Eastern India 400-1250 AD*. London & New York 2020.

— 2021–22: ID., Buddhist *Vihāras* in Early Medieval Bengal: Organizational Development and Historic Context. *Buddhism, Law & Society* 7 (2021–22): 101–143.

— https://dharmalekha.info/texts/INSBengalCharters00099.

FURUI & BRICOUT, https://dharmalekha.info/texts/INSBengalCharters00076.

FURUI & GRIFFITHS, https://dharmalekha.info/texts/INSBengalCharters00104.

GADRE 1934: A. S. GADRE, Five Vala Copper-Plate Grants. *Journal of the University of Bombay* 3 (1934): 74–91.

GHOSH 2022: SUCHANDRA GHOSH, Patronage of Buddhist Monasteries in Eastern India (600–1300 CE). *Oxford Research Encyclopedia of Religion*, published online 15 August 2022: 1–29.

GOKHALE 1991: SHOBHANA GOKHALE, *Kanheri Inscriptions.* Pune 1991.

GRIFFITHS 2018: ARLO GRIFFITHS, Four more Gupta-period Copperplate Grants from Bengal. *Pratna Samiksha: A Journal of Archaeology,* New Series, 9 (2018): 15–57.

GRIFFITHS & TOURNIER, EIAD: ARLO GRIFFITHS & VINCENT TOURNIER, *Early Inscriptions of Āndhradeśa* = http://hisoma.huma-num.fr/exist/apps/EIAD/works/.

VON HINÜBER 2012: OSKAR VON HINÜBER, Buddhistische Mönche als Verwalter ihrer Klöster. Die Entstehung des Begriffs 'vārika' in der Tradition der Theravādins. *Zeitschrift der Deutschen Morgenländischen Gesellschaft* 162, no. 2 (2012): 373–389.

KARUNATILLAKA 1980: P. V. B. KARUNATILLAKA, The Administrative Organization of the Nālandā Mahāvihāra from Sigillary Evidence. *The Sri Lanka Journal of the Humanities* 6.1–2 (1980): 57–69.

KIEFFER-PÜLZ 1993: PETRA KIEFFER-PÜLZ, Zitate aus der Andhaka-Aṭṭhakathā in der Samantapāsādikā. In: *Studien zur Indologie und Buddhismuskunde, Festgabe des Seminars für Indologie und Buddhismuskunde für Professor Dr. Heinz Bechert.* Ed. by REINHOLD GRÜNENDAHL, JENS-UWE HARTMANN & PETRA KIEFFER-PÜLZ. [Indica et Tibetica. 22]. Bonn 1993: 171–212.

— 2010: ID., review of Managing Monks: Administrators and Administrative Roles in Indian Buddhist Monasticism, by Jonathan A. Silk, *Indo-Iranian Journal* 53, no. 1 (2010): 79–84.

— forthcoming: ID., Traces of Theriyas in Āndhradeśa. Glimpses from Inscriptions and from the *Andhaka-Aṭṭhakathā.* In: *Early Āndhradeśa: Towards a Grounded History.* Ed. by ARLO GRIFFITHS & VINCENT TOURNIER, forthcoming.

KIELHORN 1884: FRANZ KIELHORN, Three Inscriptions from Kaṇheri. *The Indian Antiquary* 13 (1884): 133–137.

— 1888: ID., A Buddhist Stone-Inscription from Ghosrāwā. *The Indian Antiquary* 17 (1888): 307–312.

KIM 2024: YOUNG-JAE KIM, Constructing the Buddha's Life in Early Buddhist Monastic Arrangements at Nagarjunakonda. *Religions* 15.5 (2024): 559 (1–26), https://doi.org/10.3390/rel15050559.

KRISHNAMURTHY 2006: K. KRISHNAMURTHY, The Ikhsvāku City of Vijayapurī. Its Structures – Religious and Ritualistic: Buddhist Remains. In: *Nagarjunakonda (1954–60),* vol. 2: *The Historical Period.* Ed. by K. V. SOUNDARARAJAN. New Delhi 2006: 157–200.

LI 1995: RONGXI LI, *A Biography of the Tripiṭaka Master of the Great Ci'en Monastery of the Great Tang Dynasty. Translated from the Chinese of* Śramana *Huili and Shi Yancong.* Berkeley, CA, 1995.

— 1996: ID., *The Great Tang Dynasty Record of the Western Regions* [Taishō. 51, no. 2087]. Berkeley, CA, 1996.

— 2000: ID., *Buddhist Monastic Traditions of Southern Asia. A Record of the Inner Law Sent Home from the South Seas by Śramaṇa Yijing.* Berkeley, CA, 2000.

MAJMUDAR 1960: MANJULAL RANCHHODLAL MAJMUDAR, *Historical and Cultural Chronology of Gujarat (From Earliest Times to End of Rāṣṭrakūṭa-Pratīhāra Period, i.e. up to 942).* Baroda 1960.

MAJUMDAR 1931–32: NANI GOPAL MAJUMDAR, Nalanda Inscription of Vipulasrimitra. *Epigraphia Indica* 21: 97–101.

MARTINI 2022: KELSEY MARTINI, The Origin of *Akṣayanīvī* and the Historical Context of the *Arthaśāstra*: Convergences of Early Indian Epigraphic and Literary Data. *Indo-Iranian Journal* 65.2 (2022): 144–169.

MEHTA & CHOWDHARY 1966: RAMANLAL NAGARJI MEHTA & SOORYAKANT NARSINH CHOWDHARY, *Excavation at Devnimori: A Report of the Excavation Conducted from 1960 to 1963*. Baroda 1966.

MIRASHI 1955: VASUDEV VISHNU MIRASHI, *Inscriptions of the Kalachuri-Chedi Era* [Corpus Inscriptionum Indicarum. 4]. Ootacamund 1955, vol. 1.

— 1977: ID., *Inscriptions of the Śilāhāras* [Corpus Inscriptionum Indicarum. 6]. New Delhi 1977.

MITRA 1971: DEBALA MITRA, *Buddhist Monuments*. Calcutta 1971.

OTTER 2010: FELIX OTTER, *Residential Architecture in Bhoja's Samarāṅgaṇasūtradhāra: Introduction, Text, Translation and Notes*. New Delhi 2010.

PAL 2019: SAYANTANI PAL, Village Seals of Nalanda: Understanding Linkages between the Monastery and Its Environs. *Pratna Samiksha: A Journal of Archaeology*, New Series, 10 (2019): 95–103.

PLAESCHKE [2]1974: HERBERT PLAESCHKE, *Buddhistische Kunst*. Leipzig [2]1974.

PRADEEP & RAJANI 2025: ARYA S. PRADEEP & M. B. RAJANI, Ancient Valabhi: A Remote Sensing Perspective, *Journal of the Indian Society of Remote Sensing* 53.6 (2025): 1765–1783, https://doi.org/10.1007/s12524-024-02087-7.

RAJANI 2016: M. B. RAJANI, The Expanse of Archaeological Remains at Nalanda: A Study Using Remote Sensing and GIS. *Archives of Asian Art* 66.1 (2016): 1–23.

RAMACHANDRAN 1953: T. N. RAMACHANDRAN, *Nāgārjunakoṇḍa 1938* [Memoirs of the Archaeological Survey of India. 71]. New Delhi 1953.

REVIRE 2016: NICOLAS REVIRE, *The Enthroned Buddha in Majesty: An Iconological Study*. PhD diss., Sorbonne Nouvelle, Paris 3, Paris 2016, vol. 1.

SALOMON 1998: RICHARD SALOMON, *Indian Epigraphy: A Guide to the Study of Inscriptions in Sanskrit, Prakrit, and the Other Indo-Aryan Languages*. New York 1998.

— 2018: ID., What Happened to Buddhism in India? [Presidential Address, IABS XVIII, Toronto, August 20, 2017]. *Journal of the International Association of Buddhist Studies* 41.1 (2018): 1–25.

SANKALIA 1987: HASMUKHLAL DHIRAJLAL SANKALIA, *Prehistoric and Historic Archaeology of Gujarat*. Delhi 1987.

SANKARANARAYANAN 1967–68: S. SANKARANARAYANAN, Rentala Pillar Inscription of Siri-Chantamula I, Year 5. *Epigraphia Indica* 37 (1967–68): 29–32.

— 1977: ID., *The Vishṇukuṇḍis and Their Times: An Epigraphical Study*. Delhi 1977.

SANYAL 2018a: RAJAT SANYAL, Antichak. In: *History of Bangladesh: Early Bengal in Regional Perspectives (up to c. 1200 CE)*, vol. 1: *Archaeology, Political History, Polity*. Ed. by ABDUL MOMIN CHOWDHURY & RANABIR CHAKRAVARTI. Dhaka 2018: 131–143.

— 2018b: ID., Nalanda. In: ibid.: 291–316.

SANYAL & BOSE 2024: RAJAT SANYAL & ANUJA BOSE, Chapter VI — Epigraphic Material. In: *Śrī-Prathamaśivapura-Mahāvihāra: Excavating an Early Medieval Buddhist Monastery at Telhara in Magadh (Eastern India) 2020-2022*. Ed. by BIJOY KUMAR CHOUDHARY et al. Patna 2024: 205–244.

SARKAR 1960: HARIBISHNU SARKAR, Some Aspects of the Buddhist Monuments at Nagarjunakonda, *Ancient India: Bulletin of the Archaeological Survey of India* 16 (1960): 65–84.

— 1966: ID., *Studies in Early Buddhist Architecture of India*. New Delhi 1966.

SASTRI 1923–24: HIRANANDA SASTRI, The Nalanda Copper-Plate of Devapaladeva. *Epigraphia Indica* 17 (1923–24): 310–327.

— 1942: ID., *Nalanda and Its Epigraphic Material.* [Memoirs of the Archaeological Survey of India. 66]. Delhi 1942.

SCHMIEDCHEN 2013: ANNETTE SCHMIEDCHEN, Stiftungen zum Unterhalt buddhistischer Klöster in Indien (1. bis 10. Jahrhundert). In: *Stifter und Mäzene und ihre Rolle in der Religion. Von Königen, Mönchen, Vordenkern und Laien in Indien, China und anderen Kulturen.* Ed. by BARBARA SCHULER. Wiesbaden 2013: 99–116.

— 2014: ID., *Herrschergenealogie und religiöses Patronat. Die Inschriftenkultur der Rāṣṭrakūṭas, Śilāhāras und Yādavas (8. bis 13. Jahrhundert)* [Gonda Indological Series. 17]. Leiden 2014.

— 2018: ID., Kings, Authors, and Messengers: The Composition of the Maitraka Copper Plate Charters. In: *New Horizons in Indology: Prof. Dr. H. G. Shastri Commemoration Volume.* Ed. by BHARATI SHELAT and THOMAS PARMAR. Ahmedabad 2018: 35–41.

— 2021: ID., Buddhist Endowments by Śaiva Kings under the Maitrakas of Valabhī in Western India (6th–8th Centuries) and the Yodhāvaka Grant of Dharasena IV, [Valabhī] Year 326. *Endowment Studies* 5, nos. 1–2 (2021): 107–134.

— 2021–22: ID., Monastic Complexes for Monks and Nuns: The Social Fabric of Buddhist Monasteries under the Maitrakas in Gujarat. *Buddhism, Law & Society* 7 (2021–22): 59–99.

— https://dharmalekha.info/texts/INSMaitraka00019.

— https://dharmalekha.info/texts/INSMaitraka00020.

— https://dharmalekha.info/texts/INSMaitraka00024.

— https://dharmalekha.info/texts/INSMaitraka00025.

— https://dharmalekha.info/texts/INSMaitraka00038.

— https://dharmalekha.info/texts/INSMaitraka00039.

— https://dharmalekha.info/texts/INSMaitraka00042 (see DISKALKAR 1925).

— https://dharmalekha.info/texts/INSMaitraka00044.

— https://dharmalekha.info/texts/INSMaitraka00046.

— https://dharmalekha.info/texts/INSMaitraka00047 (see DISKALKAR 1925).

— https://dharmalekha.info/texts/INSMaitraka00048.

— https://dharmalekha.info/texts/INSMaitraka00050.

— https://dharmalekha.info/texts/INSMaitraka00055 (see DISKALKAR 1925).

— https://dharmalekha.info/texts/INSMaitraka00060.

— https://dharmalekha.info/texts/INSMaitraka00068.

— https://dharmalekha.info/texts/INSMaitraka00078.

— https://dharmalekha.info/texts/INSMaitraka00079.

— https://dharmalekha.info/texts/INSMaitraka00082 (see DISKALKAR 1925).

— https://dharmalekha.info/texts/INSMaitraka00085 (see DISKALKAR 1925).

— https://dharmalekha.info/texts/INSMaitraka00091.

— https://dharmalekha.info/texts/INSMaitraka00096.

— forthcoming: ID., Religious Patronage of the Buddhist, Śaiva, or Vaiṣṇava Kings and Queens of the Bhauma-Kara Dynasty in Odisha. In: *Śaiva-Buddhist Encounters in Early Medieval East India.* Ed. by LUCAS DEN BOER & FLORINDA DE SIMINI, forthcoming: 1–17.

SCHMIEDCHEN, GRIFFITHS & FURUI 2021–22: ANNETTE SCHMIEDCHEN, ARLO GRIFFITHS & RYOSUKE FURUI, Introduction. *Buddhism, Law & Society* 7 (2021–22): XI–XXIII.

SCHOPEN 1990: GREGORY SCHOPEN, The Buddha as an Owner of Property and Permanent Resident in Medieval Indian Monasteries. *Journal of Indian Philosophy* 18 (1990): 181–217 (reprint in: GREGORY SCHOPEN, *Bones, Stones, and Buddhist Monks. Collected Papers on the Archaeology, Epigraphy, and Texts of Monastic Buddhism.* Honolulu 1997: 258–289).

— 1994: ID., Doing Business for the Lord: Lending on Interest and Written Loan Contracts in the Mūlasarvāstivāda-vinaya. *Journal of the American Oriental Society* 114.4 (1994): 527–554 (reprint in: GREGORY SCHOPEN, *Buddhist Monks and Business Matters. Still More Papers on Monastic Buddhism in India.* Honolulu 2004: 45–90).

— 1996: ID., The Lay Ownership of Monasteries and the Role of the Monk in Mūlasarvāstivādin Monasticism. *Journal of the International Association of Buddhist Studies* 19.1 (1996): 81–126 (reprint in: GREGORY SCHOPEN, *Buddhist Monks and Business Matters. Still More Papers on Monastic Buddhism in India.* Honolulu 2004: 219–259).

— 2000: ID., Hierarchy and Housing in a Buddhist Monastic Code. A Translation of the Sanskrit Text of the Śayanāsanavastu of the *Mūlasarvāstivāda-vinaya*. Part One. *Buddhist Literature* 2 (2000): 92–196.

— 2009: ID., The Urban Buddhist Nun and A Protective Rite for Children in Early North India. In: *Pāsādikadānaṁ. Festschrift für Bhikkhu Pāsādika*. Ed. by MARTIN STRAUBE et al. [Indica et Tibetica. 52]. Marburg 2009: 359–380 (reprint in: GREGORY SCHOPEN, *Buddhist Nuns, Monks, and Other Worldly Matters. Recent Papers on Monastic Buddhism in India.* Honolulu 2014: 3–22).

SEN, RAHMAN & AHSAN 2014: SWADHIN SEN, A. K. M. SYFUR RAHMAN & S. M. K. AHSAN, Crossing the Boundaries of the Archaeology of Somapura Mahavihara: Alternative Approaches and Propositions. *Pratnatattva* 20 (2014): 49–79.

SENART 1905–06: ÉMILE SENART, The Inscriptions in the Caves at Nasik. *Epigraphia Indica* 8 (1905–06): 59–96.

SHASTRI 2000: HARIPRASAD GANGASHANKAR SHASTRI, *Gujarat under the Maitrakas of Valabhī.* Baroda 2000.

SHAW 2013: JULIA SHAW, *Buddhist Landscapes in Central India. Sanchi Hill and Archaeologies of Religious and Social Change, c. Third Century BC to Fifth Century AD.* London & New York 2013.

SILK 2008: JONATHAN A. SILK, *Managing Monks: Administrators and Administrative Roles in Indian Buddhist Monasticism.* New York 2008.

SIRCAR 1966: DINES CHANDRA SIRCAR, *Indian Epigraphical Glossary.* New Delhi 1966.

SOMPURA 1969: KANTILAL F. SOMPURA, *Buddhist Monuments and Sculptures in Gujarat. A Historical Survey.* Hoshiarpur 1969.

STRAUCH 2021: INGO STRAUCH, Money for Rituals: Akṣayanīvī and Related Insriptions from Āndhradeśa. In: *Power, Presence and Space: South Asian Rituals in Archaeological Context.* Ed. by HENRY ALBERY, JENS-UWE HARTMANN & HIMANSHU PRABHA RAY. London & New York 2021: 193–214.

TAKAKUSU 1896: JUNJIRO TAKAKUSU, *A Record of the Buddhist Religion as Practised in India and the Malay Archipelago (AD 671-695).* London 1896.

TOURNIER 2018: VINCENT TOURNIER, A Tide of Merit. Royal Donors, Tāmraparṇīya Monks, and the Buddha's Awakening in 5th–6th-Century Āndhradeśa. *Indo-Iranian Journal* 61 (2018): 20–96.

— 2021–22: ID., Kings as Patrons of Monasteries and Stūpas in Early Āndhra: Sada Rulers, the Rājagiriya Fraternity, and the "Great Shrine" at Amaravati. *Buddhism, Law & Society* 7 (2021–22): 1–58.

— 2023: ID., A 4th/5th Century *sūtra* of the Saṃmitīya Canon? On the So-Called 'Continental Pāli' Inscription from Devnimori. In: *Proceedings of the Third International Pali Studies Week — Paris 2018.* Ed. by CLAUDIO CICUZZA. Bangkok & Lumbini 2023: 403–470.

TOURNIER & SHIMADA forthcoming: VINCENT TOURNIER & AKIRA SHIMADA. Buddhism in Āndhra, forthcoming: 1–43.

VERMA MISHRA & RAY 2017: SUSAN VERMA MISHRA & HIMANSHU PRABHA RAY, *The Archaeology of Sacred Spaces: The Temple in Western India, 2nd Century* BCE *- 8th Century* CE. London 2017.

VISVANATHAN 2018: MEERA VISVANATHAN, Uṣavadāta's Akhayanivi: The Eternal Endowment in the Early Historic Deccan. *Journal of the International Association of Buddhist Studies* 41 (2018): 509–535.

Written Evidence of Buddhism in 15th-Century Eastern India: Dated Colophons of Sanskrit Manuscripts in Old Bengali Script

Shin'ichirō Hori

1. Introduction

The destruction of the major Buddhist monasteries in Eastern India, including Vikramaśīla, by Turkic Muslims around the turn of the 13th century CE delivered a disastrous blow to the Buddhist institutions. However, this did not mark the complete demise of the Buddhist faith throughout the Indian subcontinent. How long and where Buddhism continued to survive remain some of the least known aspects in its history. Dated colophons of several Sanskrit manuscripts in Old Bengali script offer important clues to these questions. In this paper I establish the exact dates of the following four manuscripts, attempt to identify the village names recorded in the colophons, and deal with personal names and their titles.

1. The *Kāraṇḍavyūha* manuscript dated 1456 CE in the Chhatrapati Shivaji Maharaj Vastu Sangrahalaya, Mumbai.
2. The *Kālacakratantra* manuscript dated 1447 CE in the Cambridge University Library.
3. The *Bodhicaryāvatāra* manuscript dated 1436 CE in the Asiatic Society, Kolkata.
4. A bound manuscript of Sanskrit grammatical texts of the Kātantra school originally owned by Vanaratna dated 1421/1422 CE in the British Library.

DOI: 10.13173/9783447124249.105

2. The *Kāraṇḍavyūha* (1456 CE)

To begin with, I shall deal with the *Kāraṇḍavyūha* (hereafter Kv) manuscript dated 1456 CE, because this is the last dated Buddhist Sanskrit manuscript most likely copied in Eastern India, as far as I know.[1] The manuscript formerly belonged to the private collection of Haridas Swali, Bombay,[2] and now belongs to the Chhatrapati Shivaji Maharaj Vastu Sangrahalaya,[3] Mumbai (hereafter CSMVS).

In CSMVS two wooden covers[4] and only 7 folios (accession number: 2004.1/2 A–G) are preserved. Since the last folio (2004.1/2 G) with a colophon has the folio number 78, it can be assumed that the original manuscript consists of 78 folios. The location of the remaining folios is unknown. The first two folios 1 and 2, the last three folios 76, 77, and 78, as well as a folio around the middle of the whole text, are preserved. The writing support of the folios can be regarded as leaves of talipot palm (*Corypha umbraculifera* L.),[5] because the folios measure 53 mm in length by 300 mm in width at maximum (folio 78: 48 × 300 mm). According to HOERNLE 1901: 94, the length of manuscripts made from leaves of another species of palm, palmyra palm (*Borassus flabellifer* L.), does not exceed 1¾ inches (≈ 44 mm). Illustrations are drawn on one side of 5 folios, among which 3 illuminated sides are reproduced by Pratapaditya Pal (PAL 1966: fig. 1). The manuscript is written in Old Bengali script.[6] Parts of the text are overwritten in thick black ink.[7] While some *akṣaras* are traced in the original script, others are overwritten in

* I am indebted to Prof. Dr. Florin Deleanu for revising my English text. This work was supported by JSPS KAKENHI Grant Number 19K00066.

1 I published an article on this manuscript, which includes a colour image of the colophon (HORI 2021).

2 CHANDRA 1971: 241; SARASVATĪ 1978: 54; WEISSENBORN 2012: 311. Pal calls it "the collection of Mr. and Mrs. H. K. Swali of Bombay" (PAL 1966: 267) or "the Swali collection, Bombay" (PAL & MEECH-PEKARIK 1988: 75).

3 The museum was called the Prince of Wales Museum of Western India from its foundation in 1905 until 2001 (CHHATRAPATI SHIVAJI MAHARAJ VASTU SANGRAHALAYA 2014: 9–10).

4 Accession number: 2004.1/1 a, 2004.1/1 b. On one side of the two wooden covers, illustrations are drawn. CHANDRA 1971: figs. 407–413, 241–242 reproduces the illuminated sides and the illustrations, adding descriptions for each illustration.

5 For physical characteristics of manuscripts made from leaves of talipot palm, see HOERNLE 1901: 94–97.

6 For the term "Old Bengali script", see DIMITROV 2002: 29.

7 See PAL 1966: fig. 1, top = 2004.1/2 E, folio 1v.

Nepalese script.[8] It can be assumed that the overwritten parts were traced for restoration later in Nepal (cf. HORI 2019: 50n6).

Fortunately, a dated colophon is preserved on the *recto* of the last folio. Although Moti Chandra transcribes the colophon in Devanāgarī (CHANDRA 1971: 241), and S. K. Sarasvatī in Bengali script (SARASVATĪ 1978: 54), their transcriptions contain many misreadings. Based upon the investigation of the original in CSMVS, I transliterate the colophon as follows:

78r2 ... || *deyadharmo 'yaṃ* ○ *pravaramahāyānayāyin*[*ā para*]*mo* || ※ || *pāsaka*
78r3 *karaṇikakāyasthaśrī«pīrokasya vadhūśrī* ○ *vāsudhā*[*syāḥ*]» *kāraṇḍavyūhamahāyānasūtraratnarāje li* ; ○ *khyāpite yad=atra puṇyaṃ ta*[*d=bha*]*vatv=ācāryopā*
78r4 *dhyāyamātāpitṛpūrvaṅgamaṃ kṛtvā* [*sa*]*kalasattvarāśe* ○ *r=anuttarajñānaphalaprāptaya iti* || *saṁ 1512 kārttikabadi* ○ *13 budhe* | *coindigrāmāvas*[*th*]*itaiḥ karaṇikakāya*
78r5 *sthaśrībhāskaradattair=likhiteyam=iti* ||

Donor

The donation formula includes several titles and personal names.

78r2–3 *deyadharmo 'yaṃ* ○ *pravaramahāyānayāyin*[*ā para*]*mo* || ※ || *pāsaka*(r3) *karaṇikakāyasthaśrī«pīrokasya vadhūśrī* ○ *vāsudhā*[*syāḥ*]»
"This is the pious gift «of *śrī* Vāsudhā,[9] the bride of» *śrī* «Pīroka», the excellent Mahāyāna follower, the best layman, the administrative scribe."

The part «*pīrokasya vadhūśrīvāsudhā*[*syāḥ*]» is overwritten in larger ductus clearly different from the other part. The hand looks awkward compared to the original scribe's hand. It can be presumed that this part was overwritten not in Nepal, but in Eastern India, because the script is Old Bengali script. Vāsudhā is a female name and Pīroka is a male name. The original personal name is illegible. Personal names ending in *-oka-* such as Pīroka are often found in colophons written in Eastern India.[10] The original donor held the ti-

8 One of the marked differences between Old Bengali and Nepalese script is an element common to the vowel signs for *-e*, *-ai*, *-o*, *-au*. While the element is placed on the left of a consonant in (Old) Bengali script (*pṛṣṭhamātrā*), it is represented as a wavy line above a consonant in Nepalese script.

9 The reading [*syāḥ*] is uncertain und tentative. A pronominal genitive singular feminine ending?

10 HORI 2019: 49n4; ALLINGER & MELZER 2010: 410–411.

tles *pravaramahāyānayāyin-*, *paramopāsaka-*, and *karaṇikakāyastha-*. The first two titles show that the original donor (and perhaps also Pīroka) was a lay follower of Mahāyāna Buddhism. He was an administrative scribe (*karaṇikakāyastha-*). The scribe of this manuscript also held the same title *karaṇikakāyastha-*.[11]

Date

Line r4 records the year, the lunar month, the lunar fortnight (*pakṣa*), the lunar day (*tithi*), and the day of the week.

> 78r4 *saṁ 1512 kārttikabadi ○ 13 budhe* |
> "in the year 1512, in the dark fortnight of Kārttika, on the 13th [*tithi*], on Wednesday"

When converting Indian dates to the Common Era, one must take into consideration whether the year is cited as expired or current (*atīta/vartamāna*), with which month the year begins (i.e., the month of Caitra or Kārttika; *caitrādi/kārttikādi*), and whether the month ends with the new or full moon (*amānta/pūrṇimānta*). The exact date can be verified on the basis of the correspondence of the day of the week. The computer program *Pancanga* developed by Michio Yano and Makoto Fushimi and based upon the *Sūryasiddhānta* is an incredibly helpful tool, which is also available online.[12] "1512" is most likely a year in the Vikrama era. If the Vikrama year 1512 is taken as an expired (*atīta*, *gata*) year beginning with the bright fortnight of the month of Kārttika (*kārttikādi*) and the month as ending with the full moon (*pūrṇimānta*), the date of the manuscript can be determined as Wednesday, October 27, 1456 CE, using the *Pancanga*.

Since no *saṃkrānti* took place between the new moon on September 30 and the next new moon on October 29, 1456 CE, October 27 fell in an intercalary period. Table 1 shows the time of the new or full moon, or the *saṃkrānti*, in the local mean time at 85.7°E calculated with the *Pancanga*, and the month names in the *amānta* and two *pūrṇimānta* schemes between the middle of August and November, 1456 CE. The scribe must have used the calendar in the scheme *pūrṇimānta* 2 in the table, in which the intercalary Kārttika (Adhika-Kārttika) preceded not the bright fortnight (*śuklapakṣa*) of Kārttika, but the dark fortnight (*kṛṣṇapakṣa*) of *pūrṇimānta* Kārttika.[13]

---

11 For this title, cf. SIRCAR 1965: 84 and 1966: 146, "*Karaṇa-kāyastha*", "*Karaṇika*".

12 For this computer program and the traditional Indian calendar, see YANO 2007. All datings in this paper are based upon *Pancanga*, version 3.14 (YANO & FUSHIMI 2014).

13 This calendar corresponds to "*Pūrṇimānta lunar months*; *By another system*; 5" in the table in SEWELL & DÎKSHIT 1896: 26. Cf. SEWELL & DÎKSHIT 1896: 30, 31, §51 and YANO 2007: 68.

Table 1

Time of the new or full moon or the *saṃkrānti* at 25.5°N, 85.7°E		*amānta*	*pūrṇimānta* 1	*pūrṇimānta* 2
Aug. 16, 3h 25m	full moon	Bhādrapada	Āśvina	Āśvina
Aug. 30, 12h 41m	*kanyā-saṃkrānti*	*kṛṣṇapakṣa*	*kṛṣṇapakṣa*	*kṛṣṇapakṣa*
Aug. 31, 10h 4m	new moon	Āśvina	Āśvina	Āśvina
		śuklapakṣa	*śuklapakṣa*	*śuklapakṣa*
Sep. 14, 12h 2m	full moon	Āśvina	Kārttika	Adhika-Kārttika
Sep. 29, 23h 16m	*tulā-saṃkrānti*	*kṛṣṇapakṣa*	*kṛṣṇapakṣa*	*kṛṣṇapakṣa*
Sep. 30, 0h 50m	**new moon**	Adhika-Kārttika	Adhika-Kārttika	Adhika-Kārttika
		śuklapakṣa	*śuklapakṣa*	*śuklapakṣa*
Oct. 13, 23h 39m	full moon	Adhika-Kārttika	Adhika-Kārttika	**Kārttika**
Oct. 27	**date of the ms**	*kṛṣṇapakṣa*	*kṛṣṇapakṣa*	***kṛṣṇapakṣa***
Oct. 29, 14h 16m	**new moon**[14]	Kārttika	Kārttika	Kārttika
Oct. 29, 20h 20m	*vṛścika-saṃkrānti*	*śuklapakṣa*	*śuklapakṣa*	*śuklapakṣa*
Nov. 12, 14h 29m	full moon	Kārttika	Mārgaśīrṣa	Mārgaśīrṣa
		kṛṣṇapakṣa	*kṛṣṇapakṣa*	*kṛṣṇapakṣa*

Place

On line r4, a village name is mentioned.

78r4 *coindigrāmāvas[th]itaiḥ*
"resident in the village of Coindi"

This phrase modifies the following personal name Bhāskaradatta. Chandra misreads the village name as *houndi* होउन्दि, and Sarasvatī as *hauṇḍī* হৌণ্ডী.

14 The *kārttikādi* expired Vikrama year 1513 began at local sunrise on October 30, 1456 CE after the new moon, regardless of whether the scheme is *amānta* or *pūrṇimānta*. Cf. SEWELL & DÎKSHIT 1896: 31, §51.

Between the *akṣaras co* and *ndi*, an independent vowel *i* is written. The first consonant of the village name is the voiceless unaspirated palatal which is usually transliterated as *ch* in the transcription of proper nouns in modern India, while the voiceless aspirated palatal is transliterated as *chh*, as in "Chhatrapati" for example. It should be noted that the *akṣara ndi* is not a retroflex, but a dental consonant cluster. Although Chandi चण्डी/चंडी derived from a Goddess name is a common village name in Bihar, it must be excluded from the candidates due to the retroflex consonant. In the transcription of proper nouns in modern India, retroflex and dental consonants are not distinguished in general. These two points, the unaspirated *ch* and the dental *ndi*, must be taken into account in order to identify the village name in modern India.

The database *India Place Finder* available on the internet and developed by the historian Tsukasa Mizushima is very convenient for searching place names of modern India. The database has two modes: "Census mode" and "Hamlet mode". In "Census mode" it is possible to search place names from approximately 600,000 villages registered in the Census of India 2001 and around 6,000 locality names in some cities. In "Hamlet mode" one can retrieve place names from around 900,000 hamlets (natural villages).[15] Using the *India Place Finder* in "Hamlet mode",[16] a candidate can be found: Chondi चोन्दी area (25°28'26''N, 85°42'8''E) in the city (Nagar Parishad) of Barh, Patna District, Bihar State. The difference between *coindi* and *condī* can be explained as follows. The Middle Indo-Aryan hiatus *oi* developed to *o* in some New Indo-Aryan languages,[17] while *oi* is preserved in others. A plain example is Sanskrit *jyautiṣiká-*, Prakrit *joisia-*, Maithili/Bengali/Hindi *josī* (see CDIAL 5302). The final short vowel *-i* is lengthened in some dialects of Hindi (KELLOGG 1938: 13, §15.b).

Chondi area is located on the right bank of the Ganga (HORI 2021: 26, Map 1, 2). According to *Google Maps*,[18] there are three Hindu temples in the area. *Google Maps* also presents a picture of the signboard of a candy shop (Ramdhani Shah, Lai Shop), which confirms the spelling of the area in Devanāgarī चोन्दी. Although there is no evidence that the manuscript was

15 For the two modes, see https://india.info-proto.com/index.php/default/howtoEn.

16 In "Census mode", no possible candidate is found in eastern India, except for the second candidate, Chaundi चौन्दी Village (26°9'0''N, 87°59'0''E), Kishanganj C.D. Block, Kishanganj District, Bihar State.

17 For Maithili see JHĀ 1958: 99, §94. For Bengali see CHATTERJI 1926: xiv, 353, §172; 379, §184; 384, §186. For Hindi see UČIDA 1977: 118, §5.2.

18 https://www.google.com/maps/place/Chondi,+Barh,+Bihar+803213,+India/?hl=en.

copied in Chondi area except for the correspondence of the toponym, it can be regarded as a tentative candidate for such a location.

Now, I should like to touch upon the limitations of identification of toponyms recorded in colophons. Place names are subject to change due to phonological or social changes. It is necessary to take into account sound changes from the time of documents to the present day. Social changes can also affect village names. Place names can be lost in changes in administrative divisions or boundaries, for example due to mergers or promotion from villages to cities. Islamic village names such as Islampur, Muhammadpur, Alipur, Ismailpur, and many more, must have formerly had different names before the Islamization. However, former place names are lost now and seem difficult to identify. Regardless of these limitations, it would be not insignificant to search for candidates for toponyms recorded in colophons.

Scribe

Line r5 contains the scribe's name.

> 78r4–5 *karaṇikakāya*(r5)*sthaśrībhāskaradattair=likhiteyam=iti* ||
> "This has been written by *śrī* Bhāskaradatta, the administrative scribe."

The scribe's name is Bhāskaradatta. He held the same title *karaṇikakāyastha-* as the donor. The plural form can be interpreted as an honorific usage (SPEIJER 1988: 15–16, §23).

As far as I know, this is the last Buddhist Sanskrit manuscript most likely copied in Eastern India which has a dated colophon. The manuscript clearly shows that Buddhist followers still survived and were copying and transmitting such Mahāyāna texts as the *Kāraṇḍavyūha* in Bihar until the middle of the 15th century CE.

3. The *Kālacakratantra* (1447 CE)

Next, I shall examine the *Kālacakratantra* (hereafter Kc) manuscript dated 1447 CE in the Cambridge University Library.[19] This manuscript is part of the collection gathered by Daniel Wright (surgeon to the British Residency at Kathmandu) in the Kathmandu Valley. According to the University Library stamp on folio 1r, it was acquired by the Library in October 1875. Cecil Bendall describes this manuscript in his catalogue of the Buddhist Sanskrit

19 I published an article on this manuscript (HORI 2015).

Manuscripts in the University Library, Cambridge (BENDALL 1883: iv, xxxvii, 69–70), drawing attention to the fact that it was written in Eastern India in the 15th century CE (BENDALL 1883: iv). Bendall's reading of the colophon includes some mistakes and he could not establish the exact date of the manuscript although he mentions the year as 1446 (BENDALL 1883: iv, 69) or 1447 (BENDALL 1883: xxxvii) CE. The manuscript is catalogued as Add.1364. A photo of folio 128r was published in PAL 1965: pl. I. High-resolution images of all the folios are now available online in the Cambridge Digital Library.[20] The manuscript has attracted special attention from art historians on account of the illustrations drawn on both sides of two wooden covers.[21]

The writing support of the manuscript can be regarded as leaves of talipot palm (*Corypha umbraculifera* L.), because the last folio measures 56 mm in length and 335 mm in width. The manuscript is written in Old Bengali script. Some folios include insertions in Nepalese script on a margin (folio 27v for example).

Based upon the investigation of the original, the colophon written on folio 128r is transliterated as follows:

128r2 ... || *deyadharmmo ‹›yaṃ pravaramahāyānānuyāyināṃ* || ||
128r3 *śrīmat*śākyabhikṣuśrījñānaśrīkānāṃ yad=atra puṇyaṃ tad=bhavatv=ācāryopā ○ dhyāyamātāpitṛpūrvaṅgamaṃ kṛtvā sakalasatvarāśer=anuttarāsamyaksaṃbodhijñānaphalalā*
128r4 *bhāyeti* || || *paramabhaṭṭāraketyādirājāvalīpūrvavat*śrī* ; ○ *madvikramādityadevapādānāṃm=atītarājye saṁ*[22] *1503 bhādrabadi 13 budhe likhyāpi*
128r5 *teyaṃ śrīmat*śākyabhikṣuśrījñānaśrīkaiḥ* | *likhiteyaṃ magadhadeśī* ○ *yakansāragrāmasāsanikakaraṇakāyasthaśrījayarāmadatteneti* || *kerakīgrāmāvasthi ;*
128r6 *tena* || *śubham=astu* || || *anena saddharmmarasāmṛtena sarvajñadoṣodbhavaśītalena* | *kleśānalaprajvalitāntarasya lokasya duḥkhaṃ praśamo ‹›stu nityaṃ* || || || ||

20 https://cudl.lib.cam.ac.uk/view/MS-ADD-01364/257.

21 For contributions by art historians, see WEISSENBORN 2012: 312. KIM 2013: 250, 268, 340n116, 343n141, 345n155, also deals with this manuscript.

22 I had transliterated this *akṣara* as *sa°*, regarding it as *sa* plus a sign for abbreviation (HORI 2015: 1326, 1327; cf. EINICKE 2009: 68–69, 274). However, this *akṣara* should be regarded as *sa* plus *anunāsika* (*candrabindu*), because the sign like a backslash with a small circle on the right of *sa* can be found also in the *akṣara oṁ* (see HORI 2018: 59, Plate 5, line 1).

Donor

The donor's name appears on lines r3 and r5 in the plural.

128r2–3|| *deyadharmmo ‹'›yaṃ pravaramahāyānānuyāyināṃ* || || (r3) *śrīmat**śākyabhikṣuśrījñānaśrīkānāṃ*

"This is the pious gift of *śrī* Jñānaśrī, the excellent Mahāyāna follower, the venerable Buddhist monk."

128r4–5 *likhyāpi* (r5) *teyaṃ śrīmat**śākyabhikṣuśrījñānaśrīkaiḥ* |

"This has been made written by *śrī* Jñānaśrī, the venerable Buddhist monk."

Here the plural form presumably includes only one personal name, i.e., "Jñānaśrī" followed by the suffix *-ka-* and conveys an honorific sense. It is also possible to interpret the compound as "people headed by the venerable Buddhist monk Jñānaśrī" on the basis of the Pāṇinian rule 5.2.78 concerning a personal name with the suffix *-ka-*, *"sa eṣāṃ grāmaṇīḥ."*[23] The donor has two titles, *pravaramahāyānānuyāyin-* and *śākyabhikṣu-*, which indicate that he was a Buddhist monk belonging to Mahāyāna.

Date

The colophon fortunately records the Vikrama year 1503, the lunar month, the lunar fortnight, the lunar day, and the day of the week.

128r4 *śrīmadvikramādityadevapādānāṃm=atītarājye saṁ 1503 bhādrabadi 13 budhe*

"in the Vikrama year 1503, in the dark fortnight of Bhādra[pada], on the 13th [*tithi*], on Wednesday"

If the Vikrama year 1503 is taken as an expired year beginning with the month of Kārttika and the month as ending with the full moon, the date of the manuscript can be determined as Wednesday, August 9, 1447 CE, using the *Pancanga*.[24]

23 The *Kāśikā Vṛtti* gives an example *devadattakāḥ*: *"grāmaṇīḥ pradhānaḥ, mukhyaḥ ity arthaḥ. devadattaḥ grāmaṇīḥ eṣām devadattakāḥ"* (SHARMA et al. 1970: 516). Cf. also Pāṇini 5.3.78 *"bahvaco manuṣyanāmnaṣ ṭhaj vā."*

24 Franz Kielhorn established the same date in an article published in the *Indian Antiquary* as early as 1890 (KIELHORN 1890: 180–181), i.e., only seven years after the publication of Bendall's Catalogue.

Scribe

Line r5 contains the scribe's name: Jayarāmadatta.

128r5 *likhiteyaṃ magadhadeśī ○ yakansāragrāmasāsanikakaraṇakāyastha-śrījayarāmadatteneti*
"This has been written by *śrī* Jayarāmadatta, the administrative scribe of the village of Kansāra in the region of Magadha."

He held the title *śāsanikakaraṇakāyastha* (administrative scribe). He seems to have been a person in charge of the village of Kansāra. The spelling *sāsanika* for *śāsanika* reminds one of Magahi (modern regional language in Magadha) *sāsan* for Sanskrit *śāsana* (VERMA 2003: 502). In Magahi the three sibilants in Sanskrit were merged to the dental *s*.

Place

On line r5, place names are mentioned.

128r5 *magadhadeśīyakansāragrāma*
"the village of Kansāra in the region of Magadha"

On the basis of the regional name *magadhadeśīya*, it would be possible to restrict the place of copying to Southern Bihar. Pal reads *magadhadeśīyaka-āra-grāma* and identifies the village as the present city of Arrah (PAL 1965: 103–104). However, this identification is based on his misreading of the *akṣara* *nsā*[25] as an independent vowel *ā* (cf. an independent vowel *a* on line r6).

128r5–6 *kerakīgrāmāvasthi* ; (r6) *tena* ||
"resident in the village of Kerakī"

This phrase probably modifies the preceding personal name Jayarāmadatta. It seems that he was a resident in the village of Kerakī as well as the administrative scribe in charge of the village of Kansāra. In this case, the two villages must have been close together.

The *India Place Finder* retrieves many villages named "Kansar". However, in the case of "Kerki", there are only two villages by this name in the whole of India. One is the Kerki केरकी Village (24°49'41"N, 84°45'11"E) located in the Guraru C.D. Block, Gaya District, Bihar State. The other is the Kerki केरकी Village (24°0'53"N, 84°24'21"E) in the Panki C.D. Block, Palamu District, Jharkhand State. The Kerki Village in Bihar is located about 25 km west of

25 For the spelling *ns* for *ṃs*, see WACKERNAGEL 1896: 185.

Gaya and has a population of 1,042 people according to the Census of India 2011.[26] Among the toponyms "Kansara" retrieved with the *India Place Finder* in "Hamlet mode", the nearest place to Kerki is about 37 km away from Kerki.[27] It seems not probable due to the distance that this Kansara is the village of Kansāra recorded in the colophon. It would be more reasonable to consider that the village of Kansāra recorded in the colophon changed its name in the last 550 years. In this connection, the village to the west of Kerki is called Dumra Ismailpur डुमरा इस्माईलपुर and there is a railway station named Ismailpur in the village. Kansāra is derived from Sanskrit *kaṃsakāra-* "a worker in bell metal; a brazier", according to SIRCAR 1966: 142.

On New Year's Eve 2016, I had the chance to visit the Kerki Village in Bihar together with the late Professor emeritus Ryōjun Satō. According to the villagers, most of the inhabitants are Hindus, with a small number of Muslims living there. We could not find any direct evidence that the manuscript was written in the village, except for the following vague information from the villagers: "When the pond in the village dried up, a Buddha statue was found there. The statue is now in a certain museum." The village can be regarded as a tentative candidate. The village name kerakī may be connected with the banana plant: Sanskrit *kadala-*, Prakrit *kayala-*, Hindi *kelā*, Maithili/ Bhojpuri *kerā* (CDIAL 2712).

Concluding verse

After *śubham=astu*, the colophon contains a verse in *upajāti* metre, which corresponds to the last stanza of the *Ratnāvadānatattva* in Kanga Takahata's edition of the *Ratnāvadānamālā* (TAKAHATA 1954: 480.28–29). Underlined parts show variant readings.

Colophon of Add. 1364[28]	*Ratnāvadānatattva*
anena saddharmmarasāmṛtena	*anena saddharmarasāmṛtena*
sarvajñadoṣodbhavaśītalena |	*sarvajñabhāsvadvadanodbhavena* ||
kleśānalaprajvalitāntarasya	*kleśānalaprahvarir āturāsu*
lokasya duḥkhaṃ praśamo stu nityaṃ ||	*prajāsu duḥkhaṃ praśamo 'stu nityaṃ* ||

26 https://censusindia.gov.in/census.website/data/population-finder

27 A hamlet in the town (Nagar Panchayat) of Makhdumpur, Jehanabad District, Bihar State (25°4'10''N, 84°58'49''E).

28 According to BANERJEE 1985: 265n9, a manuscript of the *Kālacakratantra* in the Royal Asiatic Society of Great Britain and Ireland, London (Hodgson Collection 49; COWELL & EGGELING 1876: 39), also reads this verse in its colophon.

4. The *Bodhicaryāvatāra* (1436 CE)

Next, I shall deal with the manuscript of Śāntideva's *Bodhicaryāvatāra* (hereafter Bca) catalogued as G. 8067 in the Asiatic Society, Kolkata (SHĀSTRI 1917: 21–22).[29] The writing support of the manuscript can be regarded as leaves of talipot palm on the basis of its physical characteristics, although folio 66 measures 39 mm in length by 299 mm in width and the length does not exceed 45 mm. The manuscript is written in Old Bengali script. Some folios include insertions in Nepalese script on a margin (folio 63v for example). The manuscript was brought from Nepal by Hara Prasad Shāstri (BANDYOPĀDHYĀYA 1909: 252; BANERJI 1919: 90). He describes the manuscript and transcribes its colophon in the catalogue, adding a comment that "In the post colophon statement of the present manuscript, we have a clear evidence of the prevalence of Buddhism in Bengal in the 15th century of the Christian era" (SHĀSTRI 1917: 21). R. D. Banerji presents his own transcription of the colophon (BANDYOPĀDHYĀYA 1909: 253) and reproduces folio 65r (BANERJI 1919: Plate V) and 66v including the colophon (BANERJI 1919: Plate VI). Since the surface of folio 66v is now papered with translucent paper perhaps for reinforcement, the text is more difficult to decipher than Banerji's reproduction. It is most likely that the reading can be improved, using infrared photography (HORI 2019: 49n3). The following transcription of folio 66v is tentative, although I could investigate the original.

66v1 ... || *de‹ya›dharmmo ‹'›yaṃ pravaramahāyānayāyinaḥ* | *sohiñcarīgrāmāvasthitakuṭumbikakoccha-icchamahattamaśrīmādhava*
66v2 *esutamahatta[ma]śrī[rā]madevasvārthaparārthahetave* ○ *bodhicaryāvatārapustikā likhyāpitā* | *sadbauddhakaraṇakāyasthaṭhakuraśrīamitābhena li* ;
66v3 *khitam=idaṃ ve[n]ugrāme* | *vikramādityadevasaṁ 1492 phālguṇaśudi 4 kuje* | *śubham=astu sarvajagataḥ parahitaniratā bhavantu santaḥ* ||
66v4 *likhitaṃ guṇakirttibhikṣudevapādānaṃ 15* ○ .. || ||

Donor

66v1–2 ... || *de‹ya›dharmmo ‹'›yaṃ pravaramahāyānayāyinaḥ* | *sohiñcarīgrāmāvasthitakuṭumbikakoccha-icchamahattamaśrīmādhava*(v2) *esutamahatta[ma]śrī[rā]madevasvārthaparārthahetave* ○ *bodhicaryāvatārapustikā likhyāpitā* |
"This is the pious gift of the excellent Mahāyāna follower ..."

29 I established the date of this manuscript in HORI 2015: 1325 and discussed the place and personal names in HORI 2018: 53.

The donation formula ends with *pravaramahāyānayāyinaḥ*. The following long compound includes two personal names and their titles and location. The donor's name is *śrī* Rāmadeva. He had the scribe write the manuscript of the *Bodhicaryāvatāra* for his own sake as well as for others (*svārthaparārthahetave bodhicaryāvatārapustikā likhyāpitā*). He held the title of *mahattama-* "a leading man in a village". His father held also the same title. It depends on the interpretation of the compound whether one more title *kuṭumbin-/kuṭumbika-* "a landed farmer" belongs to the son, his father, or both of them. They were probably both landed farmers. This long compound suggests that the donor as a leading landed farmer was a Buddhist layman and his family had retained the Mahāyāna-Buddhist faith from generation to generation. Although the father's name begins with Mādhava, the following part is not clear. Shāstri and Bandyopādhyāya read the name as *mādhava‹mi›tra*, restoring an *akṣara ‹mi›* and correcting an independent vowel *e* to *tra* (Shāstri 1917: 21; Bandyopādhyāya 1909: 253). Both *akṣaras* are very similar in Bengali script. I suggest a restoration *mādhava-e‹ka›-suta* "Mādhava's only son". The donor Rāmadeva and his father were residents in the village of Sohiñcarī. I shall discuss below the village name with another village name. The significance of the part *kakoccha-iccha* is not clear, which Bandyopādhyāya reads as *kakoccha-uccha*, and Shāstri as *kakocca-ucca*.

Scribe

Line v2 contains the scribe's name.

66v2–3 *sadbauddhakaraṇakāyasthaṭhakuraśrīamitābhena li* ; (v3) *khitam= idaṃ ve[n]ugrāme* |
"This has been written by *śrī* Amitābha, the true Buddhist, the administrative scribe, *ṭhakura*, in the village of Venu."

The scribe's name is Amitābha, i.e., the well-known Buddha's name. He held three titles, *sadbauddha-*, *karaṇakāyastha-*, and *ṭhakura-*. With the first title, he professed himself a true Buddhist. He copied the manuscript in the village of Venu.

Place

The following two village names are mentioned.

66v1–2 *sohiñcarīgrāmāvasthita*
"resident in the village of Sohiñcarī"

66v2–3 *li* ; (v3) *khitam=idaṃ ve[n]ugrāme* |
"This has been written in the village of Venu."

Since the first village is the donor's location, and the second the place of copying, it can be presumed that the two villages are located close together. The *India Place Finder* reveals some good candidates under the spellings of Ben, Benu, Ven or Venu. Sohiñcarī cannot be found spelled as such, using the *India Place Finder.* However, an administrative village named Sonchri सोनचरी (25°11'51''N, 85°20'9''E) is retrieved in "Census mode", and a natural village named Sonchari[30] (25°11'15''N, 85°19'51''E) "Hamlet mode". The village is located in the Parbalpur परबलपुर C.D. Block,[31] Nalanda District, Bihar State. At only 5 km to its southeast, one finds a village named Ben बेन (25°9'3''N, 85°21'40''E). The C.D. Block where it is situated is also called Ben. Bijoy Kumar Choudhary describes the archaeological finds in the village of Ben (CHOUDHARY 2015: 21), the C.D. Block of Ben (CHOUDHARY 2015: 17–29), and the village of Sonchari (CHOUDHARY 2015: 157). Since in both villages, buddha and bodhisattva statues have been discovered, both can be regarded as likely candidates for the place where this manuscript was copied and preserved.[32] As for *venu* and *ben*, there is no difference between *ba* and *va* in Bengali script, and the final short vowel *-u* is lost in Hindi, e.g. *ben* "bamboo." Since the intervocalic *-h-* is lost in Maithili (JHĀ 1958: 146, §134A) and Bengali (CHATTERJI 1926: 441, §239), *sohiñcarī* can develop to **soiñcarī*, and then to *soñcarī*, as *coindi* to *condī*. The ruins of the Nālandā Mahāvihāra are located about 8 km away from the village of Ben and 13 km away from Sonchri.

Date

The colophon records the date as follows:

66v3 *vikramādityadevasaṁ 1492 phālguṇaśudi 4 kuje* |

30 Sonchari can be regarded as an orthographical variant of Sonchri. I verified the Devanāgarī spelling सोनचरी at the village.

31 The spelling Parwalpur परवलपुर is also found in some administrative documents on the internet.

32 BANDYOPĀDHYĀYA 1909: 253 connects the two village names with toponyms in the present district of Purba Bardhaman, West Bengal: "The combination of Venugrāma with Sohiñcari shows that the Venugrāma is modern Berugrama in Pergannah Haveli. Sohincari is no doubt the Sanscritised form of Sāncar." However, his identification seems phonetically not so fit as mine.

"in the Vikramādityadeva year 1492, in the bright fortnight of Phālguna, on the fourth [*tithi*], on Tuesday"

In the case of the month of Phālguna, there is no difference between *caitrādi* and *kārttikādi* systems. As for the bright fortnight, there is no difference between *amānta* and *pūrṇimānta* schemes. Therefore, one has only to take into consideration whether the year is cited as expired or current.

1. If the Vikrama year 1492 is taken as a current year, the date should be Wednesday, February 2, 1435 CE.
2. If the Vikrama year 1492 is taken as an expired year, the date should be Tuesday, February 21, 1436 CE.

The date of the manuscript can be thus determined as Tuesday, February 21, 1436 CE.

Verse

After the date, a verse for the blessings is written.

66v3 *śubham=astu sarvajagataḥ parahitaniratā bhavantu santaḥ* ||
"Good luck to all the world! Good people should be delighted with the welfare of others."

This verse lacks the last long syllable necessary for the first half of *āryā* metre. A complete stanza in *āryā* metre is found in colophons of some Sanskrit manuscripts (GRAHELI 2012: 332; cf. YE 2009: 314n15). Although we find a parallel passage at the end of some recensions of Harṣa's *Nāgānanda* (e.g. UPĀDHYĀYA 1931: 152[33]), the last verse should be regarded as belonging to colophons rather than to Harṣa's text.

King's name

On line v4, the name of a king unknown elsewhere is found.

66v4 *likhitaṃ guṇakirttibhikṣudevapādānaṃ* 15 ○ .. || ||
"It has been written in the year 15 of His Majesty King Guṇakirttibhikṣu."

33 *śivam astu sarvajagatāṃ parahitaniratā bhavantu bhūtagaṇāḥ* |
doṣāḥ prayāntu nāśaṃ sarvatra sukhī bhavatu lokaḥ ||

In the catalogue, Shāstri adds a comment that this line was written in a later hand (SHĀSTRI 1917: 21). However, the script type is the same Old Bengali script as the other lines and no marked time difference can be observed, even if the line was written in different hand. I have never encountered this king's name elsewhere, and nothing is known except for his name itself. Although the name sounds fit for a Buddhist follower, there is no evidence that he was a Buddhist monk. A personal name ending in *-bhikṣu* reminds one of the Hindu scholar Vijñānabhikṣu from Bihar dated to the 15th–16th century CE. He was not a Buddhist monk, but a Hindu philosopher and the name may possibly mean a beggar of *vijñāna*. Guṇakīrtibhikṣu could mean a beggar of fame with his virtue. Therefore, it does not seem necessary to regard Guṇakirttibhikṣudeva as a Buddhist monk, although it is likely that the king was a non-Muslim minor local ruler. If the numeral 15 is Guṇakirttibhikṣudeva's regnal year, it suggests that his reign continued for at least 14 years.[34]

While kings' names are often found in the colophons of Buddhist Sanskrit manuscripts from Eastern India copied in the 11th–13th centuries CE (WEISSENBORN 2012: nos. 1–22, 31–33, 35–45), this is the only colophon that mentions the ruler's name among the manuscripts copied in 15th-century Eastern India. Muslim rulers' names have never been mentioned in colophons of Buddhist manuscripts. While Turkic Muslims were attacking the major Buddhist monasteries in Eastern India around the turn of the 13th century CE, Buddhists recorded the year in the gone (*gata*), past (*atīta*), destroyed (*hata*), or perished (*vinaṣṭa*) reign of Govindapāla in colophons (WEISSENBORN 2012: nos. 19–21, 42; BENDALL 1883: iii; BANERJI 1915: 110–112), instead of mentioning any Muslim ruler's name. The fact that a ruler's name is mentioned in colophons of Buddhist manuscripts would suggest that the ruler was not hostile toward Buddhists.

34 One or two *akṣaras* written to the right of the string hole are illegible and may be a decorative sign placed before two double *daṇḍas* suggesting the end of the manuscript.

5. Sanskrit Grammatical Texts of the Kātantra School Originally Owned by Vanaratna (1421/1422 CE)

As a fourth example, I shall discuss a bound manuscript of Sanskrit grammatical texts belonging to the Kātantra school.[35] The manuscript was collected in Kathmandu by Dr. G. H. D. Gimlette of the Bengal Medical Service and deposited in the British Museum. Cecil Bendall first referred to the manuscript in his article in 1888, pointing out that "it is of itself a most important fact to find Buddhism existing in Bengal in the fifteenth century" (BENDALL 1888: 552). He also describes the manuscript in a catalogue of Sanskrit Manuscripts in the British Museum (BENDALL 1902: 147–150). The bound manuscript is catalogued as Or. 3562a–e in the British Library. The writing support of the manuscript can be regarded as leaves of talipot palm, because an undamaged folio measures 47 mm long by 310 mm wide. The script of the manuscript is Old Bengali script.

Contents of the manuscript

All the texts included in the bound manuscript are Sanskrit grammatical texts belonging to the Kātantra school.

1. Or. 3562b (1v1–15r2): Durgasiṃha's *Paribhāṣāvṛtti* (PbhV), a commentary on rules concerning interpretations (edition: ABHYANKAR 1967: 49.4–66.25).
2. Or. 3562c (15r2–16v7): Sarvadhara's *Parādivyākhyāvṛtti* (PvV), a commentary on supplementary rules concerning interpretations (cf. ABHYANKAR 1967: 66n1).
3. Or. 3562d (17r1–42v5): Durgasiṃha's *Uṇādivṛtti* (UṇV), a commentary on rules concerning *uṇādi* suffixes (edition: CHINTAMANI 1934).
4. Or. 3562e (43v1–65r6): Durgasiṃha's *Liṅgakārikāvṛtti* (LkV), a commentary on the grammatical genders of nouns (edition: KOPARKAR 1952).

These four texts are supplementary texts belonging to the Kātantra school and have serial folio numbers.

5. Or. 3562a (1v1–69r5): Trilocanadāsa's *Kṛtpañjikā* (KṛP) (edition: DWIVEDĪ 2005).

35 I published an article on this manuscript (HORI 2018), where the colour images of the folios including the colophons are available.

The *Kātantra* consists of four chapters, 1. *Saṃdhiprakaraṇa*, 2. *Nāmaprakaraṇa*, 3. *Ākhyātaprakaraṇa*, and 4. *Kṛtprakaraṇa*. The *Kṛtpañjikā* is Trilocanadāsa's sub-commentary on Durgasiṃha's *Kātantravṛtti* dealing with the last chapter concerning *kṛt* suffixes.

KṛP 69r6: *vṛttitra ○ yavivaraṇapañjikā trilocanadāsavibhañjitā likhitā*

This passage suggests that the preceding three chapters were also written by the same scribe. Unfortunately, it is unknown whether a manuscript of the preceding three chapters is extant. Although the folios of the fifth text (*Kṛtpañjikā*) are numbered independently of the four supplementary texts, the format of the folios is the same as the others.

Colophons

At the end of three texts, UṇV, LkV, and KṛP, dated colophons are found. Bendall's transcriptions of the colophons contain some mistakes, such as the misreading of an important personal name as "Va**ra**ratna" (Bendall 1888: 553; 1902: 148–150).[36] Based upon the investigation of the original in the British Library, the three colophons are transliterated as follows:

UṇV 42v5 *... || || śubham=astv=iti sadā ○ || śrīmadvikramasenasyātītasamvatsarasaṁ 1478 āśvinaśudi 3 somadine kapasiāgrāme pusta*

UṇV 42v6 *kam=alekhi kāśrīvāgīśvareṇeti | śrīmanmahānubhāvamahodāra ○ caritaśrīmattathāgatoktadīkṣārakṣaṇavicakṣaṇāśeṣadoṣakṣayitaniḥkalaṅkībhūtacandramāprāyo hi*

UṇV 42v7 *bhagavānaśrīmatasthaviraśrīvanaranthamahāśayānāṃ pustakam=idaṃ nijapāṭhahetau likhāpitam=iti | svārthaparārthasaṃpadvṛddhyarthaṃ | uṇādivṛttiprakaraṇasyeti | yathādṛṣṭam=iti parihāraḥ ||*

LkV 65r6 *... || || śrīvikra ○ masenasyātītasaṁ 1479 märggaśīrṣabadi 14 śukre kapasiāgrāme pustakaṃ likhitam=i(daṃ) || ||*

LkV 65r7 *śākyabhikṣumahāsthaviraśūnyatāsarvākāravaropetāmahākaruṇāsarvālambanavivarjjitābhinnādvayabodhicittacintāmaṇipratirūpakaśrīvanaratnamahānubhāvānāṃ pustakam=i(da)[ṃ] || ɔ– ||*

KṛP 69r6 *|| || śrīmahāsthaviraśrīvanaratnamahānubhāvānāṃ pustīti | vṛttitra ○ yavivaraṇapañjikā trilocanadāsavibhañjitā likhitā kāśrīvāgīśvareṇa yathā dṛṣṭam=iti pa*

36 Although the *akṣara ra* is somewhat similar to *na* in the manuscript, the two *akṣaras* written consecutively in this name can be clearly distinguished.

KṛP 69r7 *rihāro 'tra sarvvathā śodhanīyā sadbhir=iti | jyaiṣṭhaśudi 14 som[e] dine likhitvā saṃpūrṇṇitā cātra* || ɔ– ||

Owner's name: Vanaratna

The name of the owner of the manuscript is found in the following three passages in the colophons.

UṇV 42v6–7: *śrīmanmahānubhāvamahodāra* ○ *caritaśrīmattathāgato-ktadīkṣārakṣaṇavicakṣaṇāśeṣadoṣakṣayitaniḥkalaṅkībhūta-candramāprāyo hi* (v7) *bhagavānaśrīmatasthaviraśrīvana-ranthamahāśayānāṃ pustakam=idaṃ nijapāṭhahetau likhāpitam=iti* |

LkV 65r7: *śākyabhikṣumahāsthaviraśūnyatāsarvākāravaropetāmahāka-ruṇāsarvālambanavivarjjitābhinnādvayabodhicittacintā-maṇipratirūpakaśrīvanaratnamahānubhāvānāṃ pustakam=i(da)[ṃ]* ||

KṛP 69r6: *śrīmahāsthaviraśrīvanaratnamahānubhāvānāṃ pustīti* |

In the first two passages, the owner's name Vanaratna is accompanied with very many modifiers. Among the modifiers, I should like to draw attention to the two titles, *śākyabhikṣu-* "Buddhist monk" and *mahāsthavira-* "great elder." It is worth noting the spelling *rantha* for *ratna* in the first passage.

Purpose of copying

The purpose of copying is clear from the passage: UṇV 42v7, *nijapāṭhahetau likhāpitam*, that is, Vanaratna has this manuscript written on behalf of self-teaching of Sanskrit grammar.

Scribe's name: Vāgīśvara

The colophons record the name of a scribe with his title.

UṇV 42v5–6: *pusta*(v6)*kam=alekhi kāśrīvāgīśvareṇeti* |
"The manuscript has been written[37] by Vāgīśvara, the scribe."

KṛP 69r6: *likhitā kāśrīvāgīśvareṇa*
" ... has been written by Vāgīśvara, the scribe."

37 *alekhi* is a passive aorist (cf. Pāṇini 3.1.66).

kā must be an abbreviation for *kāyastha*, the title "scribe", as recorded by SIRCAR 1966: 137. The scribe's name is Vāgīśvara, which is one of the names of Mañjuśrī. The homage at the beginning of each text suggests that the scribe is a Buddhist professing his faith in Mañjuśrī.

PbhV 1v1:	*namo buddhāya bhagavate* ||
PvV 15r2:	*namo buddhabhaṭṭārakāya* ||
UṇV 17r1:	*namo buddhāya* ||
LkV 43v1:	*namaḥ śrīmadvādirājāya* ||
KṛP 1v1:	*namo mañjukumārāya* ||

Vādirāja and *mañjukumāra* are also aliases of Mañjuśrī.

Dates

The colophons record three dates on which the scribe finished copying three texts respectively. Using the *Pancanga*, these dates can be converted to the Common Era.

1. UṇV 42v5: *śrīmadvikramasenasyātītasamvatsarasaṁ 1478 āśvinaśudi 3 somadine*
   "in the expired year of *śrīmat* Vikramasena 1478, in the bright fortnight of Āśvina, on the 3rd [*tithi*], on Monday"

The scribe overwrote the least digit 8 of the year as 9. Bendall adopted the rewritten figure 9 in his transcription (BENDALL 1888: 553; 1902: 150). However, in the case of the Vikrama year 1479, no matter what conditions we apply, Indian calendar gives no satisfactory equivalent for the day of the week "Monday". The Vikrama year 1478 is recorded explicitly as an expired year (*atītasamvatsarasaṁ*). As for the bright fortnight, there is no difference between *amānta* and *pūrṇimānta* schemes. If the Vikrama year 1478 is taken as an expired year beginning with the month of Caitra (*caitrādi*), the date should be Monday, September 29, 1421 CE. Therefore, the originally written figure 8 should be considered right. The reason for overwriting the digit is not clear.

2. LkV 65r6: *śrīvikra ○ masenasyātītasaṁ 1479 mārggaśīrṣabadi 14 śukre*
   "in the expired year of *śrī* Vikramasena 1479, in the dark fortnight of Mārgaśīrṣa, on the 14th [*tithi*], on Friday"

The Vikrama year 1479 is recorded explicitly as an expired year (*atītasaṁ*). In the case of the month of Mārgaśīrṣa, there is no difference between *caitrādi* and *kārttikādi* schemes. If the month is taken as ending with the full moon (*pūrṇimānta*), the date should be Friday, November 13, 1422 CE.[38]

3. KṛP 69r7: *jyaiṣṭhaśudi 14 som[e] dine likhitvā saṃpūrṇṇitā cātra* ||
"[It] is complete here, having been written in the bright fortnight of Jyaiṣṭha, on the 14th [*tithi*], on Monday"

This passage lacks the year. If the 14th *tithi* in the bright fortnight of Jyaiṣṭha in the ten years between 1418–1427 is calculated with the *Pancanga*, two Mondays can be found: Monday, May 24 1423 CE or Monday, May 20 1426 CE. In the period of Vanaratna's stay in Magadha from ca. 1416 to ca. 1423 CE (DAMRON 2021: 60), the 14th *tithi* in the bright fortnight of Jyaiṣṭha fell on Monday only on May 24 1423 CE, which can be regarded as the date of the colophon (cf. DAMRON 2021: 62n66).

Village name: Kapasiā

In the following two passages, a village name is found.

UṇV 42v5–6: *kapasiāgrāme pusta*(v6)*kam=alekhi*
"The manuscript has been written in the village of Kapasiā."
LkV 65r6: *kapasiāgrāme pustakaṃ likhitam=i*(*daṃ*) ||
"This manuscript has been written in the village of Kapasiā."

The manuscript was written in the village of Kapasiā. According to CDIAL 3073, Bengali *kāpāsiyā*, Odia *kapāsiā*, and so on are derived from the Sanskrit *kārpāsika-* "made of cotton". According to the *Biography of Vanaratna*, Vanaratna practiced meditation in a forest situated beyond a river called Kanakaśrotaṃ near Vajrāsana, i.e., the Mahābodhi Temple in Bodh Gaya (Źp 1: 14a6–7). According to the *India Place Finder*, the village name "Kapasia" or "Kapasiya" has many candidates in the whole of India. Four villages named "Kapasia" and one named "Kapasiya" are found in Southern Bihar (Table 2; HORI 2018: 51, Map 1). Among these, Kapasiya कपसिया Village (24°45'30"N, 84°50'30"E) in Paraiya C.D. Block, Gaya District, is the closest to Bodh Gaya and located about 16.4 km west-northwest of the Mahabodhi Temple. This village could be considered as the first candidate for the place where the manuscript was copied. Bijoy Kumar Choudhary and Abhishek Singh Amar record sculptures from the early medieval period in the village (CHOUDHARY & AMAR 2017: 299).

38 KIELHORN 1888: 168 establishes the same date.

Table 2: Villages named Kapasi(y)a in Southern Bihar.

No	Name	C.D. Block	District	Latitude	Longitude	km
1	Kapasiya	Paraiya	Gaya	24.766298	84.846157	16.4
2	Kapasia	Islampur	Nalanda	25.067053	85.293983	51.4
3	Kapasia	Aurangabad	Aurangabad	24.759207	84.466335	53.8
4	Kapasia	Akorhi Gola	Rohtas	25.050017	84.213405	88.1
5	Kapasia	Kochas	Rohtas	25.193716	83.876842	125.6

No: Numbers on HORI 2018: 51, Map 1. Latitudes and longitudes based upon the *India Place Finder*. km (kilometer): Distances from the Mahabodhi Temple measured with *Google Earth*.

The village of Kapasiya as an administrative village is divided into three zones by two rivers, Morhar Nadi in the east and Buddh Nadi in the west (HORI 2018: 51, Map 2), and has a population of 2,512 people according to the Census of India 2011.

In the year 2017 I had the chance to visit the village. According to the villagers, all the inhabitants are Hindus, without any Muslims living there. Although I could not find any direct evidence that the manuscript was written in this village, it is worth mentioning the existence of a palm-size statue of the Buddha in the *bhūmisparśamudrā* with two attendants (HORI 2018: 51, Fig. 1). The statue was shown to me by a villager who explained that it had been unearthed in the village and is now enshrined together with Hindu deities. The Buddha statue suggests that Buddhists had once lived in the village.

Vanaratna (1384–1468 CE)

The original owner of the manuscript was Vanaratna (1384–1468 CE), a scholar-monk coming from Eastern Bengal, who was called the last paṇḍita in Tibet. Franz-Karl Ehrhard (2002, 2004) deals with Vanaratna's career and works, giving an overview of 23 Sanskrit texts translated by Vanaratna in collaboration with his interpreters and 11 works of Vanaratna available in the *bsTan 'gyur* (EHRHARD 2002: 113–117). Recently, Ryan Damron published a comprehensive dissertation upon the life of Vanaratna (DAMRON 2021).

As the biographies of Vanaratna, two Tibetan documents written by his disciple, Gźon nu dpal (1392–1481 CE) are available: the *Blue Annals* (Źp 2: *tha* 21a1–24b3; ROERICH 1953: 797–805) and the *Biography of Vanaratna* (Źp 1).

According to both Tibetan sources, during his stay in Magadha Vanaratna studied with the heretical scholar Harihara the *Kalāpa*, a version which was seven times larger than the one known in Tibet. *Kalāpa* is a synonym for the Sanskrit grammar titled *Kātantra*. While the Tibetan translation of the *Kātantra* in the *bsTan 'gyur* (Peking 5775, Derge 4282) includes only the *sūtras* in 20 folios, the manuscript of the *Kṛtpañjikā* includes a sub-commentary by Trilocanadāsa. Therefore, it is reasonable that the whole Sanskrit manuscript of Trilocanadāsa's sub-commentary would be seven times larger than the Tibetan translation. Unless Vanaratna owned more than one copy of the *Kātantra*, this manuscript must be a part of the book *Kalāpa* mentioned in Vanaratna's biographies.

6. Common Characteristics Shared by the Four Manuscripts

I shall now summarize common characteristics shared by the four manuscripts and the personal names and their titles, and the toponyms recorded in the colophons.

The writing support of all the manuscripts can be regarded as leaves of talipot palm (*Corypha umbraculifera* L.), on the basis of the length exceeding 45 mm and the other physical characteristics.

All the manuscripts are written in Old Bengali script. Some manuscripts include parts overwritten in Nepalese script (Kv) or insertions in Nepalese script on a margin (Kc, Bca). This fact suggests that the manuscripts were brought to the Kathmandu Valley and preserved there, after they had been made in 15th-century Eastern India. In fact, the manuscript of Kc and the bound manuscript of Sanskrit grammatical texts were collected in Kathmandu and brought to England, and the manuscript of Bca was brought from Nepal to Kolkata. There is no doubt that the mild climate in the Kathmandu Valley in comparison to Eastern India and the careful conservation of manuscripts by Newar Buddhists contributed to the preservation of palm leaf manuscripts.

The peculiar form of the past passive participle of a causative *likhyāpita-* is found in three colophons (Kv 78r3, Kc 128r4–5, Bca 66v2), which is regarded as a blending form of the passive stem *likhya-* and the normal past passive participle form of the causative *likhāpita-* (UṇV 42v7) used in the colophon of the grammatical text UṇV.

The dates are recorded in the expired (*atīta*, *gata*) Vikrama year beginning with the bright fortnight of the month of Kārttika (*kārttikādi*) in the *pūrṇimānta* scheme (ending with the full moon), except for the date of UṇV 42v5 recorded in the *caitrādi* system.

The scribes held the titles: *kā(yastha)-* (UṇV 42v6, KṛP 69r6), *karaṇakāyastha-* (Bca 66v2), *karaṇikakāyastha-* (Kv 78r4–5), or *sāsanikakaraṇakāyastha-* (Kc 128r5). The last three titles suggest that the scribes were engaged in some administrative work. The scribe of Bca held two more titles, *sadbauddha-*, *ṭhakura-* in addition to *karaṇakāyastha-* (Bca 66v2). The names of the scribes are Bhāskaradatta (Kv 78r5), Jayarāmadatta (Kc 128r5), Amitābha (Bca 66v2), and Vāgīśvara (UṇV 42v6, KṛP 69r6).

Three donors held the title *pravaramahāyānayāyin-* (Kv78r2, Kc 128r2, Bca 66v1). The other titles held by the donors or owners are *paramopāsaka-* (Kv 78r2), *śākyabhikṣu-* (Kc 128r3,5, LkV 65r7), *karaṇikakāyastha-* (Kv 78r3), *kuṭumbin-/kuṭumbika-* (Bca 66v1), *mahattama-* (Bca 66v1,2), *mahāsthavira-* (KṛP 69r6, LkV 65r7), *sthavira-* (UṇV 42v7). The names of the donors or owners are Jñānaśrī (Kc 128r3,5), Rāmadeva (Bca 66v2), Vāsudhā (overwritten; Kv 78r3), Vanaratna (owner; KṛP 69r6, LkV 65r7, UṇV 42v7). Furthermore, the name of the donor's father, Mādhava (Bca 66v1) and the name of the donor's bridegroom, Pīroka (overwritten; Kv 78r3) are recorded.

In all the colophons, village names ending in *-grāma-* are recorded. Coindi (Kv 78r4) and Kerakī (Kc 128r5) are recorded as the scribe's location. Kansāra (Kc 128r5) is recorded as the scribe's village in charge. Venu (Bca 66v3) and Kapasiā (UṇV 42v5, LkV 65r6) are recorded as the places of copying. Sohiñcarī (Bca 66v1) is recorded as the donor's location. Using the *India Place Finder*, one can find candidates for many of these places in toponyms in the present Bihar State. This shows that Buddhists still survived in some rural areas in Bihar until the middle of the 15th century CE and they were still copying and transmitting such Mahāyāna and Vajrayāna texts as Śāntideva's *Bodhicaryāvatāra*, the *Kāraṇḍavyūha*, and the *Kālacakratantra*.

In contrast to the village names, no name of *vihāras* is recorded in the colophons. It is probable that no major monasteries (*mahāvihāras*) were functioning in 15th-century Eastern India, except for the Mahābodhi in Bodh Gaya. The Vikramaśīla was virtually destroyed as early as in the 1230s CE, as recorded in the *Biography of Dharmasvāmin* (ROERICH 1959: 64). However, it seems reasonable to consider that there were some bases for Buddhist activities, including libraries, in or near the villages mentioned in the colophons. Libraries are absolutely indispensable for copying manuscripts. Such Buddhist bases may possibly have had no name itself or have been too small to mention in the colophons. This does not seem unnatural, because also in the colophons of Buddhist Sanskrit manuscripts from Eastern India dated to the 11th–12th century CE, only such major monasteries as Nālandā, Vikramaśīla, Mahābodhi, or Uddaṇḍapura are mentioned,[39] alongside village names sometimes recorded. In the Tibetan documents describing the life of Vanaratna (ROERICH 1953: 798), a *vihāra* near Vanaratna's meditation spot is mentioned: "At the *vihāra* (*gtsug lag khaṅ*) called Uruvāsa, a stone image of Avalokiteśvara told him to go to Tibet." According to Arthur Philip McKeown, Śāriputra (c. 1335–1426) devoted himself to rebuilding the Mahābodhi Temple as the last known abbot (MCKEOWN 2018). These facts suggest that some Buddhist institutions called *vihāra* still remained in 15th-century Eastern India.

7. Historical Background

Finally, I should like to touch upon the background against which these Sanskrit manuscripts were copied. According to Joseph E. Schwartzberg (SCHWARTZBERG 1992: 39, pl. V.3 (b) "Major States of Northern South Asia, c. 1390–1450"), the territories of two Islamic dynasties overlapped in the Bihar area in the first half of the 15th century CE: namely, the Sharqī dynasty, whose capital city was Jaunpur, and the Ilyās Shāhī dynasty based in Bengal. It is more likely that the Sharqī dynasty had effective control over Southern Bihar in the 15th century CE because coins issued by the Sharqī kings at that time have been discovered in different parts of Bihar including Rajgir (DIWAKAR 1959: 393–394). Since the Sharqī dynasty came into conflict with the Lodī dynasty in 1452 and was defeated by the last Delhi Sultanate in 1479, it is likely that the Sharqī dynasty could not afford to rule Bihar in this period. Although the Ilyās Shāhī dynasty was strong enough to invade the Kathmandu Valley in the year 1349 (PETECH 1984: 124–126), the dynasty was weakened and interrupted by the Hindu Ganeśa dynasty between 1415–1435. The king's name Guṇakirttibhikṣudeva mentioned in the Bca colophon suggests the presence of a non-Muslim minor local ruler.

In connection with the transmission of Sanskrit manuscripts to the Kathmandu Valley, the achievements of the Nepalese king Jayayakṣamalla (1428–1482) described in Nepalese documents are noteworthy. During his reign, the Malla dynasty of the Kathmandu Valley reached its zenith, and he

39 See WEISSENBORN 2012: 283, nos. 2, 3, 4, 6, 10, 13, 18 (Nālandā), no. 11 (Āpanaka), no. 15 (Vikramaśīla), no. 46 (Uddaṇḍapura). In the colophon of the Pāla manuscript, MA 5161 in the Musée national des arts asiatiques – Guimet, Paris (WEISSENBORN 2012: no. 23), Mahābodhi is mentioned: "*śrīmanmahābodhau thita...*" (BÉGUIN 1990: 19, line 4 of the second figure from the bottom).

mounted a military campaign outside of the Valley (PETECH 1984: 168–180). The *Vaṃśāvalī* used by Kirkpatrick describes it as follows: "Jye Ekshah Mull, or Jye Kush Mull [Jayayakṣamalla], who is said to have annexed Morung, Tirhoot, and Gyah [Gayā] to his dominions, ..." (KIRKPATRICK 1811: 266). According to the *Narapatijayacaryyāṭīkā* composed by Jagajjyotirmalla, a king of Bhaktapur, in 1617 CE, Jayayakṣamalla conquered the kingdom of Mithila and marched as far as Gaya in Magadha with valour.[40] Luciano Petech considers that "As to his claim concerning Gayā, this is clearly an empty boast" (PETECH 1984: 178). Although the effective control over Southern Bihar by the Nepalese ruler does not seem probable, it would be possible that stable trade routes were secured between Bihar and the Kathmandu Valley and contributed to the transmission of Sanskrit manuscripts from the villages in Southern Bihar to the Kathmandu Valley during the reign of Jayayakṣamalla.

8. Conclusions

The dated colophons dealt with in this paper clearly show that Buddhist monks and lay persons were still active in some rural areas around the birthplace of Buddhism until the middle of the 15th century CE under the effective rule of a series of Islamic dynasties. This fact definitively disproves the commonly accepted hypothesis that Buddhism vanished from Eastern India at the beginning of the 13th century CE. Although the destruction of the major monasteries by Turkic Muslims around the turn of the 13th century CE had delivered a disastrous blow to the fate of Indian Buddhism, the religion had not been eliminated completely in Eastern India, including Bihar. As late as 250 years after this blow, Buddhism was still alive in the area and its followers were still transmitting their sacred texts in Sanskrit.

Symbols Used in the Transliteration

( )	restorations in a gap
[ ]	damaged or unclear (part of an) *akṣara*
‹ ›	omission of (part of) an *akṣara* without gap in the manuscript
« »	overwritten part
..	one illegible *akṣara*
=	a division of an *akṣara* into two parts for convenience's sake

40 *yo rājyaṃ mithilāṃ vijitya magadhaṃ gatvā gayāṃ pauruṣād* (ŚĀSTRI 1905: 107).

*	*virāma*
ṁ	*anunāsika (candrabindu)*
’	*avagraha*
|	*daṇḍa*
||	double *daṇḍa*
ɔ-	a sign found between two double *daṇḍas*
;	a space filler
○	a string hole
□	an illustration
⋇	a decorative sign
r	*recto*
v	*verso*
...	ellipsis

Works Cited and Abbreviations

ABHYANKAR 1967: K. V. ABHYANKAR, ed., *Paribhāṣāsaṁgraha (A Collection of Original Works on Vyākaraṇa Paribhāṣās).* Edited Critically with an Introduction and an Index of *Paribhāṣās* [Post-graduate and Research Department Series. 7]. Poona 1967.

ALLINGER & MELZER 2010: EVA ALLINGER and GUDRUN MELZER, A *Pañcarakṣā* Manuscript from Year 39 of the Reign of Rāmapāla. *Artibus Asiae* 70.2 (2010): 387–414.

BANDYOPĀDHYĀYA 1909: RAKHAL DAS BANDYOPĀDHYAYA, Saptagrāma or Sātgānw. *Journal and Proceedings of the Asiatic Society of Bengal* (New Series) 5.7 (1909): 245-262.

BANERJI 1915: R. D. BANERJI, The Pālas of Bengal. *Memoirs of the Asiatic Society of Bengal* 5.3 (1915): 43-113.

BANERJI 1919: R. D. BANERJI, *The Origin of the Bengali Script.* Calcutta 1919.

BANERJEE 1985: BISWANATH BANERJEE, ed., *A Critical Edition of Śrī Kālacakratantra-Rāja* (Collated with the Tibetan Version). [Bibliotheca Indica: A Collection of Oriental Works. 311]. Calcutta 1985.

Bca = *Bodhicaryāvatāra.*

BÉGUIN 1990: GILLES BÉGUIN, *Art ésotérique de l'Himâlaya. Catalogue de la donation Lionel Fournier.* Paris 1990.

BENDALL 1883: CECIL BENDALL, *Catalogue of the Buddhist Sanskrit Manuscripts in the University Library, Cambridge, with Introductory Notices and Illustrations of the Palæography and Chronology of Nepal and Bengal.* Cambridge 1883. Reprint: [Publications of the Nepal-German Manuscript Preservation Project. 2; Verzeichnis der Orientalischen Handschriften in Deutschland. Supplementband 33]. Stuttgart 1992.

— 1888: ID., Notes on a Collection of MSS. Obtained by Dr. Gimlette, of the Bengal Medical Service, at Kathmandu, and Now Deposited in the Cambridge University Library, and in the British Museum. *Journal of the Royal Asiatic Society of Great Britain and Ireland*, New Series 20 (1888): 549–554 (esp. 552–553).

— 1902: ID., *Catalogue of the Sanskrit Manuscripts in the British Museum.* London 1902.

CDIAL = RALPH LILLEY TURNER, *A Comparative Dictionary of the Indo-Aryan Languages*. Vol. 1: *Text*. London 1966.

CHANDRA 1971: MOTI CHANDRA, A Pair of Painted Wooden Covers of the *Kāraṇḍavyūha* Manuscript Dated A.D. 1455 from Eastern India. In: ANAND KRISHNA, ed., *Chhavi. Golden Jubilee Volume. Bharat Kala Bhavan 1920–1970*. Banaras 1971: 240–242, figs. 405–413.

CHATTERJI 1926: SUNITI KUMAR CHATTERJI, *The Origin and Development of the Bengali Language*. Part I: *Introduction, Phonology*. Part II: *Morphology, Bengali Index*. Calcutta 1926.

CHINTAMANI 1934: T. R. CHINTAMANI, ed., *The Uṇādisūtras in Various Recensions*. Part VI. *The Uṇādisūtras of Bhoja with the Vṛtti of Daṇḍanātha Nārāyaṇa and the Uṇādisūtras of Kātantra School with the Vṛtti of Durgasimha*. [Madras University Sanskrit Series. 7]. Madras 1934.

CHHATRAPATI SHIVAJI MAHARAJ VASTU SANGRAHALAYA 2014: *Treasures. Chhatrapati Shivaji Maharaj Vastu Sangrahalaya, Mumbai*. New Delhi 2014.

CHOUDHARY 2015: BIJOY KUMAR CHOUDHARY, *Archaeological Gazetteer of Nalanda District*. Patna 2015.

CHOUDHARY & AMAR 2017: BIJOY KUMAR CHOUDHARY and ABHISHEK SINGH AMAR, *Archaeological Gazetteer of Gaya District*. Patna 2017.

COWELL & EGGELING 1876: E. B. COWELL and J. EGGELING, Catalogue of Buddhist Sanskrit Manuscripts in the Possession of the Royal Asiatic Society (Hodgson Collection). *Journal of the Royal Asiatic Society of Great Britain and Ireland*, New Series 8 (1876): 1–52.

CSMVS = Chhatrapati Shivaji Maharaj Vastu Sangrahalaya.

DAMRON 2021: RYAN C. DAMRON, *Deyadharma – A Gift of the Dharma: The Life and Works of Vanaratna (1384–1468)*. Diss. University of California, Berkeley.

DIMITROV 2002: DRAGOMIR DIMITROV, Tables of the Old Bengali Script (on the Basis of a Nepalese Manuscript of Daṇḍin's *Kāvyādarśa*). In: DRAGOMIR DIMITROV, ULRIKE ROESLER and ROLAND STEINER, eds., *Śikhisamuccayaḥ: Indian and Tibetan Studies*. [Collectanea Marpurgensia Indologica et Tibetologica; Wiener Studien zur Tibetologie und Buddhismuskunde. 53]. Wien 2002: 27–78.

DIWARKAR 1959: R. R. DIWARKAR, *Bihar through the Ages*. Bombay 1959.

DWIVEDĪ 2005: JĀNAKĪPRASĀDA DWIVEDĪ, ed., *Kātantravyākaraṇa of Ācārya Śarvavarmā*. Part Four. *With Four Commentaries, 'Vṛtti' & 'Ṭīkā' by Śrī Durgasingh, 'Kātantravṛttipañjikā' by Śrī Trilocanadāsa, 'Kalāpacandra' by Kavirāja Suṣeṇa Śarmā, 'Samīkṣā' by Editor*. [Sarasvatībhavana-Granthamālā. 135]. Varanasi 2005.

EHRHARD 2002: FRANZ-KARL EHRHARD, *Life and Travels of Lo-chen bSod-nams rgya-mtsho*. [Lumbini International Research Institute Monograph Series. 3]. Lumbini 2002.

— 2004: ID., Spiritual Relationships between Rulers and Preceptors: The Three Journeys of Vanaratna (1384–1468) to Tibet. In: CHRISTOPH CÜPPERS, ed., *The Relationship between Religion and State (chos srid zung 'brel) in Traditional Tibet. Proceedings of a Seminar Held in Lumbini, Nepal, in March 2000*. [LIRI Seminar Proceedings Series. 1]. Lumbini 2004: 245–265.

EINICKE 2009: KATRIN EINICKE, *Korrektur, Differenzierung und Abkürzung in indischen Inschriften und Handschriften*. [Abhandlungen für die Kunde des Morgenlandes. Band 68]. Wiesbaden 2009.

GOODALL & ISAACSON 2003: DOMINIC GOODALL and HARUNAGA ISAACSON, eds., *The Raghupañcikā of Vallabhadeva: Being the Earliest Commentary on the Raghuvaṃśa of Kālidāsa*. [Groningen Oriental Series. 17]. Groningen 2003.

GRAHELI 2012: ALESSANDRO GRAHELI, A Preliminary List and Description of the Nyāyamañjarī Manuscripts. *Journal of Indian Philosophy* 40 (2012): 317–337.

HOERNLE 1901: A. F. RUDOLF HOERNLE, An Epigraphical Note on Palm-leaf, Paper and Birch-bark. *Journal of the Asiatic Society of Bengal* 69, Part I (History, Antiquities, &c.), No. 2 (1901): 93–134.

HORI 2015: SHIN'ICHIRŌ HORI, Evidence of Buddhism in 15th-Century Eastern India: Clues from the Colophon of a *Kālacakratantra* Manuscript in Old Bengali Script. *Journal of Indian and Buddhist Studies (Indogaku Bukkyōgaku Kenkyū)* 印度學佛教學研究 63.3 (2015): 1322–1328 (228–234).

— 2018: ID., In the Wake of a Buddhist Monk in 15th-Century Eastern India: The Manuscripts of Sanskrit Grammatical Texts Originally Owned by Vanaratna. *Bulletin of the International Institute for Buddhist Studies* 1 (2018): 45–60.

— 2019: ID., On the Exact Date of the *Pañcarakṣā* Manuscript Copied in the Regnal Year 39 of Rāmapāla in the Catherine Glynn Benkaim Collection. *Bulletin of the International Institute for Buddhist Studies* 2 (2019): 49–55.

— 2021: ID., A Sanskrit Manuscript of the *Kāraṇḍavyūha* Dated 1456 CE from Eastern India. *Bulletin of the International Institute for Buddhist Studies* 4 (2021): 21–31.

JHĀ 1958: SUBHADRA JHĀ, The Formation of the Maithilī Language (Being a Thesis Accepted for the Degree of Doctor of Literature in the University of Patna). London 1958.

Kc = *Kālacakratantra*.

KELLOGG 1938: S. H. KELLOGG, *A Grammar of the Hindí Language: in Which Are Treated the High Hindí, Braj, and the Eastern Hindí of the Rámáyan of Tulsí Dás, Also the Colloquial Dialects of Rájputáná, Kumáon, Avadh, Ríwá, Bhojpúr, Magadha, Maithila, etc., with Copious Philological Notes.* Third Edition. With Notes on Pronunciation by T. Grahame Bailey. London 1938.

KIELHORN 1890: FRANZ KIELHORN, Examination of Questions Connected with the Vikrama Era. *The Indian Antiquary: A Journal of Oriental Research in Archæology, Epigraphy, Ethnology, Geography, History, Folklore, Languages, Literature, Numismatics, Philosophy, Religion, &c. &c.* 19 (1890): 166–187. Reprinted in: WILHELM RAU, ed., FRANZ KIELHORN. *Kleine Schriften mit einer Auswahl der epigraphischen Aufsätze.* Teil 1. [Glasenapp-Stiftung. Band 3,1]. Wiesbaden 1969: 534–555.

KOPARKAR 1952: DATTATREY GANGADHAR KOPARKAR, ed., *Liṅgānuśāsana of Durgasiṁha.* [Sources of Indo-Aryan Lexicography. 10]. Poona 1952.

KIM 2013: JINAH KIM, *Receptacle of the Sacred: Illustrated Manuscripts and the Buddhist Book Cult in South Asia.* Berkeley 2013.

KIRKPATRICK 1811: WILLIAM KIRKPATRICK, *An Account of the Kingdom of Nepaul: Being the Substance of Observations Made during a Mission to That Country in the Year 1793.* London 1811.

KṛP = *Kṛtpañjikā*.

Kv = *Kāraṇḍavyūha*.

LkV = *Liṅgakārikāvṛtti*.

MCKEOWN 2018: ARTHUR PHILIP MCKEOWN, *Guardian of a Dying Flame: Śāriputra (c. 1335–1426) and the End of Late Indian Buddhism.* [Harvard Oriental Series. 89]. Cambridge 2018.

MIZUSHIMA LABORATORY 2013: *India Place Finder*: http://india.info-proto.com/, Department of Oriental History, Graduate School of Humanities and Sociology, The University of Tokyo.

PAL 1965: PRATAPADITYA PAL, A New Document of Indian Painting. *Journal of the Royal Asiatic Society of Great Britain & Ireland* (New Series) 97 (1965): 103–111, pls. I–VI.

— 1966: ID., Evidences of Buddhist Painting in E. India in the 15th C. *Journal of the Asiatic Society* (Fourth Series) 8.4 (1966): 267–270, pls. 1–2.

PAL & MEECH-PEKARIK 1988: PRATAPADITYA PAL and JULIA MEECH-PEKARIK, *Buddhist Book Illuminations.* New York, Paris, Hong Kong, New Delhi 1988.

Pāṇini = OTTO BÖHTLINGK, ed., *Pâṇini's Grammatik.* Leipzig 1887.

PbhV = *Paribhāṣāvṛtti.*

PETECH 1984: LUCIANO PETECH, *Mediaeval History of Nepal (c. 750–1482).* Second, thoroughly revised edition. [Serie Orientale Roma. 54]. Roma 1984.

PvV = *Parādivyākhyāvṛtti.*

ROERICH 1953: GEORGE N. ROERICH, *The Blue Annals.* Part 2. [Asiatic Society Monograph Series. 7]. Calcutta 1953.

— 1959: ID., *Biography of Dharmasvāmin (Chag lo-tsa-ba Chos-rje-dpal): A Tibetan Monk Pilgrim.* [Historical Research Series. 2]. Patna 1959.

SARASVATĪ 1978: SARASĪKUMĀRA SARASVATĪ সরসীকুমার সরস্বতী, *Pālayugera Citrakalā* পালযুগের চিত্রকলা. Kalikātā 1978.

ŚĀSTRI 1905: HARA PRASĀD ŚĀSTRI, *A Catalogue of Palm-Leaf and Selected Paper Mss. Belonging to the Durbar Library, Nepal.* Vol. I. Calcutta 1905. Reprint: [Verzeichnis der Orientalischen Handschriften in Deutschland. Supplementband 31; Publications of the Nepal-German Manuscript Preservation Project. 1]. Stuttgart 1989.

SCHWARTZBERG 1992: JOSEPH E. SCHWARTZBERG, ed., *A Historical Atlas of South Asia.* 2nd impression, with additional material. New York/Oxford 1992.

SEWELL & DÎKSHIT 1896: ROBERT SEWELL and ŚANKARA BÂLKṚISHṆA DÎKSHIT, *The Indian Calendar: With Tables for the Conversion of Hindu and Muhammadan into A.D. Dates, and vice versâ.* London 1896. Reprint: Delhi 1995.

SHARMA, DESHPANDE & PADHYE 1970: ARYENDRA SHARMA, KHANDERAO DESHPANDE and D. G. PADHYE, eds., *Kāśikā: A Commentary on Pāṇini's Grammar. Part II (Adhyāyas 5–8) by Vāmana & Jayāditya.* [Sanskrit Academy Series. 20]. Hyderabad 1970.

SHĀSTRI 1917: HARA PRASAD SHĀSTRI, *A Descriptive Catalogue of Sanscrit (sic) Manuscripts in the Government Collection under the Care of the Asiatic Society of Bengal.* Vol. 1: *Buddhist Manuscripts.* Calcutta 1917. Reprint: Kolkata 2005.

SIRCAR 1965: D. C. SIRCAR, *Indian Epigraphy.* Delhi 1965.

— 1966, ID., *Indian Epigraphical Glossary.* Delhi 1966.

SPEIJER 1988: J. S. SPEIJER, *Sanskrit Syntax.* Delhi 1988.

TAKAHATA 1954: KANGA TAKAHATA, ed., *Ratnamālāvadāna: A Garland of Precious Gems or a Collection of Edifying Tales, Told in a Metrical Form, Belonging to the Mahāyāna.* [Oriental Library Series D. 3]. Tokyo 1954.

UČIDA 1977: NORIHIKO UČIDA, *Hindi Phonology: Treatment of Middle Indo-Aryan Vowel Sequences in Modern Hindi.* [Intercultural Research Institute Monograph Series. 3]. Calcutta 1977.

UṇV = *Uṇādivṛtti.*

UPĀDHYĀYA 1931: BALADEVA UPĀDHYĀYA, ed., *The Nāgānanda of Śrī Harṣadeva. Edited with a New Commentary Called Bhāvārtha Dīpikā and Introduction etc.* [The Kashi-Sanskrit-Series (Haridâs Sanskrit Granthamālā). 87]. Benares 1931.

VERMA 2003: SHEELA VERMA, Magahi. In: GEORGE CARDONA and DHANESH JAIN, eds., *The Indo-Aryan Languages.* [Routledge Language Family Series]. London/New York 2003: 498–514.

WACKERNAGEL 1896: JAKOB WACKERNAGEL, *Altindische Grammatik.* Band I: *Lautlehre.* Göttingen 1896.

WEISSENBORN 2012: KAREN WEISSENBORN, Eine Auflistung illuminierter buddhistischer Sanskrit-Handschriften aus Ostindien. *Berliner Indologische Studien* 20 (2012): 277–318.

YANO 2007: MICHIO YANO, Pañcāṅga, Ancient and Modern. In: PURUSHOTTAMA BILIMORIA and MELUKOTE K. SRIDHAR, eds., *Traditions of Science: Cross-cultural Perspectives. Essays in Honour of B. V. Subbarayappa*. New Delhi 2007: 59–71.

YANO & FUSHIMI 2014: MICHIO YANO and MAKOTO FUSHIMI, *Pancanga*. Version 3.14. March 2014 (http://www.cc.kyoto-su.ac.jp/~yanom/pancanga/).

YE 2009: YE SHAOYONG, A Preliminary Survey of Sanskrit Manuscripts of Madhyamaka Texts Preserved in the Tibet Autonomous Region. In: ERNST STEINKELLNER, DUAN QING and HELMUT KRASSER, eds. *Sanskrit Manuscripts in China. Proceedings of a Panel at the 2008 Beijing Seminar on Tibetan Studies, October 13 to 17*. Beijing 2009: 307–336.

Źp 1 = 'Gos Lo-tsā-ba Gźon-nu-dpal. *Mkhas pa chen po dpal nags kyi rin chen gyi rnam par thar pa. The Biography of the 15th Century Bengali Pandita, Vanaratna by 'Gos Lo-tsā-ba Gźon-nu-dpal (1392–1481). Reproduced from a Rare Manuscript from the Goṅ-'phel Dpe-mdzod*. Thimphu 1985.

Źp 2 = Gźon nu dpal. *Deb gter sṅon po; The Blue Annals. Completed in A. D. 1478 by Ḥgos-Lotsawa Gzhon-nu-dpal (1392–1481). Reproduced by* LOKESH CHANDRA *from the Collection of Prof. Raghu Vira*. [Śata-Piṭaka Series, Indo-Asian Literatures. 212]. New Delhi 1976: 701–708.

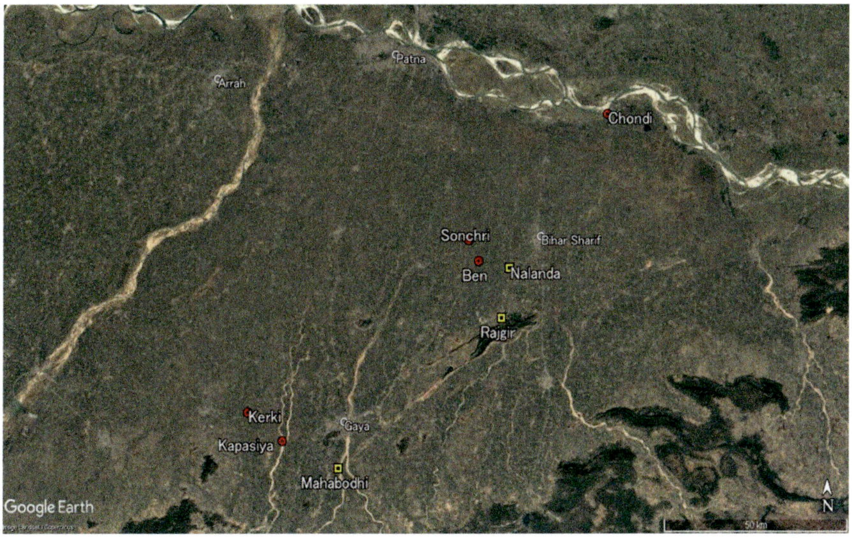

Map 1: Villages Cited.